A HISTORY OF
LONDON LIFE

A History of
LONDON LIFE
by

R. J. MITCHELL
and
M. D. R. LEYS

1724

LONGMANS, GREEN AND CO
LONDON · NEW YORK · TORONTO

LONGMANS, GREEN AND CO LTD
6 & 7 CLIFFORD STREET LONDON W I
THIBAULT HOUSE THIBAULT SQUARE CAPE TOWN
605–611 LONSDALE STREET MELBOURNE C I

LONGMANS, GREEN AND CO INC
55 FIFTH AVENUE NEW YORK 3

LONGMANS, GREEN AND CO
20 CRANFIELD ROAD TORONTO 16

ORIENT LONGMANS PRIVATE LTD
CALCUTTA BOMBAY MADRAS
DELHI HYDERABAD DACCA

First published 1958

PRINTED IN GREAT BRITAIN BY
SPOTTISWOODE, BALLANTYNE AND CO LTD
LONDON AND COLCHESTER

Dedicated to

GWYNETH CHANEY

ACKNOWLEDGEMENTS

THE authors wish to tender thanks to their predecessors in this field and particularly to Mrs. Dorothy George and Miss G. Scott Thomson. They would also like to acknowledge their debt to some who are no longer alive, to John Stow and John Norden and Daniel Defoe, and to those of more recent times—Miss E. Jeffries Davies and Miss I. D. Thorneley, and to C. L. Kingsford whose Ford Lectures inspired one of the writers to take up fifteenth-century studies.

The authors wish, in addition, to thank the librarians and officials of the Guildhall, the Institute of Historical Research, the Soane Museum, the London Museum, and the British Museum, all of whom have been most generous in their help. Mr. Arthur Gardner has given advice on the selection of the illustrations and has generously allowed the use of some of his photographs.

Special thanks are due to Professor Grimes for his supervision and encouragement, to Mr. Ivor Brown, to Sir Alan Herbert for permitting the quotation of a passage from one of his poems, and to Miss Phyllis Hartnoll, Mrs. H. T. Heath and Miss G. Chaney for their kindly criticism.

CONTENTS

PLATES

ILLUSTRATIONS IN THE TEXT

INTRODUCTION

*Let's . . . not talk gammon about the good old times without
looking fairly into them; though, when we have done this, we
may still be able to say to the rest of the world, 'Match our old
men if you can!'*[1]

1. LONDONERS

I T was a Scotsman[2] who claimed for London that she was 'the
flower of cities all', and it is a curious fact that most of those
who have been loudest in her praise were not Londoners themselves. Nor were all famous Londoners London born: the great Dr.
Johnson himself was a provincial, the son of a Lichfield bookseller,
and there he had his early education. Dick Whittington hailed from
Gloucestershire and David Garrick (and some say Nell Gwynn)
from Hereford. Yet they, among many more, identified themselves
so closely with the London life of their times that theirs are the
names that spring to mind in conjuring up the society of bygone
days. Nearly all the provincials who invaded London—Boadicea[3]
is a notable exception—had much to offer as well as to gain, and
London's strong connections with all parts of the country, from
the earliest times to the present day, have given a special quality
to her greatness.

In selecting fifteen Londoners, some of more importance than
fame, the authors have tried to choose representative figures of
their age: readers may deplore the omission of Pepys and Lamb,
and the substitution of Ben Jonson for Shakespeare, but reflection
will show that there is some process of thought behind their
choice of characters. To give one example, not everyone will
be familiar with John Taylor the Water-Poet, but no better
representative can be found of the seventeenth-century London
watermen, and no one was better acquainted than he with inn-
yards and taverns, chair-men and hackney-coachmen, highwaymen

---

[1] F. J. Furnivall: foreword to *A Booke of Precedence, etc.* E.E.T.S., 1869, p. xxiii.
[2] William Dunbar 1465?–1530?): *Poems.*, Ed. H. B. Baildon, 1907, p. 36.
[3] The authors prefer the traditional spelling, though Boudicca is accepted as more
correct.

and country carriers, or could more accurately describe their condition.

Selection must be entirely arbitrary; in writing this book the authors have been obliged to modify their choice from time to time, but they have faith in their team as it now stands, as genuinely representative of the topics with which they wish to deal.

Many subjects have had to be omitted altogether, those, for instance, that have already been treated in good and accessible books. Everything is most rigorously excluded that concerns the history of England as a whole and is not particular to London; even matters of prime importance have been left out if it cannot be shown that they had direct influence upon the London people, or a special meaning for them. That is the essence of this book; it is not a history of London—of which there are many, and will soon be more[1]—but of the London people. It is concerned not with the Court, nor Parliament, but with ordinary folk ranging from fashionable gamesters to the miserable wretches rotting in the gaols, and most particularly with those who seldom won any notice at all—the decent citizens of all classes—and the conditions in which they lived. These are drawn as clearly as the authors' hands can achieve it, from contemporary evidence of many kinds.

The book ranges from early times up to the formation of the London County Council in 1888, and as far as possible attention is focused upon aspects of London life that are usually passed by in favour of more dramatic scenes. There is less about the Great Fire than about the perplexities of those who lost their homes and goods; less about the Lord Mayor's Show than about ordinary holiday activities; less of architectural grandeur than of drains and street cleaning. Some readers may find too little of St. James's, too much of Gin Lane, but it will be easy for them to discover what they want in well-known diaries and celebrated memoirs.

The authors have tried to confine themselves to the City of London and the immediately surrounding villages, without wandering too far into the suburbs, but it has been necessary to make a few expeditions to Westminster. It should be understood, however, that Royal Westminster and the Abbey are the focus of

---

[1] The authors have omitted practically all references to topography and have sketched in the archaeological background very lightly indeed, since these subjects will be dealt with in a later companion volume by Professor Grimes.

national, not of London history, and only figure in this book where their affairs march closely with those of the City. Richard Podelicote, the Westminster burglar, is mentioned not because he was the chief character in a sensational law case, but because the property he stole was recovered in the City of London. London and Westminster were separated throughout the middle ages by more than two miles of dangerous journey, but their affairs impinged so closely upon one another that it would be as false and artificial to disregard this connection as to blur the historical outline by including the men of Westminster in a history of the London citizens.

II. PRE-ROMAN AND ROMAN LONDON

The importance of London's situation has never been in dispute. It is a natural capital, and although venerability and tradition might have made Winchester or York into England's first city, geology and geography had already combined to decide upon the site. The gravel terraces on both sides of the River Thames were there long before the Thames ceased to be a tributary of the Rhine, and here it was that the earliest settlers made their homes. As far back as the Old Stone Age the first Londoners were hunting mammoths in what is now known as Piccadilly, and there some of them dropped hand axes made of flint[1] that are now in the London Museum.

The gravel beds made possible the fording of the river, and afterwards formed bridge-heads for the earliest wooden structure that perhaps stood not far from London Bridge. It seems that from the earliest times the river was used for travel and transport, at first between the village settlements up river, and before long as a means of reaching the Continent. The Thames estuary was the main and obvious channel of approach to Britain, but nowhere along its shores—until London was reached—could gravel subsoil be found on both banks: that is, London was the lowest point at which the river could be forded and in due course bridged. The fact that the level of the Thames was at least some fifteen feet lower two thousand years ago than it is today[2]

---

[1] About 6½ inches long. They were found in 1913.
[2] R. Mortimer Wheeler: *London in Roman Times*, pp. 12–13 (London Mus. Cat., No. 3).

contributed to the advantages of the site by bringing tidal high water downstream to the city area, thus further facilitating the crossing. London's maritime character was with her from the first, and it is a happy accident that has preserved (on a bronze jug found under Threadneedle Street) the impression of an ocean deity with marine winged monsters entangled in its hair.[1]

Before the Romans came to take possession of this river-crossing, to make London the centre of their British road system and the most important of all their British towns, there had certainly been many generations of settlers along the river banks. Archaeologists may argue how great a degree of continuity, if any, can be traced between these fitful settlements: only the pottery, the weapons and the ornaments that have been found on the fringes of the river or lying in its bed tell us that men of the stone, bronze, and iron ages lived and died in this vicinity. The real continuity lies in the antiquities, often fortuitously uncovered, that stir the imagination and compel recognition of our own kinship with these men of long-past ages. Sometimes the repetitive pattern is shown in a very striking way, as recently when devotees of the new gods of power and speed were making excavations for the extension of London Airport, and happened upon the foundations of a pre-Roman temple.

If the Romans found traces of earlier habitations on their chosen site, they probably absorbed them into their new city, with the easy tolerance that accepted Celtic place-names and adapted them to a Latin form.[2] Roman Britain had no capital in the modern sense of the term, but there is strong evidence to suggest that the Romans occupied London as their chief city from quite an early date[3] and there can be do doubt at all that her greatness as a port began in Roman times. London was never primarily a military fortress: of all the relics of these years of Roman rule only two bronze shield-bosses can be certainly identified as military equipment. Retired soldiers might make their homes in this most civilized and comfortable of cities, and enjoy the contrast with their austere quarters in frontier station or fortress, but the only

[1] R. Mortimer Wheeler: *London in Roman Times*, p. 116 and frontispiece.
[2] Sir Mortimer Wheeler rejects various fanciful explanations of *Londinium* but agrees that it is probably derived from a Celtic personal name, *Londinos*. He is not a believer in King Lud. *London in Roman Times*, pp. 13–14.
[3] *Royal Commission on Historical Monuments, Roman London*, pp. 59, 170.

active soldiery that Londoners saw in their streets probably belonged to the military administration and were the equivalent of the modern Household troops.

When he was rebuilding St. Paul's, Wren's excavations revealed the remains of Roman pottery kilns, destroyed perhaps by an earlier and more disastrous fire than that of 1666. By the year A.D. 61 London had developed from a bridge-head settlement into a busy port and commercial centre. The wooden buildings flanked the wharves and quays, and stacks of merchandise of many kinds awaited distribution. The Roman armies were far away, the Roman governor was in North Wales, and Londinium lay wide open to attack. This was the opportunity for the tribe of the Iceni to come sweeping down from Norfolk under their Queen Boadicea, spurred on by cumulative rage against the slights and tyrannies of provincial officials centred in Colchester, and bent upon a revenge that was the more savage because they knew it must be brief. When news came to the governor, Suetonius Paulinus, that the tribesmen had sacked Colchester and were advancing upon London, he hastened back to his province, ahead of his troops. Realizing at once that he could not hold the unwalled city, Suetonius felt that his duty lay rather to the province as a whole than to London in particular, and withdrew, leaving the tribesmen to burn and massacre until the city was utterly destroyed.

Londinium lay in ashes: a symbol of the great destruction is the small heap of coins, all minted before A.D. 54, fused together by the heat of Boadicea's fires, that were found at the head of London Bridge Approach.[1] Soon, however, retribution came to the Iceni; London was restored and reoccupied with no less expedition than in 1666, and houses and wharves were speedily rebuilt. A couple of centuries hereafter London enjoyed peace and privilege, and in this era she reached a very high degree of civilization, wealth, and comfort. During this time (probably in the late second or early third century) the walls rose high, with their gates to admit the radiating roads that spanned the whole country. The London mint, which seems to date from 286, struck gold and silvered copper coins,[2] and there was centred here—alone among

[1] *Royal Commission on Historical Monuments, Roman London*, pp. 28, 189. There were 17 coins, 2 of Agrippa and 15 of Claudius. They are now in the London Museum.
[2] See Sir John Craig: *The Mint: A History of the London Mint from A.D. 287 to 1948*. London, 1953.

British cities—a well-organized Treasury Department. By the early years of the fourth century London had become a financial as well as a commercial headquarters for the whole British province.

In general civilization and culture the progress was remarkable. London in later Roman times had a water supply and facilities for bathing and sanitation of which any modern city could be proud. Luxuries of many kinds were brought to the quays in cargo ships that differed little from the barges seen on the Thames today. The city magnates, in their four-square houses of brick or stone, could choose subjects for their mosaic floors from all Greek and Roman mythology; such as the design of Bacchus riding on a panther that was found in Leadenhall Street and is now in the British Museum.

These pavements might withstand, wholly or in part, the ravages of later invaders, but much of the furniture supported by them was by its nature bound to perish and is only known to us through surviving fragments or chance representations. It seems that the commonest item, the wooden couch, was often uphol-stered with leather[1] and piled high with skin cushions and soft draperies. A small leather fragment, with embossed design and traces of gilding upon it, a small hole at one corner showing where it was formerly attached to a backing, came to hand during the excavations at the site of the Temple of Mithras in 1954: this is, perhaps, all that has survived of such a couch. Chairs, often made of wicker, stools of several kinds, and small 'occasional' tables, also seem to have been in general use.[2]

It is reasonable to suppose that all such household goods, and also imported foods, two-handled jars of oil and wine, and Gaulish pottery and Samian ware, as well as choice works of art, rich textiles, rugs, and fringed cushions, were on sale in the London shops. Basket chairs need not have been expensive, for they were probably made locally by native craftsmen—in the west country elaborate patterns in plaited wickerwork[3] were a commonplace before the Roman legions ever set foot in Britain—but there were also luxury articles at high prices, notably the bronze tripods and candelabra that adorned the richest houses.

[1] J. Liversidge: *Furniture in Roman Britain*. London, 1955, p. 10.
[2] *Ibid.*, p. 51.
[3] R. J. Mitchell and M. D. R. Leys: *A History of the English People*. London, 1950, p. 10.

The wide porticoes of the Roman buildings adapted themselves well to the London climate, for they could give shelter from wind and rain as well as from the sun, and the square houses with fine bathrooms and heating systems, with frescoed walls and mosaic floors, made a splendid framework for furnishings that can only be paralleled by the lush colours and textures of Victorian times. The brightly coloured veneers and inlays, the sumptuous hangings, comfortable furniture, familiar pictures on both floors and walls, all tended to make the Londoners of the fourth century completely satisfied with their surroundings. They were not attuned to listen to the rumblings that presaged the disintegration of the Empire, so that when they were left, dismayed and unprotected, on the withdrawal of the Legions, the blow seemed the heavier, the darkness denser, and the chaos more complete.

III. St. Paul's and St. Peter's

The idea that after the Romans left, 'For a while, London ceased to be', has been shown to be altogether too sweeping a generalization, and is proved by the work of recent generations of archaeologists to be unhistorical. Professor Haverfield wrote these words in 1912; since then evidence has been found that fragments of a Romano-British population lingered on, and that these people still remembered in the mid-fifth century at least some of the lessons learned from Rome. They were, perhaps, no more than groups of squatters living an uneasy life among the ruins, pale shadows of the citizens of Londinium. It may be, however, that these wraiths, in guarding what they could remember of ancient custom and tradition, laid here the foundation of that stubborn individualism that was to become so marked a characteristic of London in medieval and modern times.

Too much must not be made of Romano-British survivals, any more than the fact that there is practically no trace of the Roman street plan in medieval London should be taken to mean the total destruction of Roman civilization. Some life went on, that is clear: all else must be speculation. What did not change, and could not, although it might for a time be unrecognized, was London's natural advantage of position. This was not, however, to be exploited by the new conquerors of Britain until these Anglo-Saxon colonists had settled themselves in permanent quarters in southern England. They could then begin to take stock of their surroundings, and it was not long before they perceived the reasons why London had been, and would be again, a great trading centre. Since they were in their own country essentially farmers, the Saxons remained countrymen at heart and avoided the towns as far as they could. Some of the settlements were made in the neighbourhood of London, but were well outside the ancient walls. The only clear indication of settlement really close to the city is the pot and set of loom weights, from Savoy Hill, that are now in the London Museum. This could indicate Saxon settlements on the slopes above the river between the City and Westminster, but too firm a theory cannot be built upon so slender a foundation.

Gradually, London's population and with it her trade was built up again, so that by the closing years of the sixth century she was again a town of some importance and size. That the new London's fame had spread abroad is shown by the fact, recorded by Bede, that Augustine's mission in 597 included the foundation of a bishopric there, and that the Pope had intended London rather than Canterbury to be Christianity's headquarters in southern England.[1] Where the project failed was in underestimation of the fiercely conservative heathenism of the Londoners themselves. Never were people more intransigent or less tolerant. At first they rejected the proposed bishopric, and when Mellitus, the colleague of St. Augustine, was ultimately appointed to the new see[2] and became London's first bishop, he was faced by a task that would have daunted anyone less resolute. In the first quarter of the seventh century Londoners traded abroad, not with the Christian kingdoms of the Franks but with the obdurate heathen of the Frisian coast. Evidence of this is found in the many coins inscribed 'London' that have been found in Holland on the sites of ancient settlements, and one modern authority contends that the Frisian 'intercourse with England, which is illustrated by these coins, was already of long standing when the first of them was struck.'[3]

The conversion of London was slow and piecemeal, but Christianity triumphed in the end. It was too late, however, for

[1] F. M. Stenton: *Anglo-Saxon England* (2nd edn.). Oxford, 1947, p. 224.
[2] Founded by Aethelbert of Kent in 604.
[3] Stenton: *op. cit.*, p. 56.

London to become the Primate's see. Pope Gregory had instructed Augustine to make the transference from Canterbury when the time was ripe, and five centuries later an enterprising bishop— Richard de Belmeis[1]—petitioned the Pope to this effect, but his action called forth the strongest of protests from Archbishop Anselm and by then there was no question whatever of implementing Pope Gregory's advice. The greatest of the early Bishops was undoubtedly the fourth of the line, St. Eorcenwald, a Lincoln man.[2] He was brother to St. Ethelburga, for whom he founded Barking Abbey. In 666 he also founded Chertsey Abbey, the earliest monastic house in Surrey. Even before his consecration Eorcenwald was widely known for his piety and vigour, and after he became Bishop he made it his business to traverse all the wild forests on the fringe of London, preaching and expounding the Gospel in these last strongholds of heathenism.

London's cathedral had been begun long before, by King Aethelbert of Kent, and dedicated to St. Paul, but Eorcenwald found much still to be done, and devoted himself to the work of improving and rebuilding with as much zeal as he had shown in his missionary activities. Long after his death Eorcenwald's additions were known as the 'New Work', and an alliterative poem in his honour, written about 1386,[3] says that

> Mony a mery mason was made [ther] to wyrke,
> Harde stones for to hewe with eggit toles [edged tools].[4]

By the time this poem was written, St. Paul's had twice been burnt and twice rebuilt, in 961 and 1087, but St. Eorcenwald's burial place in the nave somehow escaped injury, according to the legends,[5] and in 1148 his remains were moved to the east side of the wall above the high altar. Here a glorious shrine was raised to the Bishop, early in the fourteenth century, and it was embellished with jewels of great beauty and value. Three goldsmiths were engaged to work upon the shrine for a whole year, and it became famous throughout Christendom.

[1] A.D. 1108–28. G. H. Cook: *Old St. Paul's Cathedral*. London, 1955, p. 14.
[2] Consecrated *c.* 675. He died in 693.
[3] *St. Erkenwald*. Ed. Sir Israel Gollancz. London, 1922.
[4] Lines 39–40. The poem is based on the legend that St. Paul's was built on the site of a heathen temple; this tale was probably derived from Geoffrey of Monmouth and does not appear to have any substance. See Cook; *op. cit.*, appendix A.
[5] Gollancz: preface to *St. Erkenwald*, p. xxvi.

One of several miracles associated with St. Eorcenwald's name occurred immediately after his death, when the monks of his new foundation at Chertsey wanted to bury the Bishop there. We are told that the people of London came with the clergy of St. Paul's and carried off the bier by force; they had to make their way through the flooded waters of the River Lea, but at the approach of the bier the stream shrank back to its original channel and the procession was able to pass with ease. There are many instances of wrangles concerning the possession of relics of saints and heroes in medieval times, but none more dramatic than this miniature battle over the body of a man whose saintliness was already manifest, who would have been the first to deplore such strife, and yet owed his canonization—at least in part—to his clergy's violent action.

Among the visitors who crowded to St. Eorcenwald's shrine and left their offerings there were many Londoners, and one of them, Richard de Preston, presented a sapphire that was believed to cure diseases of the eye. There was healing virtue, it was said, in the very dust of the saint's chapel, when it was mixed with water and applied directly to the injured part.[1] Like other fashionable cults the veneration of St. Eorcenwald fell suddenly out of favour, and Bishop Braybroke in 1386 found it necessary to re-establish the two festivals[2] of the saint as first-class feasts. The shrine remained, however, the chief asset of St. Paul's right up to the time of the Reformation; souvenirs of the saint were sold within its walls despite the protests of successive Bishops, and as late as 1537–8 there is an entry in the accounts of St. Mary at Hill: 'Paid for beryng a cope to polles on saynt Erkenwaldes day jd.'[3]

From the seventh century, then, St. Paul's was the focal point of the London people, through all vicissitudes. The great Abbey of St. Peter's at nearby Westminster did not become St. Paul's rival till many years had passed; indeed, no church at Westminster was mentioned by Bede in his *History* although persistent legend has it that one Sebert founded a church on the Isle of Thorns as

[1] As Bede put it: 'Both before and after his consecration as Bishop, Earconwald is said to have lived so holy a life that heaven still affords proof of his virtues.' *A History of the English Church and People*, A.D. 731. Trans. Leo Shirley Price. London, 1955, Bk. iv, chap. 6.
[2] I.e., his death and translation. Gollancz, *op. cit.*, p. xxvi.
[3] *The Medieval Records of a London City Church, 1420–1559*. Ed. H. Littlehales. E.E.T.S., London, 1904, p. 379.

early as 616.[1] Dean Stanley suggests that this may only have been an 'attempt of the Westminster monks to redress their balance against St. Paul's',[2] just as the tradition of a Roman temple on this site—'that ere was of Appolyn [Apollo] is now of saynt Petre'[3]—was probably a counterblast to the alleged Temple of Diana beneath St. Paul's. In later days the monks seized on a legend recorded in Ailred's *Life* of Edward the Confessor that St. Peter himself had founded the church, being ferried across the river by fishermen on the eve of the day on which Mellitus was to consecrate a monastery. On the strength of this they claimed tithes on the fish caught in the Thames, and in 1282 the Abbey actually won a law case brought against the Rector of Rotherhithe concerning tithe on fish caught between Gravesend and Staines. A hundred years later a fisherman still used to bring a salmon for St. Peter that was carried in state through the refectory.[4]

The founder of Westminster Abbey, as known to later generations, was King Edward the Confessor, who built the church on a cruciform plan in the Norman manner, and lived only ten days after its consecration in honour of St. Peter. This was on 28 December 1065, and from this day onwards the Kings of England looked upon the Church as their peculiar pride and treasure: it was far more to them than the place of their coronation, it was linked by strands of tradition with the essential character of the monarchy itself.

It is a curious manifestation of national feeling that has exalted Edward the Confessor to so high a position of veneration and esteem, for he was a man who lacked magnanimity to a remarkable degree, and the most saintly thing about him was his physical appearance. His austerity and affability were magnified into great virtues and his defects forgotten by the chroniclers who saw in Edward the Confessor the Saxon equivalent of King Arthur, the personification of Christian England as opposed to the hated heathen Vikings.

Londoners were implacable in their hostility to these invaders, and when Olaf Tryggvason, who later became King of Norway, attacked London Bridge in 994 with ninety-four of his Viking ships

---

[1] A. P. Stanley: *Historical Memorials of Westminster Abbey*. London, 1868, p. 11.
[2] *Ibid.*
[3] *St. Erkenwald*, l. 19.
[4] Stanley: *op. cit.*, pp. 19, 20.

he was astonished at the violence of the Londoners' resistance. At this time the bridge was of wood, for the first stone bridge was not completed until 1209; in some ways wood was more satisfactory for it was easy to repair, and tended to yield to the very strong pressures when the stream was running high. Twenty years after his first attack, King Olaf succeeded (at the sixth attempt) in pulling down a section of the bridge, but it was duly repaired and it was over this early version of London Bridge that King Harold led his weary men to meet their fate at the Battle of Hastings.[1] The Bridge would see the passage of many other bands of soldiers, there would be fighting and turmoil on the Bridge itself as well as at its approaches, strangers would cross it to reach the City, traders would congregate there, ships make their way perilously beneath its arches, all of them an integral part of London and of London life.

[1] R. B. Oram: 'Old London Bridge', *History Today*, August 1956, p. 546.

Chapter One

FITZSTEPHEN'S LONDON

1. The Tower of London

*And William conquered this land and he came to Westminster
and Archbishop Ealdred consecrated him King, and men paid
him tribute.*

Peterborough Chronicle, 1066.[1]

WILLIAM THE CONQUEROR received his crown in Westminster Abbey, but it was his great fortress the Tower
of London that was really symbolic of his reign. He was
a shrewd man, and sensitive to the climate of opinion. He knew
that the City had submitted with a very ill grace and that strong
fortifications would have to be put in hand immediately if the
citizens' obedience was to be maintained. As soon as the ceremony
of coronation was over, William moved to Barking and stayed
there while he perfected his defensive plans, sinking a moat and
raising a bank just inside the south-east angle of the wall, where
the White Tower was soon to rise.[2]

William saw that it was necessary for him to be present in
person at the inception of his fortress, for the same reasons that
had caused Edward the Confessor to have a house built for him
in Westminster from which he could oversee the building of
the Abbey. William did not underestimate the importance of
the coronation at Westminster—indeed, he was most careful to
observe a ceremony that so strongly emphasized the sanctity and
continuity of kingship—but since he believed also in strong and
resolute government the Tower was as important to him as the
Abbey. From his time onwards the Royal Palace might remain at
Westminster, and after his son Rufus had built Westminster Hall
the government of the country could be carried on from there,

---

[1] [Translated] W. Stubbs: *Select Charters.* Ed. H. W. C. Davis. Oxford, 1921,
p. 93.

[2] F. M. Stenton: *Norman London* (Hist. Association, 1934), p. 7.

but the Tower continued, massive and uncompromising, to be the true symbol of royal supremacy.

The White Tower, built of Norman stone from the quarries of Caen, was not the only fortress within the walls of London; there were two more lying to the west, and of these Baynard's Castle is still commemorated in the name of one of the largest of the City wards. This castle took its name from the family of Ralf Baignard who was its first custodian. The other, less important in London history, was known as Montfichet and its exact position has not yet been determined.[1]

At first the Lordship of Baynard's Castle was a position of high authority, and the Lords were also commanders of the host of the citizens of London. Within two hundred years, however, the Lordship had become a matter of honour rather than of importance and the Castle itself was no longer a fortress but a private dwelling. Indeed, in 1275 licence was given to transform it into a house for the Dominican Friars. The documents concerning this transfer throw some light upon the importance of the London army and give an outline of its organization: it is easy to underestimate the importance of this force during the civil wars of the Norman period just because so little is heard of it.[2] Only once, during Stephen's reign, is there a reference to the 'formidable and large army of the men of London,[3] this single instance however helps to explain the King's great efforts to secure the allegiance and goodwill of Londoners at this time.

Custody of the Tower brought with it a position of prime importance in London affairs. It was this office rather than his estates—extensive as they were[4]—that gave power to Geoffrey de Mandeville, Earl of Essex, so that he could menace the Crown with as much force as did Warwick the Kingmaker four hundred years later. Sometimes this position could protect a man from the consequence of his arbitrary acts. In 1378, supported by fifty armed men, the Constable Sir Alan Boxhull[5] violated the sanctuary of Westminster in pursuit of two prisoners who had escaped

[1] F. M. Stenton: *Norman London* (Hist. Association, 1934), p. 8.
[2] *Ibid.*, pp. 9–10.
[3] Henry of Huntingdon: *Historia Anglorum*. Rolls Series, 1897, p. 278.
[4] J. H. Round: *Geoffrey de Mandeville*. London, 1892, p. 113.
[5] He was also a Knight of the Garter. See G. H. Cook: *Old St. Paul's Cathedral*. London, 1905, p. 49.

from the Tower and taken refuge there. One of the prisoners was slain, and so serious was the crime considered that the Abbey was shut for four months. Clergy and laity alike were deeply shocked, but Boxhull's authority was such that when he died he was buried in St. Paul's with every mark of honour.

Geoffrey de Mandeville was succeeded by his son and grandson, but the Constable's office was not hereditary and it was often given to unexpected people at the whim of the sovereign. It might be held by a cleric; Thomas Becket was Constable at one time, and is commemorated in St. Thomas's Tower where there is an oratory dedicated to him, built by King Henry III. The Constables of the Tower did not always reside there, after the earliest days, but every holder of the office guarded his right to the perquisites that augmented the fixed salary. Payment was made for prisoners: often those of high rank had with them formidable retinues of servants for all of whom allowance was made by the Treasury. There were tolls, too, that had to be paid by passing ships—two flagons from a wine ship, for example, and a bundle of rushes from every rush-boat. All the swans below London Bridge were the Constable's, and any cattle that fell into the river while trying to cross the Bridge, and flotsam and jetsam of all kinds.

Each sovereign residing in the Tower had his own personal guard of yeomen in early days, but in time this service became continuous. At the beginning of the Tudor period two warrants are found[1] each containing several Welsh names; this suggests that the 'Yeomen of the King's Guard' mentioned there may have been Henry VII's own followers in the 'late victorieux journeye' that had brought him to the throne. The Yeomen were not known as Beef-eaters until after the Restoration; the nickname is found in the *Travels* of Cosimo, Grand Duke of Tuscany, and seems to refer to the large meat rations they drew for their daily subsistence.[2]

It was not only the Yeomen and the household that had to be supplied with rations: from an early date wild animals were kept in the Tower for the King's pleasure, and the *Liberate Rolls* have various entries concerning payments for their keep. In the time of Henry III, one William was provided with sustenance for

[1] The first is dated 16 September 1485. See Sir R. Hennell: *The History of the King's Bodyguard of the Yeomen of the Guard*. London, 1904, p. 23.
[2] *Ibid.*, p. 29.

himself and the lion in his charge, and he was reimbursed for the cost of supplying the 'chains and other things for the use of the same lion.' This king also had an elephant given him by Louis IX of France.[1] At a somewhat later date, Edward II used to keep a leopard at the Tower whose board amounted to four times that of its keeper,[2] and there were generally some exotic creatures to divert those connected with the Tower and its maintenance. Ordinary people had little opportunity of seeing these animals in early times and had to be content with representations in medieval bestiaries of tigers regarding themselves in mirrors while the huntsmen made away with their cubs, or elephants with massive castles on their backs, filled to overflowing with chain-mailed archers. There is proof that lions were still kept in the Tower in 1686 in the sad story of a Norfolk girl who was mauled to death by one of them.[3] By this time, however, they and the Tower itself had become one of the sights of London, and the White Tower, that had been built to overawe the Londoners in the Conqueror's reign, six hundred years later had become a matter for municipal pride and showmanship.

II. LIFE AND WORK

I, William, King, greet . . . all the burghers within London, French and English, friendly; . . . And I will not endure that any man offer any wrong to you. God keep you.
                    Charter of William I to the City of London, 1066–75.[4]

At this time (1250) the city of London was greatly disturbed, because the King exacted certain liberties from the citizens for the service of the Abbot of Westminster, to their great loss and injury. So far as they were able the Mayor and the whole commune opposed . . . the violence and madness of the king, who, however, proved harsh and inexorable.

                    MATTHEW PARIS: *Chronica Majora.*[5]

It is easy to overstate the number of foreigners that William the Conqueror brought with him, and it is sometimes forgotten

[1] M. A. Hennings: *England under Henry III.* London, 1924, p. 262.
[2] Sixpence a day as opposed to 1½d. Mary Bateson: *Medieval England.* London, 1903, p. 297.
[3] *A True Relation of Mary Jenkinson who was killed by one of the Lyons in the Tower on Munday the 8th of February* [1685/6]. From Misc. Pamphlets in the Ashmole Collection (Bodleian Lib. Oxford), Ashmole G.12.
[4] [Translated] Stubbs: *Select Charters,* p. 97.
[5] [Translated] Roll Series, 1872–84, vol. v, p. 127. The king was Henry III.

that London was already populated by citizens whose life and work continued with little if any interruption. There was, in fact, a considerable preponderance of English names in the generations following the Norman Conquest. 'Even in Stephen's time,' we read, 'nearly half the recorded moneyers of London have English names',[1] and this was a trade that tended to be specially attractive to foreigners. English personal names are also found strongly represented in the early charters of St. Paul's and in the lists of London citizens who presided over wards in the later years of Henry I.

That Londoners could be awkward and intransigent was very clear to William and in his relations with them he walked most warily. The strip of parchment, six inches long, on which their charter was written,[2] stated his promises briefly but unequivocally; it was left to later administrators to antagonize the Londoners by extorting from them dues that they held to be unreasonable. In this matter King Henry III was particularly inept and although he (if ever a sovereign did) needed the Londoners' support he and the Queen so offended the citizens that 'no one in London would give them a halfpenny on credit', according to the *Annals of Dunstable*.[3] On one occasion, when the Queen and her followers emerged from the Tower and started up-river for Windsor, at London Bridge they were assaulted by a rabble of Londoners who attacked them 'shamefully with base and foul words and even with stones, so that the Queen was with difficulty freed by the Mayor of London'[4] and the royal party had to return to the Tower shamed and disordered.

At other times the Londoners treated the king with deference and honour, and turned out in force to attend royal progresses, processions and occasions of pomp. They were famed, it seems, for their welcome to illustrious visitors and the 'entertainment of strangers', and the celebrations concerned with 'ratifying of betrothals, contracts of marriage, celebration of nuptials, furnishing of banquets, cheering of guests, and likewise for their care in regard to the rites of funerals and the burial of the dead'. This

[1] F. M. Stenton: *Norman London*, p. 16.
[2] Now in the possession of the City Corporation.
[3] In June 1263. Dunstable was an Augustinian House. See *Annales Monastici*, Rolls Series, 1864, p. 222.
[4] *Ibid.*, p. 223. This was on St. Mildred's Day (13 July), 1263.

passage is taken from a description of London by William Fitz-
Stephen that occurs as a prologue to his *Life* of Thomas Becket,[1]
and it shows that as early as 1180 Londoners were exhibiting their
zest for banquets and funerals, although it was not until much
later that fortunes were dissipated in providing 'pompous'
funerals for prominent citizens.[2]

Becket, like FitzStephen, was a Londoner by birth, and his
birthplace is thought to have been near the site of the chapel of
the Mercers' Company. FitzStephen contended that Becket had
adorned London 'by his rising' just as he had Canterbury 'by his
setting', and from his own position as draughtsman[3] in Becket's
chancery he was able to appreciate the dynamic force of this great
saint and to guess, from their common background, how much
Becket owed to his early upbringing.

There can be no doubt that FitzStephen was a very partial critic.
He was certain that London was the finest city in the world and
the picture he painted is in bright clear colours and conveys an
impression of spontaneous gaiety and liveliness that has seldom
been equalled. FitzStephen's Londoners are handsomer than other
men, and their wives more virtuous. There are more fish in his
Thames than anyone else has found, water in his London is
sweeter than elsewhere, the forests stretching almost up to the
walls of the city teem with the most desirable wild boars, bulls,
and 'deer both red and fallow'. When he turns from praise of the
citizens and their surroundings to a description of their daily life,
FitzStephen's prologue becomes increasingly vivid. He describes
in detail the cook-shop on the river-bank, where all sorts of
ready-cooked food could be bought by those who had to entertain
unexpected guests, and where the finest birds and venison were
provided for rich households while the poor had a choice of
humbler dishes; we are told that all was available 'at whatever
hour of night or day'; clearly an early instance of twenty-four
hours' service.

The famous account of the weekly horse-fair at Smithfield,
and the even better-known story of young Londoners fastening

[1] Written before 1183. First printed by John Stow in 1598, and trans. by H. E.
Butler, London (Hist. Assocn.), 1934.
[2] See the *Diary of Henry Machyn, 1553–63.* Ed. J. G. Nichols. Camden Society,
1848, *passim.*
[3] I.e. a drawer-up of formal letters: lat. *dictator.*

on their home-made skates and gliding swiftly over the flooded
and frozen expanse of Moorfields, have often been remarked and
quoted. A careful reading of the prologue shows also that the
pattern of London life was already becoming clear in the tendency
of different trades and tradesmen to congregate in their own special quarters—'the vendors of each several thing, the hirers out of
their several sorts of labour' were found every morning in their
own chosen place, engaged in their own particular work. Even as
early as this, Billingsgate was the place to buy fish, and it would
seem that other trades also were already localized in regions where
they are still to be found.

It is commonly supposed that 'gilds' were associations essentially connected with trade, and insufficient attention is paid to
the gilds or fraternities stemming from a benevolent or religious
basis.[1] Not nearly enough stress is laid upon the 'burial and benefit' aspect of these gilds; in them can be seen the ancestor of
modern working men's clubs, and it is possible to trace back their
origin to Anglo-Saxon times. Most parishes had their own gilds,
in London as in other towns and villages. Sometimes these were
formed for one specific purpose, as the twelfth-century gild of
St. Lazarus, for helping lepers. London Bridge was of such
paramount importance that four Bridge Gilds existed for the sole
purpose of repairing and looking after the structure. Still another
London gild, that may have had provincial imitators, was the
Pilgrims' Gild founded to enable its members to go on pilgrim-
age to distant shrines. Although none of these gilds was primarily
connected with trade, they were all founded upon community
of interest; it was natural enough for craftsmen of the same kind
to wish to join their fellows in forming such associations, and
several craft gilds had their origin in these informal friendly
societies.

The history of these craft gilds differs little if at all from the
normal development of such institutions, but in one respect
London's economic organisation was singular. The 'gild merchant' that was in one sense the parent of the craft gilds (though
it would be an over-simplification to claim that all these sprang
from the larger, earlier, and more general association of traders)

[1] See D. M. Stenton's summary in *English Society in the Early Middle Ages*. London,
1951, p. 182.

never existed in London. This was not because she was too weak
to demand privileges from rulers anxious to placate the powerful
townsmen, but perhaps because she was too strong to need this
institution. From the first, London has had the wish and the will
to manage her own affairs, and by Norman times the more prominent craftsmen such as the Goldsmiths and the Weavers were
beginning to form their own associations. The oldest surviving
document concerning the history of a city company is the charter
of the Weavers of London,[1] granted them by Henry II, which
confirmed to these craftsmen all the privileges they already
enjoyed, and forbade anyone outside their gild to practise weaving
in London or Southwark. At about the same time the Bakers'
Gild had come into being, and possibly others whose early records
have been lost.

The impression gained from FitzStephen's description is one
of great well-being and solid prosperity, and he had good grounds
for taking this view of London life; but it would be a great
mistake to suppose that Londoners had exchanged their character of strong independence for a supine and easy-going tolerance.
There is violence and rioting in the annals of medieval London,
suspicion of the encroachments of the King, or his representatives
in the Tower, and a sturdy antagonism to the infiltration of
foreigners. At the same time, Londoners were beginning to
extend their outlook to include trade with all Europe, and by the
end of the twelfth century they had not only consolidated their
strong position but had also extended their horizon. In this, as in
other ways, London was some fifty years ahead of her main rivals
among English cities.

London became in the next half century an example also of the
new standards of living and behaviour. During the first decades
of the twelfth century Ramsey Abbey owned a two-storied house,
said to have been built of stone,[2] and the Abbey of Abingdon had
a large house and a chapel on the north bank of the Thames, on
the road between London and Westminster.[3] Other religious
foundations also had property in or close to the City, and all

---

[1] Printed by F. Consitt: *The London Weavers' Company*. London, 1933, vol. i,
pp. 180–1.
[2] Mary Bateson: *Medieval England*. London, 1903, p. 135.
[3] *Chronicon Monasterii de Abingdon*. Rolls Series, 1858, vol. ii, p. 15–16. See F. M.
Stenton: *Norman London*, p. 23.

through the middle ages these prelates' houses were the best and finest in London. In the fourteenth and fifteenth centuries they were often rented or borrowed on behalf of ambassadors and their suites, for not only were they capacious, but in many instances they were furnished with great magnificence.

These, and other rich men's houses, were in strong contrast to the rickety huts and hovels where the poorest classes lived. The city authorities were empowered to demolish dangerous buildings and to improve others where overhanging projections impeded free passage, but little was done and the streets in the poorest quarters remained narrow, dark and dangerous. Well-to-do shopkeepers, however, were beginning to imitate the good houses of the clergy and nobility, and by the fourteenth century the richer tradesmen were living in conditions that would have astonished their grandfathers, and some of them dissipated in ostentatious grandeur the fortunes carefully amassed by an earlier generation.

The fact that it was thought necessary in the year 1281 to pass a sumptuary law in London suggests that men and women— particularly women—had been indulging to a great extent in rich clothes that were beyond their means. Henceforward no female hucksters, nurses, servants or loose women would be allowed to dress in the guise of their betters, and only those who could afford furred capes would be allowed to sport also fur-trimmed hoods. Although there had to be a distinction between rich and poor in dress, all could join on the same level in festivities, and all could drink red wine from the conduit in Cheapside at times of special celebration. When a prince was born in 1312 the mayor and aldermen led the ring-dances or 'carols' in St. Paul's cathedral,[1] and everyone was free to join in the festivity although there was not room for all of them to dine in the Guildhall. Londoners worked hard, and played hard too, in the earlier middle ages; there were many accidents and sudden deaths and life was crude by modern standards, but FitzStephen summed up the position as he saw it, with his customary felicity, when he wrote: 'The only plagues of London are the immoderate drinking of fools and the frequency of fires.'[2]

[1] M. Bateson: *op. cit.*, p. 408.
[2] F. M. Stenton: *Norman London*, p. 30.

III. Men and Women of Religion

*[The Friars] They illuminate our whole country with the
bright light of their preaching and teaching . . . Oh, if your
holiness could see with what devotion and humility the people
run to hear from them the word of life.*

Robert Grosseteste's letter to Pope Gregory IX, 1238.[1]

*At this time certain of the Friars minor and some of the
preaching friars . . . secretly pushed themselves into the domain
of some noble monastic communities and . . . they celebrated
masses secretly . . . and received many confessions, to the
prejudice of the parish priests.*

Matthew Paris: Chronicle, 1235.[2]

The oldest of all monasteries in or adjoining London—with the
one exception of the Benedictine Abbey at Westminster—was a
college of secular canons at St. Martin le Grand, which was
founded about two years after the Norman Conquest. This was
followed in rapid succession by the Cluniac Priory of St. Saviour
in Bermondsey, by three priories of Augustinian Canons, and an
Augustinian nunnery at Holywell. Parish churches were built and
rebuilt, enlarged and improved, and the Hospital of St. Bartholomew was established for the sick and needy.[3] In all this London
conformed to the pattern of the country as a whole and there is
little to distinguish her religious foundations from those of
any other city, except that they were more numerous and on the
whole richer in endowments. This was in keeping with London's
position and significance, and was not due to any singularity of
religious feeling.

With the coming of the Friars, however, London immediately
became one of their most important bases. It was the practice of
these early Friars, particularly the Franciscans, to seek out the
most congested districts and to do everything in their power to
alleviate the misery, want, and disease that they inevitably found.
That they deliberately chose poor and unhealthy areas for their
dwellings is probably not true; they had to accept, from necessity,
whatever happened to be available. Those sites that were unattractive and undesirable were naturally those that were cheapest and
in least demand.[4] In London the Grey Friars settled in Stinking

---

[1] [Translated] *Roberti Grosseteste Epistolae.* Rolls Series, 1861, no. viii.
[2] [Translated] *Chronica Majora.* Rolls Series, 1872–84, vol. iii, p. 332.
[3] In 1123. The Knights Templar were established five years later.
[4] A. G. Little: *Studies in English Franciscan History.* Manchester, 1917, pp. 10–11.

Lane, near the shambles of Newgate, and although it might be thought that no one of any sensibility and with the means to live elsewhere would have chosen that locality as a dwelling place, their nearest neighbours were 'prelates and noblemen',[1] who were apparently quite satisfied with their quarters.

When the Franciscans first arrived in London in 1224 they were only four in number. One of the sheriffs granted them a lease of his house in Cornhill, and there they stayed until a mercer named John Iwyn gave them the land in the shambles where they built their first house.[2] Their numbers increased, and so did their influence. Many citizens helped them with gifts and many too, showed goodwill and sympathy with the Friars' aims. When, in 1239, they wished to turn the chapel into the choir of a new church the Mayor had the work done at his own expense, and a few years later another Mayor, Sir Henry Waleys, paid for the building of the nave. A third benefactor built them a chapter-house, and this generous man was practical also, for he made the Friars a present of 'all the brazen pots necessary for the kitchen, infirmary, and other offices'.[3]

It is easy to understand the jealousy and indignation aroused among the conventuals—who had at first welcomed the Friars and given them hospitality—by the success of the new movement. The Franciscans also showed a lack of tact in their relations with the parish clergy. These were offended by the Friars' encroachment upon their duties and privileges, and thought that the Franciscans had gone far beyond the General Constitutions of their Order for 'the edification of others by example, counsel, and wholesome exhortation'.[4]

In their earliest days the Grey Friars had concentrated upon deeds rather than words, helping the poorest citizens, the sick, and the vagrants, and encouraging them to new hope and new energy, but as time passed the 'exhortation' developed into the preaching of sermons expressed in homely phrases and illustrations drawn from everyday life. Some Franciscan sermons in a collection known as the *Fasciculus Morum* refer to the games and pranks of children, and familiar household processes like the lighting of a

---

[1] Riley: *Memorials of London, etc.* London, 1868, pp. 339, 358.
[2] *Chronicle of the Grey Friars of London.* Ed. J. G. Nichols. Camden Society, 1852, p. x.
[3] *Ibid.*, pp. x–xi.　　　　[4] Quoted A. G. Little: *op. cit.*, p. 1.

fire with 'flint, steel, and sulphurated thread',[1] in forceful and racy terms. The writer of these sermons also shows close familiarity with the practical problems of the ordinary business man, and a clear knowledge of the intricacies of partnership and of the temptation to quibble about matters of usury, as distinct from charitable loans, and their attempted justification.

Much of the preaching was done at Paul's Cross, and it was here that a remarkable disputation took place in the mid-fifteenth century between Franciscans, Carmelites, and secular clergy. The first force of the Friars' enthusiasm had long been spent and the movement had fallen away from its early ideals, but on this occasion, in 1465, the disputation flared into life. Charges of heresy were made on all sides, and appeals to Rome resulted which were not finally resolved until long after the original debate was forgotten and the protagonists had relapsed into obscurity. Many laymen of London attended the disputation and took a keen interest in its result; this was shown by the number of city men who laid bets on the various issues and on the result of the appeals.[2] Whether this showed a genuine interest in religion on the part of city magnates, or merely that they welcomed an opportunity for having a little flutter, it is clear that the disputation was no merely academic exercise and that the crowds it attracted were moved by interest as well as by curiosity.

IV. THE LONDON JEWRY

Among other things I think that the slaughter of the Jews which was perpetrated at that time in London should not be passed over in silence . . . Rushing . . . in unexpected tumult on the Jews, of whom a very great multitude dwelt with all confidence in London, little thinking that harm would happen to them, they, enticed not by the zeal of the law, but by the lust of temporal good, most cruelly slew as many as they could find in the city . . . nearly four hundred Jews of both sexes and all ranks being killed. And although they were not signed with the mark of our faith, it seemed an inhuman and impious deed to slay them without cause.

THOMAS WYKES: Chronicle, 1264.[3]

By the time of William Rufus a considerable number of Jews lived in London. If there were any Jews in England before the

[1] Quoted A. G. Little: *op. cit.*, p. 147.
[2] William Gregory: *The Historical Collections of a London Citizen in the Fifteenth Century.* Ed. Jas. Gairdner. Camden Society, 1876, p. 230.
[3] [Translated *Annales Monastici*. Rolls Series, 1864–9, No. iv, p. 141.

Conquest, they were only scattered individuals;[1] it was not until it became the clearly defined policy of the early Norman kings to encourage Jewish immigrants that they settled in the towns, particularly in Oxford and in London, and began to practise their art of money-lending.

Since usury was forbidden to Christians, and the King and the nobles and all those concerned in the great building enter-prises of the time were chronically short of money, there was no difficulty in finding clients, and the Jews fulfilled a very useful purpose. They were, however, liable to exceptional taxation at any time; they had no political rights, could not hold estate of inheritance in land, and were subject to expulsion at the whim of the sovereign and at a moment's notice. They might make a good living, if they could induce the borrower to pay the high rate of interest that they asked, but they had no social or political security of any kind.[2]

So long as the Jews conformed outwardly with the behaviour required of them, and refrained from actions or the expression of opinions that might inflame their Christian neighbours, they generally lived peaceably enough, but when London was per-turbed and emotions were running high, the ordinary Londoners were liable to turn against the Jews and to attribute to their presence in the city every misfortune that occurred. Quarrels that were in no way their concern often led to blows, looting, and even to massacres in which the Jews were always the victims; after 1181 they were not allowed to bear arms even for their own defence. Attacks upon the Jewish quarter, the Old Jewry in London, were made without warning and with the flimsiest excuse. One such took place because some Jews had attended the coronation of Richard I, and the attack in 1264 described by Thomas Wykes in his Chronicle[3] was due to the indignation excited by the mis-rule of Henry III and had nothing whatever to do with the Jewish colony.

In reply to baseless charges, particularly those concerned with clipping coin of the realm, some liberal-minded men raised their voices in defence of the Jews, but not to much effect. In some

---

[1] *Select Pleas, Starrs, and other Records from the Rolls of the Exchequer of the Jews, A.D. 1220–84.* Ed. J. M. Rigg. Selden Society, London, 1902, p. x.
[2] *Ibid.*, p. ix.
[3] See the heading to this section.

ways, however, their lot became more tolerable as restrictions were relaxed and they were given small concessions. After 1177, for instance, they were allowed to bury their dead outside the walls of the towns where they dwelt, instead of bringing all bodies to London for interment in the Jews' burial ground at Cripplegate.

Some Jews were able to make a living as doctors of medicine although this profession had its special dangers—when one of the London practitioners had the misfortune to lose a patient the Jews of London were fined collectively the large sum of £2,000 'for a sick man whom they killed'.[1] Others won respect and admiration by their profound scholarship; one of the most famous of these learned Jews was Master Elias of London, who died in 1264. He was renowned on the Continent for his erudite writings and other members of his family also wrote Hebrew books that were venerated by scholars.[2]

The Jews had to be supple and adaptable in their business methods, and were expected to accept a great variety of goods offered as pledges: one Jew was sued for the return of a psalter, a book of medicine, and a saddle.[3] Accounts of the royal household mention furs, silks, and even cushions deposited as security for loans from Jewish money-lenders, as well as the more conventional pledges of jewellery and manuscripts.

King Henry III, poor as he was, was moved by his compassion to found a home for converted Jews, on the site of the present Public Record Office in Chancery Lane. Any Jews who were converted and took a Christian name, and who gave up their property in exchange for an allowance of 1½d. a day, or 8d. a week for women, could find a home here.[4] Many years earlier Archbishop Anselm had written, 'Let no poverty or any other cause which we can avert make him regret leaving his Kin and his Law for Christ's sake', and the House of Converts was intended to fulfil this particular purpose of welcoming Jews ready to abandon their faith. There were, however, very few who were ready to do this, so that in the end the House of Converts had to be closed for

[1] In 1130. Quoted by D. M. Stenton: *English Society in the Early Middle Ages*. London, 1951, p. 193.
[2] *Ibid.*, p. 197.
[3] C. Roth: *A History of the Jews in England*. Oxford, 1941, p. 274, n. v.
[4] D. M. Stenton: *op. cit.*, p. 198.

want of inmates, and in 1377 it was turned over to the use of the Master of the Rolls.

Edward I, more practical than his father Henry III, imposed *chevage*, or a poll-tax, on all Jews in England from the age of twelve years, and entrusted its collection to 'John le Clerk, goldsmith, and William le Convert', both members of the London House of Converts[1] on whose behalf the *chevage* had been devised. Converted Jews were called in when the corpse of a boy was exhumed in London and found to bear signs of ill-usage and puncture marks thought to resemble Hebrew letters. These they were asked to read, and although they could make little of the marks, certain enemies of the Jewish community construed the alleged letters into evidence suggesting a ritual murder of a Christian boy, comparable with the cases of twelve-year-old William of Norwich and 'little St. Hugh' of Lincoln. The corpse of this unknown boy was re-buried in St. Paul's, and the London Jewry had to pay a fine of 60,000 marks, spread over five years.[2]

These penal levies impoverished the rich and ruined the poorer Jews; for the time being the Exchequer was replenished, but it soon became clear that the Crown had squeezed the Jews nearly dry and it was thought that they had outstayed their usefulness. Already in 1288 Edward I had expelled the Jews from Gascony,[3] and two years later the Jewry of England was consigned to perpetual banishment, without warning and without pity. It was not until the time of the Commonwealth that they were suffered to return, and even so Cromwell's enlightened policy was not fully implemented for another two hundred years, when Baron Lionel de Rothschild took his seat for the City of London in the Parliament of 1858.[4] The Jews had to wait a long time for recognition, but in the end it came: it is appropriate that the first Jew to sit in Parliament should have been elected by the citizens of London, whose ancestors had given the Jews of their own day little of respect and less of toleration.

---

[1] *Select Pleas, etc*, p. 113.
[2] *Ibid.*, p. xxviii.
[3] C. Roth: *op. cit.*, p. 265.
[4] *Ibid.*, p. xl.

Chapter Two

CHAUCER'S LONDON

1. LONDONERS' PASTIMES

They spent all Monday at a joust and dance
And the high services of Venus. Yet
Because they knew that up they'd have to get,
And early too, to witness the great fight,
They went to bed betimes on Monday night.

GEOFFREY CHAUCER: *The Knight's Tale.*[1]

IT may be argued that Geoffrey Chaucer transcended the times in which he lived. He was, nevertheless, a fourteenth-century Londoner, who represented his city as clearly as the sculptured Cockney craftsman who looks down with mocking good humour upon the congregations gathered in Westminster Abbey.[2] Although the history of the Chaucer family is obscure, there is no doubt that they were Londoners. It matters little whether Geoffrey's father really was a vintner, but the fact that the poet sprang from the solid middle class established in a prosperous city is one clue to his poise and confidence as well as to his wide experience of men and women.

Chaucer's career led him to mix with many different types and classes, for he was a man of affairs long before he was a poet. In considering Geoffrey Chaucer the writer, it is easy to forget Chaucer the Member of Parliament,[3] Chaucer the comptroller of petty customs in London, and Chaucer the citizen living for twelve years (1374–86) over Aldgate and drawing his 'fees, robes, annuities and butts of malmsey'[4] in return for his services as a civil servant. Like Thomas Hoccleve he composed his poems and lived an interesting life out of business hours, but at a higher level

---

[1] Part iv, lines 4–8. Rendered in modern English by Nevill Coghill: *The Canterbury Tales*. London, 1951, p. 92.
[2] See illustration 'Londoners at Work and Play.'
[3] For Kent, in 1386.
[4] H. S. Bennett: *English Books and Readers, 1475–1557*. Cambridge, 1952, p. 7.

than that raffish verse-making clerk in the office of the King's
Privy Seal. Hoccleve shared exuberantly in the pastimes and
pleasures of young Londoners, and Chaucer too was no stranger
to sport: to imagine him as a grave customs officer would be as
absurd as to represent him as a solemn poet. No man ever had
more sympathy with sportsmen and revellers, or was more
tolerant of the indiscretions of light-hearted pleasure-seekers.

When Moorfields was frozen over, mere skating was not enough
to satisfy London boys; they fastened bone skates securely to their
feet, armed themselves with sticks shod with iron, and set out to
tilt at full speed with their friends and rivals. It was a rough and
hazardous game, leading to bloody noses and sometimes broken
limbs, but it made for boldness and hardihood—or so FitzStephen
said.[1] From his time onwards, all through the middle ages, Moorfields provided the training ground for the apprentices and their
younger brothers; and when they reached manhood they still spent
their holidays here in wrestling and racing and fighting and archery.

The young citizens were joined by young courtiers and pages,
boys 'not yet invested with the belt of knighthood', all anxious
to exercise themselves with lance and shield, or to win honour in
athletic contests. FitzStephen tells us of races run on summer
feast-days, of putting the stone and throwing the javelin, of fighting with sword and buckler, of mimic battles on horse and on foot,
and of the 'naval tourneys' at Easter when a shield was fastened
to a strong pole set in midstream and young men aimed lances at
it from the prows of boats rowed swiftly with the current. Crowds
gathered to watch this sport, to cheer when the lance was shattered
and to laugh when the inaccurate marksmen fell into the river and
had to be dragged up the muddy bank to safety.

Commonest of all was the practice of archery, so common
indeed that it is seldom mentioned. It was taken for granted that
all able-bodied men and boys would be drawing their bows or
caring for their gear whenever they had any time to spare, during
long summer evenings or on public holidays. An accident occurred
on the Feast of the Epiphany, in 1280, when a spectator named
William was watching John de Burton and some of his neighbours
of Fleet Street shooting at a mark. They were using cross-bows
in place of the more usual long-bows, and one of John's shots

[1] F. M. Stenton: *Norman London*, pp. 30-1.

went wide of the mark; the bolt[1] glanced off the branch of a pear tree, and hit and killed the unfortunate William.[2] At the ensuing inquest a verdict of misadventure was returned, as it was in the case of a little girl trampled to death by a horse that swerved from the quintain, and when a ten-year-old boy was killed during a game of hockey.[3]

Teams of Londoners played games among themselves and also against the neighbouring suburbs; in the summer of 1222 a wrestling match with the youths of Westminster had a disastrous sequel. The city men won, and a return match was fixed for a week later, but this time the Steward of the Abbey armed the home side so that the Westminster men set about the Londoners and caused many casualties. The irate Londoners went home to gather strength and, ignoring the advice of the Mayor, rushed to Westminster and pulled down the Steward's house. When the Abbot came to complain they seized his horses, beat his servants and stoned him out of the City. Matters had by this time become so serious, that the Mayor and chief citizens were held responsible for the uproar and were summoned to the Tower by the Justiciar, Hubert de Burgh. The ringleader of the rioters and two other men were hanged next morning, and some were punished with the loss of feet or hands; moreover the City had to pay an enormous fine to the King for breaking his peace.[4] All this trouble had grown from a small beginning; many games were played with good sportsmanship and without rancour, but there was always tension between London and Westminster, each jealous of the other's position and privileges.

This tendency of Londoners to rush to arms when any quarrel broke out led in 1281 to the prohibition of the carrying of swords and bucklers in the City by night,[5] but there were still fights occasioned by trifling insult or thoughtless gesture, very often arising from some contest of strength or skill. A violent affray broke out on Ascension Day, 1327, between the City saddlers on the one side and the joiners, painters, and lorimers on the other.[6]

---

[1] In the original the word appears to be 'ball', but 'bolt' makes better sense.
[2] *Calendar of Inquisitions (Miscellaneous)*, vol. i, no. 2233.
[3] *Ibid.*, nos. 2099, 2209.
[4] J. G. Noppen: *Royal Westminster*. London, 1937, p. 27.
[5] *Calendar of Letter Books* (A) (1275–98). Ed. R. R. Sharpe. London, 1897, p. 213.
[6] Lorimers were bit-makers, working either in copper or in iron.

Some blows were exchanged, and then they seized arms and all 'manfully began to fight' in Cheapside and thence to Cripplegate. Many other tradesmen were drawn into the struggle so that the greater part of the City became involved. Some were killed, others wounded, and it was a long time before the King's peace could be restored.

The 'arms' may have been makeshift weapons—sticks or tools of their trades—but all Londoners understood the use of sword and lance, and this made them knowledgeable and critical spectators of the jousts and tourneys held at Smithfield and elsewhere. There were frequent prohibitions of tournaments by the Church, and also by the King: on 18 June 1230 the arrest was ordered of 'all persons who shall attend tournaments throughout the realm' —but they continued to be held and to attract large crowds.[1] In early times the tournament was looked upon simply as training for warfare; as it became more of a stylized entertainment, it became decreasingly useful from a military point of view, but the magnificence of the court of Edward III, so brilliantly described by Froissart, revived past glories and initiated a new age of the tourney as a courtly pastime and display of heraldry. The commons attended in festival spirit, as much to witness the pageantry as to applaud the skill and courage of the participants.

As the elaboration grew, and the rules of conduct became more technical and formal, so did the armour become heavier and increasingly intricate. This meant good business for the London armourers, lorimers, spurriers and saddlers, and these craftsmen were still finding employment in Tudor times in spite of German competition. For tournaments, immensely thick and heavy armour was worn, much more solid than could have been used upon the battlefield, and with far more gilding, engraving and embossing. Although much armour came from abroad, London armourers produced some of the best work, and in 1396 the will of Symon Wynchcomb shows that he possessed six *bacinettes*[2] of London make.

'Hors harneys' for the protection of the shire horses that had to carry all this weight in the lists was also very elaborate and sumptuous.[3] When their saddles became worn and shabby, the

---

[1] For the tournament as a spectacle see the authors' earlier book: *A History of the English People*. London, 1950, pp. 151–4.
[2] These were flattish helmets.
[3] Viscount Dillon: Armour notes in *The Archaeological Journal*, June 1903, p. 97 ff.

nobles used to give them to their grooms, who would send them to the London saddlers to be re-conditioned; they were then sold as new, to the great annoyance of the members of kindred crafts who had no such perquisites themselves.[1]

It seems certain that all the best armour was made to measure, and in this respect London armourers held the pre-eminence afterwards accorded to London tailors. Generally, they made provision for letting out the armour at crucial points, should the wearer's size increase. In comparing the stature of the ordinary man today with those of his medieval counterpart it appears that the former exceeds the latter in the girth only of his thighs; in most other respects medieval armour would fit the modern man quite well. He might, however, be oppressed by its weight—the engraved suit in the Tower made for King Henry VIII weighs 63 lb. 11 oz. without the gauntlets. The armoured knight of the later middle ages clearly had more to fear from suffocation or exhaustion than from blows of lance or sword.

II. MEN AND MONEY

A fiddler, a ratcatcher, a Cheapside raker,
A rider, a rope-seller, dish-selling Rose,
Godfrey of Garlickhithe, Griffin of Wales;
And a heap of upholsterers, early assembled,
Gave Glutton, with glad cheer, a treat of good ale.

> LANGLAND: *The vision of William concerning*
> *Piers Plowman* (14th cent.).[2]

Then went I forth by London Stone,
Thrwghe out all Canwicke [Candlewick] Strete;
Drapers to me they called anon,
Grete chepe of clothe they gan me hete.
Then came there one and cried, 'Hot shepes fete!'
'Rushes faire and grene!' another gan to grete.
Both melwell and makarell I gan mete:
But for lacke of money I myght not spede.

> ANON: *The London Lickpenny.*[3]

There is a great difference between the company depicted by Chaucer in the Tabard Inn in Southwark and the miscellaneous people so vividly described by Langland in a tavern of a much

---

[1] See the Petition of the Joiners, Painters, and Lorimers against the Saddlers, in *Calendar of Letter Books* (E), 1327.

[2] Ed. and modernized by Prof. W. Skeat. London, 1922, p. 80.

[3] There are several versions of this work, which has been (erroneously) ascribed to John Lydgate. This rendering is from the Brit. Mus. MS. Harley 542, fo. 102 ff. Printed by H. S. Bennett: *England from Chaucer to Caxton*. London, 1928, p. 127.

THE TOWER OF LONDON

The Craftsman

LONDONERS AT WORK
AND PLAY

A Tournament

Armourers

The Bakehouse

Children's Pastimes

lower and coarser type. Chaucer's pilgrims are, as Blake once said, 'characters which compose all ages and nations'. Langland's low-life Londoners consist of street cleaners, rat-catchers, and low-grade workmen of various crafts. Not all of them are London born, but it is in London that they find their livelihood. Some might be runaway villeins, some might well have Lollard sympathies; all would welcome the anonymity they could find in a great city and scratch a living there by rough manual work. Some craft gilds refused as members those of servile birth, but were ready to make use of them as casual labourers. The common belief that a serf could secure his freedom by remaining unmolested in a borough for a year and a day was not always true,[1] although he would find a measure of toleration in most towns.

A Cheapside rakyer, more or less contemporary with Piers Plowman's boon companion, who made a practice of pushing the dung and filth from his own ward into the neighbouring one of Coleman Street, was prosecuted for his anti-social activity;[2] he and the Billingsgate man said to be 'a common dicer and nightwalker' and 'a corrupter of the wives, daughters, and maidservants of his fellow citizens'[3] are of the very clay of Langland's low-life Londoners. There were also rogues of great ingenuity, who flash for a moment through the records and do much to illuminate the dark places of London life in Chaucer's day. There was William who pretended to be a serjeant and arrested two bakeresses from Stratford who were constantly in trouble for selling short-weight loaves; he let them go with a warning, after they had paid him a fine. Alice, an ale-wife who laid a false bottom in her quart pot, sealing it with pitch and decorating the surface with sprigs of rosemary, found herself set on the 'thewe', the special pillory for women, with her fraud exposed beside her. Again, there were the two able-bodied men who pretended to have lost their tongues and worked on the charitable impulses of passers-by, 'making a horrible noise, like unto a roaring'.[4] These two also were set in the pillory—on three different days for an hour at a time.

[1] H. S. Bennett: *Life on the English Manor*. Cambridge, 1937, pp. 297–302.
[2] *Calendar of Patent Rolls*, 1381–1412, p. 71.
[3] Ibid., 1363–81, p. 139.
[4] These cases, from the fifteenth-century *Letter Books* (G and H), are included in Riley's *Memorials of London Life*, etc.

3

Another woman, not fraudulent but a virago, was made to stand in the thewe as a common scold. Apparently she had greatly molested her neighbours by her malicious words, 'sowing envy among them, discord and ill-will, and repeatedly defaming . . . and backbiting many of them, sparing neither rich nor poor'.[1] It is difficult to feel sympathy with this offender; on the other hand it is hard not to be attracted by the 'common bawd' who had the appropriate name of Joan Jolybody.[2]

It has been remarked that the importance of London is nowhere better shown than in the fact that all moneyers had to go to London for the dies with the King's image used in striking the silver pennies that were the universal coins of the middle ages.[3] There was, however, still a certain amount of barter, or payment in kind. For instance in 1360 the Guildhall Archives show that a certificate was issued declaring that Walter de Bixtone had received in part exchange for his barrel of 'wyldewerk' (the fur of wild rabbits?), as approximately half the value, a cross of alabaster and silver, a chess-board and pieces, a breast-plate and 'other arms of iron'.[4] From about the time of Edward III the dependence for capital upon foreign merchants, which had been so marked a feature of earlier trade, had greatly diminished and English dealers were becoming rich enough to provide and equip their own ships.[5]

A very difficult matter in medieval times was the recovery of lost or stolen property. The surprising thing is not that so much was lost as that such a high proportion of the stolen goods was found. John atte Wharf, a citizen of London, sought his linen and woollen cloths, 'pots, pails . . . basins, and other things of great value' in many towns before he located them at St. Albans, but he got them all back in the end.[6] Runaway servants were often at fault, as was Margaret de Marcherne who decamped to Oxford with her master's silver spoons, and other goods to the value of £10,[7] or the pewterer's servant Agnes, who broke open his

---

[1] In 1375.
[2] In 1420. *Calendar of Plea and Memoranda Rolls*, 1413–37. Ed. A. H. Thomas. Cambridge, 1943, p. 124.
[3] D. M. Stenton: *English Society in the Early Middle Ages*, pp. 159–66.
[4] *Letters from the Mayor and Corporation of the City of London, c.* 1350–70. Calendared by R. R. Sharpe. London, 1885, no. 229 (p. 105).
[5] G. H. Unwin: *The Gilds and Companies of London*. London, 1908, vol. i, p. 78.
[6] *Calendar of Letters from the Mayor and Corporation*, no. 39 (p. 21).
[7] *Ibid.*, no. 83 (pp. 40–1).

coffers while he was away at the Fair of St. Ives and fled to Dublin with all his gold and jewellery, clothes, linen, and two amber rosaries.[1] A number of these objects seem to have been recovered in due course, but not many were so promptly found as the countryman's hood in the *London Lickpenny*. This was stolen in Westminster and the owner recognized it the same day exposed for sale on a stall in Cornhill.[2]

London merchants were greatly incensed when their goods were seized in other towns on suspicion that they had been stolen; and they complained very bitterly. A letter was sent to the sheriffs of Cambridge and Huntingdon on behalf of a London fishmonger, three of whose horses ('one being white, another black, and the third bay') had been seized from the hands of one of his servants.[3] The following year two hireling horses, together with their saddles and bridles, were arrested in Cambridge, and letters had to be sent to the mayor and bailiffs before the owners could recover them. In Reading also two young horses that had been hired from a London 'hakeneyman' were thought to have been stolen.[4] Goods, too, might be summarily taken from their owners, as were the coverlet, pair of sheets, linen cloths, shoes, and hoods belonging to Gilbert the servant of a prominent London citizen, the Mayor of Guildford having taken the view that Gilbert was 'disloyal and of a bad character'.[5]

Housebreaking was more difficult than casual pilfering, and was not lightly undertaken. Most famous of all medieval burglaries is the one that took place at Westminster Abbey in 1303;[6] and since most of the stolen property was afterwards recovered from different parts of London, it may be claimed as in part the City's concern. The culprit was named Richard Podelicote, or Pudlicott, who had originally been a clerk but preferred to act as an itinerant dealer in wool, cheese, and butter. He had a real grievance, since he had been imprisoned in Flanders for debts incurred there by Edward I, and on his escape had failed to secure redress from the

---

[1] *Calendar of Letters from the Mayor and Corporation*, no. 138 (p. 63).
[2] H. S. Bennet: *England from Chaucer to Caxton*, p. 128.
[3] *Calendar of Letters from the Mayor and Corporation*, no. 274 (p. 131).
[4] *Ibid.*, no. ii, 8 (p. 140); no. 179 (p. 83).
[5] *Ibid.*, no. 275 (p. 131).
[6] Recounted by Prof. T. F. Tout at Manchester on 20 January 1915, and printed in the *Bulletin of the John Rylands Library* in October of that year. Some inaccuracies have been corrected in J. G. Noppen's *Royal Westminster*, London, 1937, pp. 57–60.

King's Court at Westminster. Podelicote determined to help himself to some of the valuable plate stored in the Chapter House. He found an open window, swung himself in by the window-cord and out by the same means, having picked the lock of the refectory and taken six silver cups and thirty silver spoons. After selling his booty and living on the proceeds for nine months, Podelicote persuaded the Abbey Sacrist, the Keeper of the Palace and his deputy, and a craftsman to make the necessary tools, to join in a new enterprise. This was to break into the crypt through the outside wall and steal the treasure stored there: the task took weeks of endeavour but was at last successful. The King, Edward I, acted with the greatest energy as soon as news of the crime was brought to him in Scotland; he sent out writs and directives in all directions and Podelicote was caught and hanged, with five accomplices. Those who had accepted some of the treasure were naturally very frightened and got rid of it as best they could. A linen-draper who had received a pannier-full from one of the monks gave it to a young shepherd to hide in the fields of Kentish Town,[1] a fisherman caught in his net a silver goblet that had been thrown into the Thames, and finally, the inventory was all but complete.

After all these evidences of fraud and duplicity, it comes as something of a shock to find that 'conscience-money' has an older history than might be supposed. Among the London Bridge records[2] of the early fifteenth century is an entry concerning five shillings paid to the wardens 'by a certain unknown man from a movement of conscience' in settlement of an old debt. There is, however, no reason to suppose that the action of this unknown is any less typical of the times than the deceits and robberies we have had occasion to mention: as always, the records are silent about all those who paid their debts honourably, kept their word, and gave good value in services and goods.

[1] Noppen: *op cit.*, p. 60.
[2] In the Guildhall archives. See *Transcripts of the Bridge House Rentals*, 1404–21, p. 139.

III. THE SCAVENGERS

And whereas the watercourse of Walbrook is stopped up by divers filth and dung thrown therein by persons who have houses along the said course, to the great nuisance and damage of all the city . . . punishment may be inflicted upon the offenders . . . But it shall be fully lawful for those persons who have houses on the said watercourse, to have latrines over the course, provided that they do not throw rubbish or other refuse through the same, whereby the passage of the said water may be stopped.

Ordinance of 1383, from *Letter Book* (H).

In 1421 William atte Wode is presented '*for making a great nuisance and discomfort to his neighbours by throwing out horrible filth, on to the highway, the stench of which is so odious that none of his neighbours can remain in their shops*'.

Plea and Memoranda Rolls, 1413–37.[1]

The term 'scavenger' is used today in a limited or specialized sense; in the middle ages it covered a wide range of duties and the London scavengers were responsible officials of very considerable importance. Originally they were customs officers, in the same category as Chaucer, on duty at the hithes and quays to inspect the unloading and unpacking of imported goods. Next, they were asked to supervise the cleaning of the streets, then the condition and repair of the pavements, and finally they were held responsible for precautions against fire in the construction of new buildings.[2] In the latter part of the fourteenth century there is mention of a new official, the Serjeant of the Channels, who first appears in the *Letter Books* in 1385; his function was to survey the streets and lanes of the whole City, and he was given power to fine defaulters. But the scavengers continued to control all arrangements for safety and cleanliness; they were responsible to the Aldermen of the wards and ultimately to Common Council and to the Lord Mayor himself.

Householders were expected to collect their own slops and filth and carry them to the gutter or kennel that ran down the middle of the street, but it was natural enough for dwellers on the upper floors to empty slops out of the windows to the peril and discomfort of passers-by. Complaints of this practice were still being

---

[1] Translated from the French. See *Calendar, etc.*, Ed. A. H. Thomas. Cambridge, 1943, p. 129.
[2] E. L. Sabine: 'City Cleaning in Medieval London', *Speculum*, January 1937, p. 22, n. ix.

made in the seventeenth century, so it is not surprising that many offenders were presented on this charge all through the middle ages. In the widest streets there might be a gutter on either side and some of the dirt would be washed away by rain water from the roofs, but with kitchen garbage helping to cause obstruction, dwellers at street level often found a foul flood running in to their houses by the door: many of them put up wooden boards for protection as they still do in low-lying country districts today.

By the fourteenth century there was at least one public latrine provided for each of the city wards, and the scavengers had to see that these were kept in working order. Two complaints that occurred within three years are typical of many more: one concerned the common latrine at Baynard's Castle, the other that in Ludgate ward. The first was 'very ruinous', and watermen had apparently fastened their boats to one of its posts, so that it had become very shaky, and persons unnamed had made great heaps of firewood on either side of the frail structure.[1] The privy of Ludgate, however, was in even worse case; it is described in the Plea and Memoranda Rolls as 'ful defectif and perlus, and the ordur therof rotith the stone wallys and makith other while an orrible stench and foul sight, to grete disese and . . . a desclaunder to all this citee . . . and oft hit hath be presentyd and no remedye yit is ordeined.'[2]

The unsatisfactory condition of the latrines and the open sewers running through the streets were the prime cause of the stench that became insupportable in hot weather, but the disposal of other sorts of rubbish added to the scavengers' difficulties, and had it not been for the kites and crows that carried off and consumed great quantities of offal, the street cleaners would have been powerless to deal with the problem.

Another bulky although comparatively harmless obstruction was formed by the rushes which were thrown out of the houses when floor coverings became too matted and sticky to be of further use. More troublesome were the dung heaps and dirty straw from the stables, for these sometimes completely blocked the narrow lanes leading to the Thames, and in this region of the

[1] In 1421. *Calendar of Pleas, etc.,* 1413–37, p. 132.
[2] Printed in *A Book of London English, 1384–1425.* Ed. R. W. Chambers and M. Daunt. Oxford, 1931, pp. 134–5.

waterfront were kept not only horses but also cattle, pigs, and poultry. There was builders' rubbish too, old laths, rotten wood, decayed plaster, and the earth from excavations. Most offensive of all were the rejected offal thrown out by the butchers and the mounds of stale fish from the fishmongers' stalls. It was difficult to know how to check this annoyance, and although tradesmen were not supposed to throw their garbage into the Walbrook, or the Thames, they used to do so secretly, generally by night. When, however, the cooks in Bread Street kept dung and garbage under their stalls, they were presented and duly fined.[1]

The only means of cleaning the streets of rubbish that had not been washed away, or slipped into the river, or carried off by birds of prey, was to rake it together and load it into tumbrils with high tail-boards[2] that could be taken down when the carts were tipped to empty the rubbish into the appointed laystalls in the suburbs. There were only twelve of these carts for the whole city,[3] but boats were sometimes used as well, to collect the rubbish from riverside districts. At times of crisis or epidemic sickness when this street-cleaning could not be carried out, matters became very bad indeed, as in 1349 after all arrangements had been dislocated at the time of the Black Death.[4] Normally, however, the dung-cart and dung-boat collections worked fairly well, and by the end of the century special days were appointed for rubbish to be put outside the doors for the rakyers to scoop up into their carts and trundle away to the laystalls.[5]

There was not much for the scavengers to do to the roads, beyond making sure that irresponsible people did not dig holes there for some purpose of their own, for in these early days highways were only of trodden earth or sometimes cobbled. A much more difficult task was to take precautions against fire that could spread with terrifying rapidity among the thatched timber-built dwellings. Efforts were made to force people to tile their roofs instead of thatching them with reed or straw, and fire-hooks were kept hanging in the churches ready for use in pulling

[1] *A Book of London English, 1384–1425*, p. 127.
[2] They had to be two and a half feet high.
[3] A. H. Thomas: 'Life in Medieval London', *Journal of the Brit. Arch. Assoc.*, new series, vol. xxxv (1929), p. 127.
[4] Sabine: *op. cit.*, p. 26. In the further outbreaks, from 1361 to the end of the century, the city and suburbs again became very foul.
[5] *Ibid.*, p. 38.

down woodwork that was already burning or—in extreme cases —to make a fire-break across which the flames could not leap. There were many disasters, with loss of life and property, but it was hard to persuade Londoners to change their traditional mode of building, and the scavengers found it impossible to enforce the tiling of roofs, despite the many ordinances that were issued.

There were many other kinds of transgressors against the common good. Sometimes their stalls impeded passers-by, or the signs projected too far and became a public danger. More culpable were those who kept their goods too long and allowed them to rot, for they might cause one of the outbreaks of disease that from time to time ravaged the City with terrible mortality. A minor nuisance was the cloud of feathers that filled the air when poulterers plucked geese and hens in the street; they were forbidden to do this in an ordinance set out in 1366, but paid small attention to the prohibition.

The fishermen who brought oyster boats to the wharves had a custom of fastening their ropes across the footway ('of evell will, and scornyng ye peple')[1] at such a height that passers-by were bound to trip over them, although repeated complaints were made against this practice. A sharp lookout was kept for misdoings by these oyster-boatmen, for they had a tendency to take their boats down river in the evening with an unsold catch and to return next day with a 'freshing' of new oysters among the old.[2] The work of overseeing the oystermen had been entrusted to John of Ely, and he appears to have delegated or farmed out this office to ignorant women who would not know a fresh oyster from a stale —or so the presentment stated.

Towards the end of the thirteenth century the smell from the Fleet river, or ditch, was so bad that the Carmelite Friars complained of it to the King. It was caused less by the fishmongers' dirty water, that was thrown there by permission, than by the habits of the butchers of the St. Nicholas shambles. These were allowed to use a special wharf, just opposite the Fleet prison, for cleaning their carcasses after each weekly slaughtering, and here they threw their offal into the water at ebb tide.[3] But the unfortunate prisoners in the Fleet became so ill from the stench that the butchers' privilege had to be withdrawn.

---

[1] *A Book of London English*, p. 128.   [2] *Ibid.*, p. 129.
[3] Sabine: *op cit.*, p. 35.

From these accumulated instances, selected from a great mass of presentments and ordinances, it might be argued that medieval London was consistently squalid, filthy and stinking, but the very fact that people protested against the abuses, that the nuisances were recognized as such, and that real efforts were made to correct them, proves that they were certainly not regarded as inevitable. If throwing out slops on to the heads of passers-by had been considered proper behaviour it would not have excited rebuke; 'Marjery', who was well-known also as a scold, was indicted less for her anti-social manners in speech than because 'by day and night [she] throws out of her house stinking ordure to the very great nuisance of the neighbours'.[1]

A proclamation, which was issued in both Latin and Norman French in the year 1375, appealed to everyone to keep the streets clean. This echoed the King's admonitions of some eighty years earlier, and it shows clearly that people were still allowing their pigs to wander in the streets and were still building projecting pent-houses and hanging dangerous signs. It must, however, be remembered that the population was still very small, and that many of the problems of health and sanitation that have so vexed later ages had not even begun to exist. There are many who deride William Morris's vision of medieval London as 'small and white and clean', but fewer who realize how wholesome it was compared with the Augustan age which has so dazzled posterity by its brilliance that it has obscured the horrifying conditions of the poor and inarticulate.

IV. THE PEASANTS' REVOLT

We be all come from one father and one mother, Adam and Eve; whereby can they say or shew that they be greater lords than we be, saving that they cause us to win and labour for that they dispend. They are clothed in velvet and camlet furred with grise, and we be vestured with poor cloth: they have their wines, spices, and good bread, and we have the rye, the bran, and the straw . . .

John Ball's speech to the Peasants, 1381.[2]

Froissart referred to John Ball as ' a crazy priest in the county of Kent' (although it seems that most of his preaching was done in the region of Colchester), and the words he attributed to him seem

---

[1] *Calendar of Pleas and Memoranda, etc.*, p. 127.
[2] As given by Froissart in his *Chronicles of England, France and Spain*, chapter ix. Trans. by Thomas Johnes. Everyman edn., London, 1906, p. 208.

more likely to be Froissart's own. There can be no doubt, however, that the sentiments were John Ball's, nor that he had an
inflammatory effect upon the minds of his hearers, most of them
already attuned to such teaching. The idea of revolution was already in the air; it was due mainly to the social changes of the
time that were sweeping over the continent of Europe. It is not
surprising that many Englishmen were affected. The causes of the
Peasants' Revolt in 1381 were nation-wide; it cannot be claimed
as a particularly 'London' happening, for districts as remote from
the capital as the Scottish border, Cheshire, Hampshire and Norfolk were simultaneously affected. It was in London, however,
that it came to its climax, and London people were to some extent
involved in the disturbance.

Resentment against the weakness and incompetence of the
central government combined with political, social and religious
grievances to induce a dangerous frame of mind among the
peasants and a smouldering disaffection that was quickly kindled
into flame by the imposition of the poll-tax. This tax was unwise,
unfair and exceedingly unpopular, since it pressed most hardly
upon the poorest and least resilient classes. Lollardy contributed
very little, if anything, to the Revolt[1] except in so far as Lollard
teaching affected men like John Ball who in turn influenced the
peasants to make their voices heard.

The fumbling and ineffective behaviour of their rulers tempted
the peasants to come to London to lay bare their grievances, and
it was through the treachery of two London aldermen that the
Kentish men were allowed to march across London Bridge, while
those from Essex surged in through Aldgate. The relationship
between Government and City at this time could hardly have been
worse, and there was also a bitter feud between the 'victuallers'
gilds and the 'non-victuallers' who were trying to break down the
formers' trade monopoly and the policy by which they excluded all
strangers.[2] A divided and subdivided London could not offer resistance and, indeed, many apprentices and others hastened to throw
in their lot with the rebels. The greater part of these came from the
lowest classes and had not any particular motive beyond getting

[1] A. R. Myers: *England in the Late Middle Ages*. London, 1952, p. 71.
[2] This conflict is admirably described by Miss Ruth Bird in *The Turbulent London
of Richard II*. London, 1949, *passim*.

rid of personal grudges and an obscure idea that they were striking a blow for freedom. One Roger Lyett, a man who was notorious for having set dangerous iron booby traps in the fields where the chancery clerks and apprentices were accustomed to play, had his property burned by the rioters and he himself was dragged from the sanctuary of St. Martin's-le-Grand and cruelly murdered.[1]

This violation of sanctuary was a very sinister manifestation of the lawless and leaderless condition of the rebels. As in the Evil May Day riots,[2] much of their fury was turned against peaceful foreign traders; seven Flemings were murdered at St. John's, Clerkenwell, and thirty-five more in St. Martin's Vintry.[3] The climax came when Archbishop Sudbury, whom only a few years earlier the Mayor and Commonalty had described as 'much beloved' when they begged the Pope not to translate him from the see of London to that of Worcester,[4] was seized in the Chapel of the Tower and dragged to his death. At the same time John Imworth, warden of the Marshalsea, was taken from Westminster, where he was clinging to the very pillars of St. Edward's shrine.

Both Court and City seemed powerless; the young King Richard II showed more initiative and certainly more courage than all the rest of his councillors in riding to meet the peasants and listening to their claims. Opinion is divided as to how Wat Tyler their spokesman met his death. Where discipline was so slight and hardly any of his followers knew where they were going or what they wanted, Tyler could not very accurately be called their leader, but there was no one else to fill this position. The facts are difficult to discern. Even those who were eye-witnesses could not agree upon what happened, but it was generally supposed that Wat Tyler had drawn a weapon—idly, perhaps—when he was speaking with the King, and that the Mayor of London, William Walworth, struck him down, declaring that he did so in the King's defence. The rebels were shocked and dismayed by the sudden violence, but at this crisis Richard II had a moment of greatness. Riding forward and striking an attitude, he promised the peasants that their demands would be met, and pardons given. He

---

[1] *The Turbulent London of Richard II*, p. 53.
[2] See below, Chapter Four, § iii.
[3] Isobel D. Thorneley: 'Sanctuary in Medieval London', *Journal of the Brit. Arch. Assoc.*, new series, vol. xxxviii (1930), p. 299.
[4] *Calendar of Letters from the Mayor and Corporation, etc.*, no. 211 (p. 299).

was only thirteen years old, and completely in the power of his Council, but the pledge was given in all sincerity. Afterwards, however, promises were broken on both sides; the rebels did not go quietly home, and vindictive measures were taken against them. The reaction came quickly and in the end the peasants found that far from improving their position their revolt had worsened it, so that their emancipation was delayed, not hastened, by these protestations.

London soon returned to normal. Signs of fighting were cleared away; the dead were buried. John of Gaunt returned to the city to view the ruins of the Savoy, lately his palace; Walworth was knighted; and the champion of the lesser gilds—John of Northampton—was elected Mayor in the following October. As far as London was concerned, this was one of the most important results of the rising, for John was a resolute and honest man, who during his two mayoral years did his utmost to break down the monopoly of the great capitalist traders. He would never have been made Mayor had not the city feared the weakening of authority should there be a disputed election following closely upon the Revolt. In the end, however, vested interests proved too strong for John of Northampton, and he was imprisoned until his patron, John of Gaunt, secured him a pardon.[1] The fact was that the Mayor of London had become an important character simply by virtue of his office and this became increasingly apparent in the following century, when the position was held by several citizens of outstanding ability.

[1] R. Bird: *op. cit.*, pp. 65-84.

Chapter Three

DICK WHITTINGTON'S LONDON

1. THE APPRENTICE

*There is a young man, a mercer in the Chepe, the which a(t)
Michaelmas purpose(s) to sett up a shop of his owne . . .
Jeffrey hath proferred to lend him for iiij yeare a hundreth merce
(marks), the which mony is ready in a bag if they agre.*

Plumpton Correspondence, 1464.[1]

O F all those who came as boys to London and stayed on to become illustrious citizens, none is more famous than Richard Whittington. Little is known of his character at first hand, and the only thing that most people remember about him—apart from his mythical cat—is that he was three times Lord Mayor of London. The layers of legend that have encased his memory cannot, however, obscure the fact that Whittington really was a very remarkable man and that he completely fulfilled the ambition that must have inspired many an enterprising apprentice upon his enrolment.

A son commonly, but not always, followed his father's trade. As a rule the father could help his boy, not only by teaching him the rudiments at an early age, but also by putting him with a good master and persuading his own gild to accept the lad as an apprentice. Without strong family connections, or influential backing, it was by no means easy to secure apprenticeship, and in the important trades practically impossible.

In the first instance, apprenticeship was instituted to make sure that craftsmen had the necessary skill and experience to turn out work of a really high standard. The craft gilds were very jealous of their good name and every member felt humiliated if one of their number produced a piece of work that was shoddy or incompetent. Ideally, this was admirable, but in practice the gilds became both tyrannical and restrictive; individuality was discouraged and enterprise virtually outlawed. The eager young apprentice, fired

---

[1] Ed. T. Stapleton. Camden Society, 1839, p. 11.

with zeal for his new job, soon found himself obliged to conform
to established practice and had to travel the long road to independence step by step. When he became a master he would still have
to accept without argument the decisions of the gild wardens: if
he defied them he faced the risk of expulsion and this would mean
ruin for himself and his household. Even if he left the town and
went elsewhere he would never be able to practise his craft as a
master; the most he could hope for, after due admission of his
fault, was to work as a hireling for some master-craftsman more
conformable than himself.

In London the gilds were particularly strong; by the fifteenth
century they were on the way to becoming the all-powerful City
Companies that held power and property to a formidable extent
well into the age of mercantilism.[1] In Dick Whittington's day,
however, they still retained much of their original character as
an association of craftsmen to promote the well-being of the
members and to maintain a high standard of workmanship. There
were, of course, battles between the various crafts; feuds and old
rivalries and sudden quarrels; but the pattern of these ran upon
familiar lines and seldom involved questions of principle.

The number of apprentices who could be admitted was limited
most strictly, and sometimes they were made to serve longer than
their normal term of seven years before they were presented to the
freedom. In 1496 the London Grocers ordained that boys must
serve ten years or more, so that at the age of twenty-four or five
they were still in their apprenticeship, although capable of doing
skilled work.[2] It has been estimated that not more than half of
the apprentices who were enrolled ever became freemen, and the
suggestion is that the boys who paid no premium for their articles
were never intended to qualify, but to stay on with their masters
as workmen or servants. In theory, however, there was nothing
to prevent any apprentice who had served his term, and could pay
his fee, from becoming a freeman.

Normally, the boys would be about fourteen years old, but
in the *Early Chancery Proceedings*[3] John Hill, draper, is found to

---

[1] G. H. Unwin: *The Gilds and Companies of London*, 2 vols. London, 1908, *passim*.
[2] S. Thrupp: 'The Grocers of London', in *Studies in English Trade in the Fifteenth Century*. Ed. E. Power and M. Postan. London, 1933, p. 255.
[3] Public Record Office, 19/466. See A. Abram: *Social England in the Fifteenth Century*. London, 1909, p. 144.

have enrolled an apprentice at the age of eleven, in defiance of the City ordinance that laid down thirteen as the minimum age. Girls, as well as boys, could be admitted to apprenticeship at a similar age. In early days it was sometimes customary to pay the premium in instalments; a woman—perhaps a widow—agreed in 1275 to pay the 20*s.* for the apprenticeship of her son William in four sums of 5*s.*[1]

The master of course had his obligations: to feed, clothe and teach the apprentices who had paid him their fee. One Fishmonger had to return the whole of the premium paid, less an agreed charge for board and lodging, on the ground that he had not properly looked after and instructed the boy.[2] It was, of course, to the master's interest to give his apprentice thorough instruction in his own craft, but he sometimes undertook to provide general education as well. The *Early Chancery Proceedings*[3] mention a London Haberdasher who took a boy for twelve years, agreeing to put him to school for two of those to learn writing and grammar. The *Plea and Memoranda Rolls*[4] also have a case of a master—in this instance a Barber—who had failed in such a duty. Here, the boy was taken away and apprenticed to another master.

Occasionally parents made difficulties, as did the father of Katherine Lightfoot, who complained that the girl had bound herself apprentice to a carpenter without his consent, although she claimed to be fourteen years old and so free from parental control. At this time, 1429, no birth certificate could be produced to settle the matter, so the Mayor had to send for Katherine to interview her and decide her age. The court determined that she must be younger than fourteen; she was therefore returned to the care of her father.[5]

Most master craftsmen were intent upon getting all the work they could from their apprentices, but not all of them treated the children harshly; often apprentices were accepted as part of the family and the relationship was very happy. Some masters continued to interest themselves in their apprentices long after they had become journeymen or set up shop for themselves. Often they

[1] *Calendar of Letter Books* (A) (1275–98). Ed. R. R. Sharpe. London, 1899, p. 5.
[2] Thrupp: *loc. cit.*
[3] P.R.O. 19/491.
[4] 1413–37. Ed. A. H. Thomas. Cambridge, 1943, p. 41.
[5] *Ibid.*, p. 229.

bequeathed the boys money in their wills. A stockfishmonger and
alderman named John Mitchell, who died in 1441/2, left five marks
'to Henry my apprentice' and a further sum to Phoebe his servant, after he had made provision for his widow and bequeathed
considerable sums to charities.[1]

Some boys hated their work and left it as soon as they could,
some ran away,[2] some died, but there cannot have been many who
had so strange an apprenticeship as did Simon Eyre. As an apprentice he served his master for seven years before he discovered
that the business was that of an upholsterer and not, as he had
imagined, of a draper. Eyre succeeded in transferring himself to
another master—this time a full member of the Drapers' Company
—but the matter was complicated and very expensive. In the end
he became rich and successful, owning a splendid house in
Lombard Street, and became Mayor in 1445.[3]

Occasionally a master pretended to a skill he did not possess in
order to secure a premium from a would-be apprentice: one such
instance occurred in 1422 when Alice, an embroiderer, induced
two girls from Northumberland to bind themselves to her for
seven years. As it turned out, Alice had no skill or knowledge, nor
was her husband the freeman he had represented himself to be,
and the young Northumbrians took the matter to court.[4]

Such imposition engendered bitterness and strife, and this was
increased by the attitude of certain of the masters who did everything in their power to try to prevent the journeymen from setting
up in business. Some even exacted an oath from their apprentices
that they would never do so. Among the *Early Chancery Proceedings* is a petition from an apprentice whose master brought an
action against him designed to prevent him from setting up his
own shop.[5] The master was a London Girdler (or girdle-maker),
member of a gild of some importance. The boy's petition was successful; he was more fortunate than many, for the masters could
—and often did—make unfair use of their influence to prevent

---

[1] From MS. collections made by F. J. Mitchell in 1893.
[2] During the twenty years 1350–70 we read of London masters trying to recover
their apprentices from Lincoln, Leicester, Winchester, Doncaster, Penrith, and even
as far as Ireland. These were all from different crafts. See *Calendar of Letters from
the Mayor and Corporation, etc.*, Ed. R. R. Sharpe. London, 1885, *passim*.
[3] Thrupp: *op. cit.*
[4] *Calendar Pleas and Mem. Rolls*, 1413–37, pp. 146–7.
[5] 67/169. See Abram: *op. cit.*, p. 121.

Judge More

St. Thomas More

Cecily Heron

John More

THE MORE FAMILY

THE ROYAL EXCHANGE

THE TRAIN BANDS

the loss of a skilled employee who might become a dangerous rival. In this and other ways the power of the masters, backed by the Corporation, waxed stronger and stronger as the century progressed.

In later centuries, when the problem of poor relief had become more acute, the parishes often found themselves responsible for the maintenance of boys or girls who had no parents or friends able to provide for them. Generally these were orphans, or their parents were in gaol, or they were found lost or abandoned in a starving condition. Those that were old enough were apprenticed to some trade and the premium was paid by the parish officer. Theoretically, this gave them a good start in life; in practice, however, they had small chance of gaining their freedom and almost certainly would have to continue all their lives as low-grade workers and household servants, with no one to protect their interests or to inquire about possible ill-treatment and under-nourishment. Occasionally a kind and charitable master might be found, but as a rule those who had room for a 'parish apprentice' were not the best craftsmen or the best characters, for any first-rate master would already have been approached by a number of parents anxious to put their children in his charge.

The worst and most startling instances of ill-treatment did find their way into the Courts, and during the eighteenth century there were several cases that resulted in the death of some of these friendless children in circumstances of cruelty and horror.[1] In the fifteenth century, however, London was still small enough and the trading community sufficiently compact to allow practical supervision, and the system of apprenticeship by the parish had not yet become general.

An order of the Mayor in 1479 sought to forbid 'all labourers, servants and apprentices of any artificer or victualler' to play tennis or football, or to use cards or dice, on pain of six days' imprisonment, but they were encouraged to practise shooting 'or other semblable games which be not prohibet nor forboden by the Kynge'.[2] A previous proclamation (1418) had forbidden them to take any part in Christmas mumming that involved the wearing of false beards or 'disfourmyd or colorid visages'.[3]

[1] M. D. George: *London Life in the Eighteenth Century*. London, 1930, chapter v, *passim*.
[2] *Letter Book* (L) (1461–97). Ed. R. R. Sharpe. London, 1912, pp. 163–4.
[3] Riley: *Memorials of London, etc.*, p. 669.

4

From this it would seem that the London apprentices were condemned to a life of austerity and dullness, but in practice things were very different. They might be forbidden to wrestle within the sanctuary of St. Paul's,[1] but there was merrymaking on the vigils of the great feasts, with dancing in the streets, and the houses decorated with flowers, and oil lamps burning throughout the night. On Midsummer Eve the well-to-do citizens set out tables with wine and bread and biscuits, and invited all passers-by to drink with them as they had done for generations past. If the prohibitions ever did have any weight, they were forgotten on such occasions, and young Londoners continued to dance and sing and play rough games as they had done in FitzStephen's day and would continue to do until Puritan efficiency firmly stopped their revels.

II. THE MERCHANT

Some cits have I seen, in the City of London,
Wear chains on their necks of the choicest gold,
Or collars of crafty work . . .

LANGLAND: *The Vision of William concerning*
Piers Plowman (14th cent.)[2]

God give you good winning.

Letter to John Sebol from his brother, 1471.[3]

The damsel with high-heeled boots, who romps her way through the traditional pantomime of 'Dick Whittington', bears about as close a relationship to that admirable citizen as does a Nordic Santa Claus in a London store to St. Nicholas of Bari. In only one respect did Richard Whittington conform to legend; he was, indeed, the third son of his father. Sir William Whittington was a country gentleman in Gloucestershire, and it was a normal thing for people like him to apprentice a younger son to a London Mercer. The connection was valuable, the boy was receiving an excellent start in life, and the close connection between trading interests and the landed gentry was being maintained.

Certainly there was nothing derogatory in alliance with trade; members of the aristocracy were bidding against each other to secure successful tradesmen as sons-in-law, and the rich widows

---

[1] *Memorials of London, etc.*, p. 580.
[2] Ed. and modernized by Prof. W. W. Skeat. London, 1922, p. 10.
[3] [Translated] *Calendar of Close Rolls*, 1468–76. London, 1953, p. 194.

of London merchants were matrimonial prizes for ambitious younger sons of noble families.[1]

In the following century the practice continued and developed; many employers grumbled because their apprentices were too independent and apt to be pre-occupied with aristocratic interests. As Philip Massinger has it in his play *The City Madam*,[2]

> . . . The masters never prospered
> Since gentlemen's sons grew 'prentices: when we look
> To have our business done at home, they are
> Abroad in the tennis-court.

Many of the most famous London merchants of the fifteenth century came from country stock; Stephen Browne was the son of a Newcastle merchant, and Robert and John Chichele, brother and nephew of the Archbishop, derived from Northamptonshire yeomen. Sometimes they rose from humble beginnings with great speed, but not so fast that they forgot their origins. Many successful countrymen who had done well in London kept up their connection with their native parish by founding local schools or chantries, and sometimes retired there to end their days.

Not many citizens could trace back their connection with London for more than one or two generations; few could claim, as did Thomas Usk, to be a Londoner born and bred—'forth growen in London, the place of his kindly engendure'.[3] In his maturity, however, London was less than kind, for Thomas was executed for treason in 1381 at Tyburn and his head exhibited at Newgate 'to the great shame of his family who inhabited thereby'.[4]

It is often forgotten that the traffic between London and the country was two-way: provincials came to the capital to seek their fortunes, and Londoners who had accumulated a little wealth tended to invest it in land, if possible in a small country estate. Even the lesser merchants, or well-to-do artisans, might hold property outside the city: in the Court Rolls of the Manor of

---

[1] On this point see the letters that passed between members of the Plumpton family concerning one Agnes Drayate, aged forty, who was 'beautiful, womanly, and wise', who had 20 marks of good land within three miles of the City, and was 'called worth £1000 beside her land'. *Plumpton Correspondence*, Ed. T. Stapleton. Camden Society, 1839, p. 125.

[2] Act v, sc. ii. *Massinger's Plays*, Mermaid edn., vol. i, p. 487.

[3] *A Book of London English*, p. 21.

[4] R. Higden: *Polychronicon.* Ed. J. R. Lumby. Rolls Series, 1882, vol. ix, p. 169.

Tooting Bec, butchers and carpenters are found among the tenants in 1440.[1] At a higher level, men like Thomas Knolles, Nicholas Wotton, and Geoffrey Boleyn, all of whom served at least one term as Mayor in the first half of the fifteenth century, bought lands in the country and founded families that soon became illustrious.[2] Essex in particular was sprinkled with Londoners' estates.

At this time the government of London was strongly oligarchic: this is a characteristic of other towns too, but perhaps the tendency to depend upon certain prominent families is more marked in London than elsewhere. Typical of these are the Chicheles, whose provincial origin has already been noted. These held sway for several generations.[3] The two younger brothers of Henry, Archbishop of Canterbury, were both prominent Grocers, Sir Robert becoming Mayor in 1411 and again ten years later, and William acting as Sheriff for a number of years up to his death in 1425.

It was William's son, John Chichele, who held the important office of Chamberlain in addition to serving as Sheriff. In 1443 his re-election as Sheriff was expected to be merely a matter of form, but when the time came 'a great number of inferior citizens who had not been summoned entered the gates of the Guild Hall, through the negligence of the gate keepers', and, 'with loud voice and uplifted hands'[4] clamoured for the election of another candidate. The interruption was as unexpected as unwelcome. The Mayor and Aldermen at once ordered the city serjeants to find out if all these voters had been properly summoned. The Mayor then produced a writ of the time of Edward II stating that only notable citizens should vote, and when it was found that the poorer citizens had not in fact been summoned, the re-election of Chichele went smoothly forward and the common citizens were discomfited and their right to vote denied.

The opposition to Chichele may or may not have been aimed at him personally; at all events his colleagues were determined to keep him within their ranks. His position in the City was unshaken,

[1] Abram: *op. cit.*, p. 97.
[2] C. L. Kingsford: *Prejudice and Promise in Fifteenth Century England*. Oxford, 1925, p. 121.
[3] *Stemmata Chicheleana*: Oxford, 1765, with additions by Dr. Buckler, pp. x–xiv.
[4] *Calendar of Letter Books* (K), pp. 286–7.

and there is evidence too that he stood well with the King and Queen. Henry VI and Margaret of Anjou, like all sovereigns who were chronically short of money, found it wise to show friendship towards the City magnates even if they did not go so far in this direction as did Edward IV. Both of them wrote letters to the Marquis of Ferrara on behalf of Reynold, the ninth of John Chichele's ten sons,[1] who proposed to go to Ferrara to study in the University. Indeed, their letters were so enthusiastic, and their praise of the young Reynold so high, that he was immediately elected Rector although he had not hitherto given any particular indications of ability.

Chaucer's merchant, who talked always of his winnings, was surely drawn from life; he must have been an intolerable bore, not necessarily typical of the best tradesmen of the day. Any business man who had not only made a great success of his own affairs but had reached the eminence of Sheriff or Mayor must have had far wider interests than merely buying goods cheaply and selling them as dear as possible. All the best and most liberal-minded of fifteenth-century Mayors left some permanent mark upon the city, although few of them became widely known outside its boundaries. Richard Whittington, however, had clearly become a legend within ten years of his death, for in the *Libelle of Englyshe Polycye*[2] he is named as the 'chefe chosen floure' and 'sonne [sun] of marchaundy'.

The writer was thinking, no doubt, of Whittington's great benefactions to London, but three English kings also had occasion for gratitude—Whittington personally made loans to Richard II, Henry IV, and Henry V. To the last of these he lent 700 marks (to be repaid from the wool customs) to help finance the French wars.[3] The City had already provided a loan of 10,000 marks on the security of 'a great collar of gold', for the same purpose.

One of Whittington's executors, who carried out his many charitable bequests—for the rebuilding of Newgate, both prison and gate,[4] almshouses for the poor, and conventual buildings at

[1] R. J. Mitchell: 'English Students in Early Renaissance Italy', *Italian Studies*, vii (1952).
[2] Written *c.* 1436. Ed. Sir G. F. Warner. Oxford, 1926, p. 25.
[3] On 2 September 1415. *Syllabus of Rymer's Foedera*, compiled by T. Hardy. London, 1873, p. 589.
[4] Whittington's prison was used until 1767.

Greyfriars—was John Carpenter, the famous Town Clerk of London, like him an enlightened philanthropist. His executors interpreted Whittington's wishes with great care; this is well seen in their furnishing of the Guildhall Library after it was rebuilt with his money. Desks, settles, and wainscotting were provided; Stow tells us there were twenty-eight desks there, and that Whittington's bequest also provided a pavement of 'hard stone of Purbecke' and glazed windows bearing his arms.[1] A librarian was chosen, and given the use of the garden; he was appointed for life so as to ensure him 'his lyflode housyng and easement'.[2]

Many people found 'easement' through Whittington's benevolence; of all countrymen who have come to London in search of fame and fortune none have more richly deserved success or carried it better; he has every right to be accepted as a national figure and needs no accretion of legend to emphasize his virtues.

III. THE LORD MAYOR

> . . . *with yn London he ys nexte unto the Kynge in alle maner thynge.*
>
> *Gregory's Chronicle,* 1463.[3]

It was, in the later middle ages, quite common for a successful Mayor to be given a second year of office, and Richard Whittington was not unique in being Mayor three times.[4] Indeed, Sir John Pulteney of the Drapers' Company was four times Mayor and was still a comparatively young man when he died during the Black Death in 1349; had he lived he might well have served yet another term.[5]

Reviling the Lord Mayor was an offence that could be purged only by a term of imprisonment, as a London vintner found when, 'quite losing his senses', he defied the Mayor's authority 'with abusive and horrible words'.[6] It should be noted that the title 'Lord' Mayor was used only intermittently in the fourteenth and fifteenth centuries and did not become regular until after 1545,

---

[1] John Stow: *Survey of London.* Ed. C. L. Kingsford. London, 1908, vol. i, p. 272.
[2] *Calendar of Letter Books,* (K), p. 295.
[3] *The Historical Collections of a Citizen of London in the Fifteenth Century.* Ed. Jas. Gairdner. Camden Society, 1876. p. 223. (Hereafter quoted as *Gregory's Chronicle.*)
[4] In 1397/8, 1406/7, and 1419/20.
[5] E. Power: *The Wool Trade in English Medieval History.* Oxford, 1941, p. 117.
[6] In 1355. See M. Phelps' translation in her *Extracts from Riley's Memorials, etc.* London, 1912, p. 17.

but the 'worship' due to his position was with him from the first.
John Russell, who was usher to Duke Humphrey of Gloucester,
drew up an order of precedence in which he set the Mayor of
London on a level with viscounts and mitred abbots, and it is
significant that his expenses allowance was never less than double
that of mayors in smaller cities.[1] He had a great position to maintain and his dignity was very dear to him. In the City he preceded
all other subjects of the King, even Archbishops and the royal
family, and as chief magistrate he also had strong judicial power.

The worship that was accorded to the Mayor was, then, no
empty thing, and it is not surprising that so high a position was
attractive to ambitious aldermen. During his year of office the
Mayor would hold a position of great responsibility and renown,
and ever afterwards—even if he were not elected for a second
term—some of the glory would cling to his name.

Any alderman who had served as Sheriff was eligible for
election: this had been decided upon by 1385, and within twenty
years it was customary for two such persons to be nominated by
the ancient assemblies now grouped together and known as
'Common Hall'. One of the two candidates was then selected by
the aldermen, but royal approval was necessary to confirm his
appointment. When Whittington was chosen for the second time,
in 1406, his rival was a goldsmith named Drew Barentyn. Common Hall chose these two men 'peacefully and amicably, without
any clamour or discussion', a fact remarkable enough to be
recorded in the official account. Whether the Mayor and aldermen
had rancorous discussion we do not know, for their debate was
behind closed doors, but they claimed, as was customary, to have
been guided by the Holy Spirit.

By the time Whittington came to serve his third term, in 1419,
he was already established as a man of ability, integrity, and great
benevolence. In taking a stiff attitude towards the Brewers'
Company he ordered them to mark their vessels properly and to
comply with the ordinances fixing the price of their liquor, and
forbidding them to go out into the country to buy up malt below
the London price.[2] This firmness was, of course, resented by the

[1] M. Bateson: *Medieval England*. London, 1903, p. 397.
[2] From the *Brewers' First Book*, printed in *A Book of London English*, 1384–1425.
Ed. R. W. Chambers and M. Daunt. Oxford, 1931, p. 141.

Brewers, who thought Whittington had an animosity towards them because (their clerk said) they had fatter swans at their feasts than he could get at the Guildhall. The Brewers fared better with two subsequent Mayors: William Crowmer (1423–4) was 'a good man and a lovynge to ye craffte of Brewers', and John Mitchell, elected in 1425, who was 'meke and softe to speke with', accepted presents at their hands and did the craft 'no harme ne desese'.[1]

This matter of bribery runs like a dark thread through the fabric of the records. 'Entreat the sheriff as well as ye can by reasonable rewards', wrote Sir John Fastolf to his man of business;[2] and when the suppliant Mayor of Exeter sought to win favour from the Lord Chancellor he plied him with presents of tench and pilchards expressly sent to London from the West Country.[3] Occasionally, bribes were offered not to obtain office but to avoid it. In 1416 there were some well-to-do citizens who wanted to evade responsibility, so they persuaded a crowd of people to make an uproar in the Guildhall and demand that so-and-so should be made sheriff or mayor in order to escape election to office themselves.[4] This might be described as inverted bribery; it is very rare in these early days, for most people were anxious to secure for themselves the power and perquisites of office.

The Lord Mayor's Show, with all its 'drumes and flutes and trumpettes blohyng',[5] did not reach its full flavour for another hundred years, although the custom of water pageants with decorated barges was established by the middle of the fifteenth century. The feast in the Guildhall, however, was already traditional. According to Fabyan's *Chronicle*, the Guildhall began to be 'new edyfied' in 1411 and transformed from 'an oylde and lytele cotage' into ' a fayre and goodly house'[6], Whittington and other citizens giving or bequeathing large sums of money towards its embellishment. It was not, however, at a Guildhall feast that the Lord Mayor suffered injury to his dignity, but at Ely House on the occasion of the admission of new members to the Order of the

[1] From the *Brewers' First Book*, printed in *A Book of London English*, 1384–1426, pp. 182, 189.
[2] *Paston Letters*, ed. Jas. Gairdner, 6 vols. London, 1904, vol. ii, p. 235.
[3] *Letters and Papers of John Shillingford, Mayor of Exeter*, 1447–50. Ed. S. A. Moore. Camden Society, 1871, pp. 9, 23.
[4] Riley: *Memorials, etc.*, p. 637.
[5] *The Diary of Henry Machyn*. Ed. J. G. Nichols. Camden Society, 1848, p. 294.
[6] R. Fabyan: *The New Chronicle of England*, Ed. H. Ellis. London, 1811.

Coif, in 1464. This banquet was given by the Serjeants at Law, and since Ely House was within the precincts of the City, the Mayor was of course the principal guest. He was Matthew Philip, a noted Goldsmith who had recently made the garter presented to Richard Duke of Gloucester. On arrival at the banquet the Mayor found that the seat of honour had already been appropriated by the Lord Treasurer, whereupon Matthew Philip left the hall 'with owte mete or drynke,' deeply displeased by his reception. The stewards, appalled at what had happened, hastened after the Mayor and tried to placate him with presents of 'mete, brede, wyne, and many dyuers soteltys' and begged him to return. This he would not do, but the story has a happy ending in that the Mayor and some of his aldermen made an excellent meal at home from tit-bits of the feast, cygnets and all, and many 'mervelyd how ale thynge was done is so schort a tyme'. The chronicler adds: 'And . . . the worschippe of the cytte was kepte, and not lost . . . And I truste that nevyr hyt shalle, by the grace of God'.[1]

As representative of the City, the Mayor, supported by his aldermen, took a leading part not only in civic functions, but on such occasions as royal funerals and weddings, and of course at the coronation of the sovereign. When Henry V was buried on 7 November 1422, with great solemnity, the Mayor headed the officials all robed in black, and members of the 'craftes of London' clad in black or russet.[2] Ten years later the City welcomed the young King Henry VI when he returned to London after his coronation in Paris. This time the mourning robes were exchanged for scarlet and blue, and there was much pageantry. Two 'olde men lyke hevynly folke, the whyche were Ennocke and Ely', saluted the Kyng 'whythe the wordys of grace and vertu', and maidens representing 'Mercy, Grace, and Pytte', who drew wine from the great conduit in Cheapside, offered it freely to all comers.[3]

Jack Cade's rebellion, in 1450, with the discord that followed, belongs rather to the history of England as a whole than specifically to London. Cade did secure support from Londoners, but it seems that this was due to general discontent with the existing

[1] *Gregory's Chronicle*, p. 223. The Lord Treasurer at his time was Lord Hastings, not, as is often stated, the Earl of Worcester. See R. J. Mitchell: *John Tiptoft*. London, 1938, pp. 93–4.
[2] *A Book of London English*, p. 146.
[3] *Gregory's Chronicle*, p. 174.

government and ought to be regarded as an early expression of
the Yorkist sympathy shown in the 'strange and wonderful bills
. . . set in divers places about the city'.[1]

There was strife and bloodshed in London at this time, as
William Gregory noted in his *Chronicle*: . . . 'they were ever
fyghtynge upon London Brygge, and many a man was slayne and
caste in Temys, harnys, body, and alle',[2] and Londoners could
not but be affected by the troubles of the times. The presence of
the bodyguards, or retainers, of the great nobles caused the citizens
to arm themselves secretly in case of need; the Mayor and Sheriffs
kept watch and rode about the city daily to make sure that peace
was kept.[3]

When civil war in fact broke out, most of the leading merchants
tended to be Yorkist in sympathy, but there was a strong Lancas-
trian element among the poorer citizens. These seem to have been
backed by Richard Lee who was Mayor in 1460, for he admitted
Warwick and his followers to the City with some unwillingness.[4]
The shops were shut and the great majority of citizens stayed
indoors for fear of becoming involved in a quarrel that was none
of their seeking.[5]

Once Edward IV was established upon the throne, and comparatively good order succeeded chaos and muddle, the citizens
gave him active support, and he won their goodwill towards his
marriage with Elizabeth Woodville by making five aldermen
Knights of the Bath. This certainly was, as Gregory said, 'great
worship in the City'.[6] The friendly relations, both personal and
political, that existed between King Edward and the chief citizens
of London persisted throughout his reign and were not disturbed
by Henry's transitory return to the throne in 1470. Typical of this
easy friendship was the hunting party at Waltham to which the
King invited not only Mayor and aldermen, but a number of the
lesser citizens as well. Each guest enjoyed good sport and a good
dinner, and carried home to his wife venison and wine as a present
from the King.[7]

---

[1] C. L. Kingsford: *Prejudice and Promise in Fifteenth Century England*. London,
1905, p. 168.
[2] *Gregory's Chronicle*, p. 93.
[3] *Chronicles of London*. Ed. C. L. Kingsford. London, 1905, p. 168.
[4] *Ibid*., p. 117.
[5] *Calendar of State Papers*. Milan, vol. i, p. 49.
[6] *Gregory's Chronicle*. p. 28.   [7] *Chronicles of London*, p. 189.

If Philippe de Commynes is to be believed,[1] Edward IV had more to offer the merchant's wives than wine and venison, and he says that they influenced their husbands to grant the King loans of money and loyal support against his enemies. This easy-going ruler, who could relax his dignity sufficiently to dine domestically with townsmen in their own homes, was astute enough to realize the value of such contacts and to foster them assiduously. Edward IV misjudged many situations and consistently underestimated his enemies, but he had a very sound judgement on the importance of the goodwill of the Mayor and aldermen of London.

IV. SHOPS AND HOUSES

[John Pekker, carpenter, to make a bay window] *yn the same fourme of werke of carpentrie as be the wendowes yn the new corner rente of the Chartre hous yn Cornhill of London with vj bayes like as it is yn the same rente with a vawte to be made be the same Carpenter underneth the same wendowe yn the said two other plain wendowes euerych of ij bayes yn the same same south side with lyntell abouen.*

Indenture for repairing the Brewers' Hall, 1423.[2]

John Pekker the carpenter came from Cambridge. He was brother[3] to another John Pekker, a vintner, who acted as surety for him, and, since Brewers and Vintners had close association, it can hardly be doubted that it was on his brother's recommendation that Pekker of Cambridge was given the work of repairing the Brewers' Hall. This building was, their clerk said, likely to fall down 'yn defawte of reparacion', and Pekker promised that he would undertake no other work until he had strengthened the rickety structure, inserted two great beams on the south side, and made bay windows to the requirements set out in his indenture. This was dated 8 June, and the time for completion was given as 14 August, part of the price being paid in advance. It seems that the work was finished punctually and to the Brewers' satisfaction, for they made the carpenter an additional payment above his charge, and gave him a gown of the Brewers' own livery as a practical reward and graceful compliment.

[1] *Mémoires*. Ed. J. Calmette. Paris, 1924, vol. i, p. 213.
[2] *A Book of London English*, p. 162.
[3] This habit of calling several members of the family by the same name became still more common in the sixteenth and seventeenth centuries. The authors give a number of instances in their *History of the English People*, London, 1950, p. 263.

The Brewers of London were good employers, and they were well served by their clerk, who kept most detailed accounts of the money spent and added personal touches that make them exceptionally interesting to the social historian. Moreover, these are some of the earliest records written in English—with occasional lapses into Latin or French—and so form a landmark in the history of the English language.[1]

When, in 1423, the Brewers decided to build an almshouse 'for powr Britheren Soosteren of ye craffte and Fraternite', very full accounts were kept of wages paid and materials used, so that a good idea can be formed of costs and conditions of labour at this time, and also of the general standard of living conditions. Wages ranged from the 8d. a day given to masons, and sometimes to carpenters,[2] to the 3d. that seems at this time to have been the standard labourer's wage. Plasterers, tilers, glaziers, and so on, generally had 5d. to 6d.: everyone expected his 'noonchyns' (mid-morning and mid-afternoon draughts of ale) to be supplied by his employer. Women, who were brought in to do the more menial cleaning work that was beyond the power or beneath the dignity of 'old Stephen' the regular cleaner, were also given ale.[3]

Very often wages were partly paid in kind, or special allowances were made. The masons who were working on London Bridge at almost the same time as those who were re-pointing the Brewers' Hall, were provided not only with gloves and boots, that were regularly repaired and oiled for them, but with hats as well. They were also given special rates for overtime.[4]

Wages in London were, it seems, considerably higher than elsewhere. A special rate might be paid to an individual, a highly skilled craftsman doing some particular job, as to Richard Russell who worked for nineteen days carving the angels and fixing them to the ceiling in Archbishop Chichele's new buildings at Lambeth. This work was done in 1434; it was so cold a winter that sixteen bundles of straw had to be bought to protect the new masonry against the frost. It is worth noting that among these English

---

[1] *History of the English People*, pp. 138–80.
[2] *Ibid.*, pp. 153, 157.
[3] *Ibid.*, p. 160.
[4] P. E. Jones: 'Some Bridge House Properties', *Journal of the Brit. Arch. Assoc.*, vol. xvi (1955).

labourers were two Dutchmen, specially employed as 'cement-makers' but given the same wages as the others.[1]

The Brewers' almshouse provided a chamber for each inmate, and a parlour is mentioned that was perhaps shared by several people.[2] We read of locks for the doors, and gardens allotted to individuals. The privy, which was later made more secure and provided with a new lead gutter, had its lock mended at the cost of 2*d.*, and for the price of one penny there was bought 'j Erthen potte, for to kepe ye water yn of ye privie yn an chaumber of ye seide Allmershous'.[3] This was generous provision for the Brewers' pensioners; these almshouses must have been model dwellings when they were built, and by current standards they offered a very high degree of comfort.

Much of the timber, the Baltic 'estrisshboard' (or deal) in particular, came from abroad, imported through the Hansa merchants.[4] Probably the glass also had to be brought from overseas. These two materials were the main components of the projecting bay windows that were the great feature of new building at this time, and were frequently inserted as improvements to the old. They illustrate the new tendency towards a more humane and leisured life, and the possibility of observing and sharing the life of one's neighbours instead of guarding fearfully against them.

Shopkeepers and their families lived mostly above—or sometimes below—the place of business, making their home among the stock-in-trade, but those who had succeeded in making good profits were putting the money into building 'fair houses'. These were still in the vicinity of their work, but thought was not now of convenience only; the new houses were to be comfortable and beautiful, and if they demonstrated their owner's wealth as well as his taste, so much the better for his business.

John Stow tells us in his *Survey of London*,[5] compiled towards the end of the next century, of the many grand houses built by merchants, who tended to congregate in certain districts as they had done in the days when their shops were only market stalls.

[1] D. Gardiner: *The Story of Lambeth Palace*. London, 1930, p. 53.
[2] *A Book of London English*, p. 155.
[3] *Ibid.*
[4] Members of the Hanseatic League, who had a monopoly of Baltic trade, with depots or 'factories' in many cities. In London their headquarters was the Steelyard. Sometimes they were known as Easterlings.
[5] Ed. C. L. Kingsford, 2 vols. London, 1908.

In Aldermanbury, for instance, 'be diuerse faire houses on both sides, meete for marchants or Men of Worship',[1] and he has a very interesting passage in his description of Fish Street where he traces the development from covered stalls made from movable planks on trestles to 'tall houses, of three or four stories in height'[2] where the Fishmongers dwelt in the reign of Elizabeth I.

One very handsome house in Harp Lane, at first a private dwelling, afterwards became the hall of the Bakers' Company. Here they dined and had their meetings from the year of its purchase, 1506,[3] until its destruction in the recent war.[4] The Bakers bought it from John Chichele the Grocer, whose activities as Chamberlain of the City have already been described. Here he lived, and fathered his family of twenty-four children, and entertained his friends in great style and comfort.

Some of these merchants' houses had private chapels[5] and gardens as well as several chambers clustered round the great hall that remained the centre of family life. The hall in the house of Stephen Browne, in Thames Street, measured 40 feet by 24 feet; others were content with halls less than half that size, but most had a small, snug parlour, with window seats at a convenient height, whence one could overlook the garden plot. Damask roses from this garden might stand in pots of earthenware, or in brass bowls from Dinant; boughs of greenery and bunches of herbs decorated the room and gave out a useful aroma. Cushions of skin and worsted hangings provided comfort and warmth, while the glazed windows let in a sufficiency of light through their latticed panes. Here the tired business man could relax when his day's work was done, and enjoy games or music in the company of his womenfolk, or simply sleep before the fire.

Few citizens were as wealthy as these merchant princes; most people had to be content with a few rooms over the shop, their goods stowed away in the vaults below. One of the Hustings Rolls of the thirteenth century mentions fifteen shop-fronts occupying a site of 150 feet: this was in the area between the Old Jewry and

---

[1] *Survey of London*, vol. i, p. 292.
[2] *Ibid.*, p. 346.
[3] S. Thrupp: *A Short History of the Worshipful Company of Bakers of London*. London, 1933, p. 163.
[4] W. Kent: *The Lost Treasures of London*, London, 1947, p. 93.
[5] C. L. Kingsford: *Prejudice and Promise, etc.*, pp. 138–9.

Ironmonger Lane,[1] and there must have been many in Whittington's day still built upon this scale. Artisans and labourers occupied even narrower quarters; for the most part they lived in one or two rooms in a tenement house generally known as someone's 'Rents'. Access to the upper floors would probably be by an outside ladder; this was common also in quite good houses. Internal staircases, spiralling their way upwards, were reserved for houses of the great.

Among the Bridge Records at the Guildhall there have lately been discovered some very interesting examples of pre-fabricated houses, that were erected at the turn of the century (in 1505) in Rood Lane.[2] Local bricks, made in Whitechapel and Limehouse, were used to build substantial walls on which the timber frames were set. These frames were made by carpenters at Maldon, Essex, and sent to London ready for erection. Presumably they came by water: since each of the four houses was three stories high, their transport must have presented something of a problem. Another instance of pre-fabrication is the storehouse that was 'framed', ten years later, at Charlwood, in Surrey; this was designed for the Bridge House at the end of London Bridge.[3]

When considering these London shops as dwelling-houses, their main purpose must not be forgotten. Here the goods were stored, displayed, and sold. In many instances they were made also on the spot, but as trade expanded and demand grew, shopkeepers tended more and more to include in their stock goods made wholly or in part by other craftsmen. Someone wrote of a Cheapside mercer in 1464 'what he is worth in goods I cannot wytt. Mercers deals nott all together with their owne proper goods'.[4]

Some of the fifteenth-century letters that survive in the Public Record Office and elsewhere throw strong light upon the relations between the London shopkeepers and their country customers. The Stonor papers are particularly rich in this material: at one time we hear of Dame Elizabeth Stonor unable to return home because she has no money to settle the small bills of tradesmen

---

[1] A. H. Thomas: 'Life in Medieval London', *Journal of the Brit. Arch. Assoc.*, new series vol. xxxv (1929), p. 125.

[2] P. E. Jones: 'Some Bridge House Properties', *Journal of the Brit. Arch. Assoc.*, vol. xvi (1955).

[3] *Ibid.*

[4] *Plumpton Correspondence*. Ed. T. Stapleton. Camden Society, 1839, p. 11.

who call upon her every day to ask for payment,[1] and then, in 1479, she received a most delightful letter from a London mercer named William Bradbury. He sent Dame Elizabeth 38 yards of green 'sarcenet', with a covering letter that has the true accent of salesmanship. Bradbury says that the stuff is well worth the 5*s.* a yard he is obliged to charge, for it is very fine in quality and will last her all her life and her child's after her, whereas an inferior material 'of 40*d.* or 44*d.* a yard' would not last for two seasons. 'Therefore for a little more cost me thinketh most wisdom to take of the best'.[2] He assures Dame Elizabeth that his advice is disinterested for he wins 'never a penny' in selling it to her. This mercer's letter might well have been written yesterday instead of nearly five hundred years ago.

[1] *Stonor Letters and Papers*. Ed. C. L. Kingsford. Camden Society, 2 vols., 1919, no. 229.
[2] *Ibid.*, no. 252.

Chapter Four

THOMAS MORE'S LONDON

1. THE INNS OF COURT

... Master More, being ... occupied in the study of the common laws, openly read in the Church of St. Lawrence in London the books of the said St. Augustine 'de Civitate Dei', to his no small commendation, and to the great admiration of all his audience. His lesson was frequented and honoured with the presence and resort ... of ... the chief and best learned men of the City of London.

NICHOLAS HARPSFIELD : *The Life and Death of Sir Thomas More.*[1]

The student in the Inns of Courts turns over 'Ployden' with more alacrity, and tugs with that crabbed study of the law, because he hopes one day to become a judge.

JAMES HOWELL : *Familar Letters, c.* 1646.[2]

ONE of the articles in Magna Carta directed that 'common pleas shall not follow our court but shall be held in some fixed place', and the Court of Common Pleas was in fact fixed at Westminster. That is, suits between subject and subject, concerning real property, would henceforward be heard in this Court and it would not be necessary to pursue the King to York, or Woodstock, or to one of his hunting lodges, before gaining a hearing. The author of the *London Lickpenny* made his way to Westminster Hall 'To a man of law to make my complaynt,' in the earlier half of the fifteenth century. He had little difficulty in finding a lawyer to attend to him, but unfortunately could not pay his fee—'I would gyve sylvar, but my purs is faynt'—so that the doleful refrain of his poem has to be:

> For lacke of money, I may not spede.[3]

This concentration of judges and lawyers led naturally to a demand for quarters within easy reach, and hostels began to spring

[1] Ed. E. V. Hitchcock, London, 1932, with notes by R. W. Chambers, who quotes this passage on p. 83 of his *Thomas More*, London, 1938.
[2] London, 1903, vol. iii, p. 136.
[3] H. S. Bennett: *England from Chaucer to Caxton.* London, 1928, p. 127.

up near the village of Holborn. 'Chancellors' Lane', which became Chancery Lane, led from this village to Fleet Street, and the Templars' Church and mansion were close at hand. It so happened that when the Templars were disbanded[1] lawyers from Holborn leased their riverside estate from the Knights of St. John of Jerusalem and formed societies of the Inner and Middle Temple. Other lawyers secured the Bishop of Chichester's palace in Chancery Lane, and set up their quarters there. Others, again, took over some of the Earl of Lincoln's property and founded 'Lincoln's Inn'. In the same way, 'Gray's Inn' was named from the Grey de Wilton houses which also came into the lawyers' hands.

The distinction between the Middle and Inner Temple was already clear by 1440, for in that year, on All Saints' Day, one Robert Repps urges John Paston to 'resorte ageyn on to your college, the Inner Temple'.[2] There were other Inns of Chancery, such as Furnival's, which for some reason failed to achieve permanent renown. Thavie's Inn, however, went on into the seventeenth century and is associated with the names of several famous lawyers. The charges made by the great Inns were very high, and various lesser ones offered accommodation at lower rates, but failed to gain more than a temporary footing and were soon lost to sight. It has been reckoned[3] that during the Tudor period there were no fewer than a thousand students resident during term-time in the Inns of Chancery, and nearly as many in the four Inns of Court. Here, the new students learned the elements of jurisprudence and practised nightly their exercises in mooting and in disputation.

The deep interest taken in legal matters by ordinary people has often been remarked, and the easy familiarity with legal processes that attracted families like the Pastons and the Plumptons into litigation with their neighbours. A less well-known instance, showing good knowledge of procedure, is an ingenious fraud that was exposed in 1423/4. To give his forgery an air of verisimilitude, Thomas Corbet had sealed his parchment with 'a seele of Armes ... pulled from an olde dede, And, to blynde the people ...

[1] That is, their lands were expropriated.
[2] *Paston Letters*, ed. Jas. Gairdner, no. 27.
[3] R. O'Sullivan: *Edmund Plowden, 1518–85*. Cambridge, 1952, p. 3.

endorsed hit on the bakke as it hadde be enrolled in the Kynges-
bench'. Corbet's professional skill did not in this case save him
from exposure and he had to stand in the pillory to expiate his
deceit.[1]

This enthusiasm for legal studies and for the language, idioms,
and processes of the law shows itself in many of the young noblemen and country gentry who came to the Inns of Court for their
education. These seldom had any serious idea of practising as
lawyers, but found the life congenial and the company pleasant,
and the legal knowledge that they absorbed almost incidentally
did in practice prove very useful when they returned to their
homes and were called upon to act as justices of the peace. The
social life at the Inns was delightful, a prolongation of the most
agreeable elements of life in an Oxford or Cambridge college, with
better quarters, better fare, and more scope for acting and dancing.
The masques acted by the 'young active gallant gentlemen'[2] of
the four chief Inns were often very ambitious, as on the occasion
of the marriage of Princess Elizabeth, daughter of James I, in
February 1613. The celebrations included several masques, and
in devising them the actors had employed 'the best wits and the
skilfullest artisans' to create the necessary properties and to compose delicate music. Edmond Howes described the scene at length,
with the Shrove Monday procession that included the Master of
the Rolls, an 'antic or mock-masque of baboons, attired like
fantastic travellers in a very strange and confused manner, riding
upon asses or dwarf jades', and other masquers disguised as
Barbary princes with every extravagance of jewels and gold
embroidery.

In some cases plays were written specially for the students to
act; indeed, it has been suggested[3] that Shakespeare's *Troilus and
Cressida* was written for the students of the Middle Temple and in
fact played by them.

It is not surprising that there were complaints from the genuine
law students; these social occasions were so frequent and so
costly that the judges said the Inns were being disparaged and

[1] *A Book of London English.* Oxford, 1931, pp. 104–5.
[2] E. Howes: *Annales*, 1615. Quoted by J. Dover Wilson: *Life in Shakespeare's
England.* Cambridge, 1915, pp. 198–202.
[3] By Dr. Leslie Hotson. See his essay 'Love's Labour's Won', in *Shakespeare's
Sonnets Dated.* London, 1949. The authors owe this reference to Mr. Ivor Brown.

turned 'from Hospitia into Diversoria'.[1] Sometimes an important personage thought (often with good reason) that he was being satirized by the masquers—Wolsey was deeply offended by a Gray's Inn masque in 1521, and the author and chief actor were sent to the Fleet Prison. Students might also behave obnoxiously towards the City authorities, and at all times tended to show arrogance and extreme independence. Perhaps the climax was reached when there was a serious fire in the Temple in the year 1678. The fire broke out in Pump Court and spread rapidly, for there was a hard frost to make the woodwork dry and brittle, and all the water was frozen. It was only twelve years since the ravages of the Great Fire, and the Lord Mayor and sheriffs hastened to the scene in understandable alarm. But the members of the Inner Temple confronted the Mayor and refused him admission, preferring that their Inn should be burnt rather than accept the City's help.[2]

The high spirits of the students led to some flouting of discipline, but this was maintained at a fairly high level by the Masters of the Bench. They composed strict rules concerning dress, forbidding extravagances of shape and colour, and such fripperies as velvet shoes, double cuffs on shirts, and feathers and ribbons on the cap. A first offence occasioned a fine of 3s. 4d., a second meant expulsion. Nor might the students carry swords or rapiers when in Commons, and no one was allowed a beard of more than three weeks' growth.[3]

There were of course many serious students, like Thomas More, who desired a genuine career as a lawyer and hoped for real distinction in civil life. For them, previous experience at a university was unnecessary, and the Inns of Court had their own examinations by which a student could become a barrister: to do this he would not only have to pass rigorous tests but also defend a thesis.[4] The reputations of the different Inns varied according to the brilliance and lucidity in exposition of leading lawyers attached to them, who acted as Readers or 'Preachers'. Lady Harley in 1641 wrote to her son Edward that she was glad he had 'changed

[1] This was in 1630. Sir Plunket Barton, C. Benham, and F. Watt: *The Story of the Inns of Court.* London, 1924.
[2] *Ibid.*, p. 202.
[3] R. O'Sullivan: *op. cit.*, pp. 97–8.
[4] R. W. Chambers: *Thomas More.* London, 1938, p. 67.

the Tempell to Linconsine, because theare is a better preacher'.[1]
This anxious mother was less glad of her son's change of quarters
only a fortnight later, when she found that his chambers were
not in Lincoln's Inn itself but in 'the laine over against it; those
lains weare the unsweatest places in Loundoun, and allways the
sikness is in those places': for this reason Lady Harley wished that
'Ned' would change to Gray's Inn for that, she said, was 'a fine
place'.[2]

The reputations of the Inns of Court might vary relatively to
one another, from decade to decade, but their general standing
was unassailable. Their fortunes might vary too; Gray's Inn might
be suspected of Popish tendencies and the harbouring of Catholic
priests, a censorious foreign visitor might complain of a filthy
tablecloth in the hall of the Middle Temple,[3] but they upheld
traditions that were venerable when the Tudors were petty Welsh
squires, and the aristocracy of the Law was more to them than
changing dynasties.

II. THE FAMILY

> *. . . And seeing you have at Chelsea a right fair house, your
> books, your gallery, your garden, your orchard, and all other
> necessaries so handsome about you, where you might in the com-
> pany of me your wife, your children, and household, be merry, I
> muse what a God's name you mean here still thus fondly to
> tarry.*
>
> Dame Alice More to her husband in the Tower prison.[4]

Dame Alice, Sir Thomas More's second wife, had a sharp tongue,
but she was a very efficient housekeeper. The household at Chelsea
had expanded to include as well as More's own children, William
Roper who had married the cherished eldest daughter, his son
John's girl-wife,[5] Margaret Gigs the foster-child, and a variety of
tutors and secretaries, attendants, servants, and the fool Henry
Pattenson. It was a patriarchal assembly, and all visitors to the

---

[1] *Letters of the Lady Brilliana Harley.* Ed. T. T. Lewis. Camden Society, 1854,
p. 127.

[2] *Ibid.*, p. 130.

[3] Zacharias Conrad von Uffenbach: *Travels in England in 1710.* London, 1934,
p. 57.

[4] William Roper: *The Life of Sir Thomas More.* Ed. E. V. Hitchcock. London,
1935.

[5] Anne Cresacre; she was betrothed to John More in 1527, before she was fifteen,
and married him two years later. Chambers: *Thomas More*, p. 184.

Chelsea house were astonished by the harmony that prevailed there and the delightful conversation and civilization of all its members. These visitors included some of the greatest scholars in Europe, and they were received immediately into a congenial atmosphere of intelligence, deep knowledge, wit and merriment.

Sir Thomas frequently rose at two in the morning for study and religious contemplation, and the hair shirt he always wore was a symbol of the austerity of his private life, but no one knew better how to take part in family jokes, agreeable music, and charades or plays. Ball games Sir Thomas did not care for, and he would not allow even the youngest of his circle to play at dice or cards. In the London home at Bucklersbury their quarters had been cramped, but when More moved to Chelsea his family were able to enjoy all the country pleasures, gardening and so forth, and to increase their number of pets. Even their animals seem to have been more intelligent than other people's: Erasmus reported that the family monkey had prevented a weasel from breaking into the rabbits' hutch, and drew from this exploit the moral that monkeys are fond of rabbits.

It would be a mistake to suppose that the household of Sir Thomas More was typical of his times. The household first at Bucklersbury and later at Chelsea shows an ideal translated into practice, and we are fortunate in being able to reconstruct it in such detail from the writings and letters of More and his circle of friends. Other people had intelligent children, other children learned Latin, kept rabbits, observed their religion with genuine devotion, and bore cheerfully the scolding and discipline of a strict stepmother, but no other household can show so complete a picture of daily life in the first half of the sixteenth century.

There was nothing particularly distinctive about the Mores' diet or manner of dress. Sir Thomas cared little for appearances and did not encourage his children to take much interest in fine clothes. Nor did he care for elaborately cooked food and strong drink, preferring milk, fruit, and eggs, with small beer or water, to wines and choice meat. According to his own account, in a playful letter to his children,[1] he fed them with fruit and cakes (and beat them —if he had to—with peacock's feathers). More had lived in the King's court, at Lincoln's Inn, New Inn, and at Oxford—that is

---

[1] Quoted by Chambers: *op. cit.*, p. 179.

to say, at four different levels of diet, and when he set up house on a small income, before preferment had come his way, he chose to live at Lincoln's Inn standard for the first year. If this could not be maintained, they would have to descend 'to New Inn fare, wherewith many an honest man is well contented'. Should they find themselves unable to afford this, then they must descend to Oxford fare,[1] where dinner might consist of broth and oatmeal and a penny piece of beef among four persons.

More's four children[2] all grew up, and in this the family showed some singularity. There were few households that did not at some time or other mourn the loss of a baby or small child unable to face the rigours of its early upbringing. There is nothing to show that infantile mortality during the sixteenth century was any greater in London than anywhere else in the country, but it was certainly no less. A citizen and merchant tailor of Southwark, in designing his own tombstone, required an inscription to be carved on the marble slab 6 feet by 4 feet that was to be erected in the church of St. John the Baptist. 'And under this scripture fyve men children and fyve women chyldren' were to be shown: ten of his children who had predeceased their father;[3] this does not seem to be an exceptional case. Generalizations on this subject are unsatisfactory where the evidence is so sparse. The impression remains, however, that the death rate was very high.[4]

There were renewed complaints at this time that London tradesmen were marrying their children into the families of country gentry; certainly fathers tried to do the best they could for the security of their children and the furtherance of their family fortunes. More himself chose his sons-in-law with great shrewdness, and his one daughter-in-law came from a family with a far more distinguished pedigree than the Mores'. This alliance between tradesmen and gentry seemed to most men natural and desirable, but there was always a minority to raise objection, which in Puritan times became much more pronounced or at any rate more vocal. Robert Crowley, who today might be called a

---

[1] Chambers: *op. cit.*, p. 67.
[2] Margaret was born in 1505, Elizabeth in 1506, Cecily in 1507, and John in 1508 or 1509.
[3] The will of John Aunsell of London, 9 October 1516. P.C.C. Holder 23.
[4] Some contemporary instances are given by R. J. Mitchell and M. D. R. Leys: *A History of the English People*. London, 1950, p. 208.

'sour-puss', wrote in *The Voyce of the Last Trumpet* (1550) his
advice to London merchants:

> Let it suffice the to mary
> Thy daughter to one of thy trade:
> Why shouldest thou make hir a lady,
> Or bye for her a noble warde?
>   And let thy sonnes, euery chone,
> Be bound prentise yeres nine or ten,
> To learne some art to lyue vpon:
> For why should they be gentelmen?[1]

Those who had risen higher in the social scale did not necessarily forget their old family connections. The London Grocer's
apprentice, George Stoddard, who lived in the middle of the
sixteenth century, came from very humble stock. He was known
as a singularly hard-headed and not too scrupulous business man,
but in his private account book there are many entries that show
regard for his mother and sister (to whom he gave boots, shoes,
and dresses) and for his niece and godchild. Among other items,
he paid the expenses of the confinement at his godchild's birth, and
gave her a gilt spoon, costing 14s. 8d., as a christening present.[2]

In a household like the Mores' the servants were an integral
part, and in merchant's houses too where the apprentices lived
with the family and performed domestic duties, full responsibility
was accepted for their well-being. Much was expected of them;
sometimes they may have been starved or ill-treated, but generally
speaking the line drawn between them and members of the family
was very thin, if, indeed, it existed at all. We have to turn on to a
further passage in Robert Crowley's *Works*[3] before we find the
foreshadowing of the attitude of later centuries:

> Se thou kepe them styl occupyed
> From morne tyl it be nyght agayne.

These lines carry a suggestion of the segregation of servants in
the cellars and attics of great houses, or their enclosure beyond
the green-baize door in lesser dwellings, rather than the medieval
truckle bed beside their master's and the companionship of the
housewife in the kitchen. Their lot was sometimes very hard, and

[1] *The Select Works of Robert Crowley*. Ed. J. M. Cowper, E.E.T.S., 1872, p. 89.
[2] H. Hall: *Society in the Elizabethan Age*. London, 1892, p. 159.
[3] Page 101.

they might encounter cruelty and neglect, but at least in the sixteenth century they were thought to be of the same species as
their employers, and no one doubted that the servants, even the
least of them, were indeed a part of the family life.

III. EVIL MAY DAY

Londoners have such fierce tempers and wicked dispositions that
they not only despise the way in which Italians live, but actually
pursue them with uncontrolled hatred. They look askance at us
by day, and at night they sometimes drive us off with kicks and
blows of the truncheon.

A Journey to London in 1497.[1]

The strong resentment felt by Londoners against alien merchants,
expressed as it was in the events that culminated in Evil May
Day in 1517, was not a new thing; it was far older and had its roots
deep in national history. It was closely connected with the growth
of national feeling, and the strong prejudices against the transference
abroad of British assets which animated those who objected to
alien priories and the payment of Peter's Pence. That is to say, it
was a general rather than a personal animosity, and individual
foreigners in practice found considerable toleration.

A wide variety of aliens had made London the most cosmo-
politan of cities. Other towns, such as Bristol, had their foreign
quarters too, but in London the aliens were an integral part of the
population, and some of them, for example, the 'Easterling' merchants of the Steelyard, were regarded as permanently resident
although they were likely to go back to their native land when
they retired from business, and few of them troubled to become
naturalized.

By the mid-fifteenth century the annual rate of taxation on
alien householders had risen to forty shillings. The authorities
cannot have hoped that this punitive taxation would bring a really
large sum into the Exchequer, for such aliens were comparatively
few; it must, then, have been intended to discourage them from
residence. It has been estimated than in 1437 there were only 540
registered aliens in London, although by 1583 the number had
increased to 5141.[2]

---

[1] [Translated] *A Journey to London in 1497*. Ed. C. V. Mulfatti. Barcelona, 1953,
p. 36.
[2] G. H. Unwin: *The Gilds and Companies of London*. London, 1908, vol. i, p. 246.

Many foreign traders and craftsmen concealed their origin and so escaped the register. One of the most unpopular things that a London tradesman could do was to give cover to an alien by 'colouring' his goods, that is, by selling them under his name. As a freeman the Londoner would not have to pay the taxes imposed on foreigners, and the alien no doubt would recompense him for the favour. One craftsman in the middle years of the fifteenth century was fined for being a 'maintainer and receiver' of foreign men, and another at about the same time was accused of habitually colouring the goods of strangers.[1] Sometimes, too, Englishmen would lend their names to aliens who wished to keep food shops or taverns, and if they were found out their punishment was severe.

The foreign wool merchants, those who came to sell their wares and to buy English fleeces, brought also new ideas and kept Londoners in touch with their fellows in the Low Countries, France, Spain, and Italy. The Genoese of Mincing Lane, the Dutchmen of Billingsgate, the Venetian captain and crew of the galley laden with exotic merchandise from the Levant, all these contributed to the kaleidoscopic pattern. As the anonymous author of *The Libelle of Englyshe Polycye* has it:

> The grete galees of Venees and Florence
> Be wel ladene with thinges of complacence,
> All spicerye and other grocers ware,
> Wyth swete wynes, all manere of chaffare,
> Apes and japes and marmusettes taylede,
> Nifles, trifles, that litell have availed,
> And thynges wyth whiche they fetely blere oure eye,
> Wyth thynges not endurynge that we bye.[2]

Often these aliens lodged with English families; one of the Venetian captains married his landlord's daughter and took her back to Padua, where she made a home for Englishmen studying in the University.[3] It is clear that, particularly in earlier times, Londoners fraternized to a considerable degree with alien traders, despite frequent brawls between individuals and the quarrels that flared up between particular groups.

---

[1] The first was a wire-drawer, the other a shearman, both highly specialized trades. *Calendar of Plea and Memoranda Rolls*, 1413–57. Ed. A. H. Thomas. Cambridge, 1945.
[2] Ed. Sir G. F. Warner. Oxford, 1926, pp. 18–19.
[3] R. J. Mitchell: *Italian Studies*, vol. vii (1952), p. 70.

As for the ordinary foreign visitors, they for the most part thought little of English manners and singled out the Londoners for their most unfavourable criticisms; the strictures quoted at the head of this section are an early example of what became a commonplace sixty years later. Most visitors were agreed that London was 'a large, excellent, and mighty city of business', but tended to add 'its inhabitants are extremely proud and overbearing; and because the greater part, especially the tradespeople, seldom go into other countries, but always remain in their houses in the city attending to their business, they care little for foreigners, but scoff and laugh at them'.[1] Emanuel von Meteren, an Antwerp merchant living in London at the beginning of the reign of Elizabeth I, found the Londoners fairly agreeable, but 'inconstant and desirous of novelties',[2] and thought the women very poor housekeepers. The Frenchman Stephen Perlin,[3] at a rather earlier date, dismissed Londoners as given 'only to vanity and ambition and to all sorts of merchandise', but he did not find them as quarrelsome and antagonistic to foreigners as did many Italians.

The most striking manifestation of this dislike of foreigners occurred in London and was very much a Londoners' affair. By Easter week, 1517, their antipathy had become very marked, and the apprentices jostled aliens in the streets and frequently pushed them into the gutter, so that the authorities thought it wise to command every man to stay indoors with his servants and apprentices from nine in the evening till seven next morning on the eve of May Day, just the time when young men and maidens were counting upon holding their customary May Day Revels.

The apprentices were often unruly towards their masters and the City authorities; it was a notorious characteristic of these London youths, but they seldom carried their insolence to the length of open defiance. On this occasion, however, they refused to go indoors as the clock struck nine, and when ordered to do so by an alderman who tried to arrest one of their number, resorted to kicks and blows and finally drove the alderman back to his

[1] Frederick, Duke of Wurtemberg. Trans. by W. B. Rye: *England as seen by Foreigners in the days of Elizabeth and James I*. London, 1865, p. 7.
[2] *Ibid.*, p. 71.
[3] Description of England and Scotland, Paris, 1558. Trans. by W. Grose: *The Antiquarian Repertory*. London, 1809, vol. iv, pp. 501–20.

house. Thereupon he gave the alarm and reported that the apprentices were in open revolt. It is true that the mob of rioters did swell to some hundreds; there was much noise and some stone-throwing and breaking of windows, even the forcing open of prison doors, but nothing to justify the panic measures that were immediately set in motion.

Ostensibly the rioters were demonstrating against aliens, but the foreigners sensibly stayed indoors and suffered no injury at all: the riot was, in fact, without motive and unpremeditated. It was in essence nothing more than a crude outbreak of high spirits and rough behaviour, but those who repressed it treated the 'revolt' as something very much more serious. Enemies of the City, particularly the Court party, seized upon the occasion and turned it to their own advantage, greatly exaggerating the disorders and spreading wild rumours to the discredit of the Mayor and Corporation, who were supposed to have lost all control over a savage and dangerous mob. It was represented to the King, Henry VIII, that the rioters had committed treason in violating his amity with foreign nations, and he was urged to take strong repressive measures. Volunteers from the Inns of Court were called for to help restore order, and the Lieutenant of the Tower was warned to prepare his artillery for action. He did in fact order some shots to be fired, but they did little harm.

In the meantime, Sir Thomas More had sought out the rioters and reasoned with them during the night;[1] their ardour was soon spent and within a few hours the apprentices were willing to disperse to their houses. This, however, they were not allowed to do until a number of them had been arrested and lodged in gaol. Even then, few people expected that there would be any serious consequence, but at a special court on 4 May a charge of treason was brought against the boys. Thirteen of these 'poor younglings', as the chronicler called them, were executed forthwith, to the consternation of their parents and friends. Some of the boys were scarcely in their teens, and the whole City was shocked and deeply distressed. Sir Thomas and some of the aldermen pleaded with the King for mercy towards the offenders not yet sentenced, and arranged for the Mayor to present his apology for the happening. Many more 'younglings' were paraded with halters round their

[1] Chambers: *Thomas More*, pp. 147–51.

necks, although ultimately they were pardoned. It was three weeks
before the King was satisfactorily appeased, but there were no more
hangings; the gallows were taken down and normal life resumed.

The apprentices were shaken and subdued, the kinsfolk and
friends of the victims of King Henry's ruthlessness nursed their
sorrow, and outwardly serenity returned to London. The foreigners suffered nothing but temporary fright. As the Venetian ambassador wrote smugly to his Senate: 'This has been a great
commotion, but the terror was greater than the harm.' Harm
there was, however, to those who had seen their friends suffer a
cruel death in punishment for a moment's folly, and Londoners
had a foretaste of the judicial barbarities that were to become a
commonplace in their lives.

IV. THE LONDON BOOK TRADE

Unto the noble auncyent and renommed Cyte, the Cyte of london
in Englond, I william Caxton Cytezeyn . . . of the same, . . .
owe of ryght my seruyse & good wyll . . .

Caxton's dedication to the City of London of his
translation of the book called *Caton*, 1483.

Although Caxton was born in the Weald of Kent, he dated his
birth from the year in which the 'whether cocke' was set up on
the steeple of St. Paul's[1] and no one of his generation could have
been a more devoted Londoner.[2] This mercer's apprentice, who
learned the new craft of printing while he was representing his
master's interests in Bruges and Cologne, not only became England's first printer, but was also translator, editor, bookseller, and an
excellent judge of public taste. He was, indeed, a great pioneer and
a great Londoner, and a man too of singular modesty and charm.

William Caxton set up his press not in London, but in Westminster,[3] yet he had many contacts with the London merchants
who were his clients and patrons, and his business transactions
were conducted in the City. It has only recently come to light that
Caxton was a considerable importer of foreign books, an activity
revealed by a careful study of the Customs accounts in the Public

---

[1] In 1422. *Ibid.*, p. xxvii.

[2] Caxton was apprenticed in 1438 to Robert Large, who became Mayor in the
following year. See E. Gordon Duff: *Early Printed Books*. London, 1893, p. 126.

[3] For the exact siting of his press see Lawrence E. Tanner; 'William Caxton's
House at Westminster,' *The Library*, Sept. 1957.

Record Office for the years 1460 to 1492.[1] In 1488, for instance, Caxton brought 1161 books and 'one container with books' to the port of London within the space of two months. In the same year he exported 140 French books: it has been suggested that these may have been remainder copies dating from the time when he was printing in Bruges,[2] where he produced at least four books in the French language.

Several foreign merchants, notably Peter Actors and Henry Frankenbergh, had been importing printed books to England well before this date, and at some time between 1466 and 1468 John Tiptoft, Earl of Worcester, arranged with one of the Hansa merchants at the London Steelyard to bring him two printed Bibles, presumably from Germany. Gerhard von Wesel, of Cologne, was the London representative of the Hansa at this time, and he mentions in his accounts that he has received the Bibles on behalf of 'my lord Worchester'.[3] Some idea of the scale of their business may be gained from the fact that of the two dealers named, Henry Frankenbergh imported about five hundred books including 'divers histories' in the year 1479–80, and at the same time Actors received at least seven hundred volumes.[4] Books were classed as general merchandise and duty had to be paid on them at the rate of threepence in the pound.[5]

Sometimes binding material, such as linen or 'red skins', was brought to England, so it seems probable that at least some of the binding was done in London. Paper was being brought in long before the days of printing; most of it came from Italy although some confusion is caused by the habit of French paper-makers at Troyes of copying the early Italian watermarks. When a Genoese ship was wrecked in the Bristol Channel in 1380 there were twenty bales of paper in its cargo,[6] destined for the English book trade. Towards the end of the fifteenth century increasing quantities were coming from France, and later on paper was sent also from the Rhine countries.

[1] Nelly J. M. Kerling: 'Caxton and the Trade in Printed Books', in *The Book Collector*, Autumn 1955, pp. 190–9.
[2] *Ibid.*, p. 197.
[3] *Hansisches Urkundenbuch*, ed. W. Stein, vol. ix. Leipzig, 1903, art. 439, no. 27.
[4] H. R. Plomer: 'The Importation of Books into England in the Fifteenth and Sixteenth Centuries', *The Library*, September 1923, pp. 146–7.
[5] Nelly Kerling: *op. cit.*, p. 191.
[6] E. Heawood: 'Sources of the Early English Paper Supply', *The Library*, vol. x (1929–30).

Of Caxton's aristocratic patrons much has been written; less attention has been paid to his middle-class public. From the first, Caxton was quick to recognize their needs. It was not for him to compete with the continental printers of classical texts: when he printed an author like Cicero he did so in a popular English translation, and concentrated upon 'small storyes and pamphletes' instead of producing English editions of works already well known and available upon the Continent. When he wanted to offer his public a large and sumptuous book he chose such a work as the *Golden Legend,* and it is no accident that one of the earliest and most successful of all his products was *The Game and Playe of Chess.* On occasion he wrote explicitly for a particular class: the *Order of Chyvalry* 'is not requysyte to euery comyn man to have',[1] but *Reynart the Foxe*[2] was meant 'for alle good folke' among 'marchantes and other comone people'.

It was on the suggestion and with the encouragement of one of the London aldermen[3] that Caxton translated *The Mirrour of the World* in 1481, and for two London mercers he made further translations in 1487 and 1488.[4] The well-to-do citizens of London were now able to leave their heirs more varied and interesting books than the merchant tailor who in 1468 could only bequeathe to his daughter Joanna his primer, bound in blue velvet with 'a clasp of silver gilt ornamented with a cross and three barley sheaves', and to his son his other primer, this one in 'blood coloured velvet'.[5]

In his prologue to the *Polychronicon* (1482) Caxton shows very clearly his conception of the duties of an editor. Caxton would have been the last person to claim scholarship, but he treated his authors with real respect. His over-riding idea was to make his books both useful and palatable to his readers and, in the word he would probably have chosen, 'seemly'. Here he succeeded most triumphantly and without the specialization found necessary by his successors, who limited their output to a particular field.[6]

[1] *The Prologues and Epilogues of William Caxton.* Ed. W. J. B. Crotch. E.E.T.S., London, 1928, p. 82
[2] First edition, 1481. See *ibid.,* p. 60.
[3] Hugh Bryce; he, too, was a Kentish man.
[4] For William Praat, *The Book of Good Manners,* and for 'a synguler frende of myn', *The Royal Book.* See *Prologues, etc.,* pp. 99, 101.
[5] H. R. Plomer: 'Books Mentioned in Wills', *Bibliographical Society Transactions,* vol. vii (1904), P.C.C. 24 Godyn.
[6] H. S. Bennett: *English Books and Readers, 1475–1557.* Cambridge, 1952.

In the year 1500 Caxton's late apprentice, Wynkyn de Worde, moved his business from Westminster to London, and henceforward London became the great centre of the book trade and St. Paul's Churchyard its principal mart. Wynkyn de Worde printed his books in his house in Fleet Street 'at the sygne of the Sonne', and every printer had his own sign hung outside his premises so that they could be easily identified. Caxton's 'Red Pale', Roger Madeley's 'Star', the 'blewe Garland' of John Wayland—all these signs guided customers in their search for the books they wanted, and the fact that booksellers were now beginning to concentrate their shops and stalls around St. Paul's made the task easier. In some cases the signs on the shops differed from that on the printing house; Julian Notary, however, employed his 'Three Kings' for both premises.

At first Caxton had a clear field and during his whole lifetime he was troubled very little by competition. The foreigners John Lettou (of Lithuania) and his partner William de Machlinia held to school and law books and did not venture into Caxton's field, and the books imported from abroad were chiefly missals and legendaries.[1] After Caxton's death de Worde and Richard Pynson brought out a large number of books, many of them small and of transient interest, but when Pynson was appointed King's Printer in 1509 he was obliged to print books of statutes and Year Books and greatly developed his business on the legal side. On the other hand, de Worde showed realism in printing a large number of school books to suit the new curriculum of the grammar schools —old-established grammars and also the new ones by Colet, Lily and Erasmus.

The English printers had good reason to fear the competition of foreign books, better printed and better bound, and they were fortunate in having the support of official opinion. The Church and the King wanted to control the heretical literature coming into the country, and Henry VIII was very sensitive to criticism of his divorce proceedings, so an Act was passed in 1534 which in effect prevented any importation of foreign printed matter.[2]

Provincial booksellers generally expected to order their goods from London printing houses, although there were presses in

[1] Bennett: *op. cit.*, p. 182.
[2] *Ibid.*, p. 31. The preamble to the Act speaks of 'a marvellous number of printed books' that had been brought into the country since 1484.

various towns, notably in Oxford and St. Albans. Some Londoners moved to the provinces and started new businesses; one such was Henry Jacobi, who went to Oxford between 1512 and 1514, and there set up his shop under his old London sign of 'The Trinity'.[1]

It is very difficult to make any general statement about the prices of books, for not all booksellers were as businesslike as John Dorne, of Oxford, who kept a day-book in which he entered particulars of more than eighteen hundred and fifty book sales during the year 1520. Broadsheets of ballads seem to have cost as little as a halfpenny or a penny, as they still did in 1647 when Henry Peacham wrote his *Worth of a Penny*.[2] On the other hand, solid books like the *Golden Legend* might cost 3s. 4d., or more if they were specially bound. The less educated London public often proved unwilling to spend money on books, then as now. The customer described by the printer Robert Copland is probably typical of most ages.

> Hast thou a boke of the wydowe Edith[3]
> That hath begyled so many with her words . . . ?

asks the customer. Copland tells him the price will be one groat, whereat the customer replies:

> Ye syr, somuche ? Nay, that I shorowe my cote.
> A peny I trow is ynough on bokes.
> It is not so soone goten, as this world lokes.

v. LONDON SCHOOLS

Every man strains his fortunes to keep his children at school. The cobbler will clout it till midnight, the porter will carry burdens till his bones crack again, the ploughman will pinch both back and belly to give his son learning, and I find that this ambition reigns nowhere so much as in this island.

JAMES HOWELL; written in the Fleet prison, 1647.[4]

London schoolboys pass fleetingly through the records of pleas and memoranda: they play fives against church towers, lose their

---

[1] E. Gordon Duff: *op. cit.*, p. 156. The whole subject is well summarized by S. H. Steinberg: *Five Hundred Years of Printing*. London, 1955 (Pelican Books).
[2] Printed by A. Lang in *Social England Illustrated*. London, 1903, p. 363 ff.
[3] A famous jest-book of the time. Quoted by Bennett: *op. cit.*, p. 186.
[4] *Familiar Letters*, 3 vols. London, 1903, vol. iii, p. 16.

6

balls in lead gutters and damage buildings, cause accidents in the streets, and themselves suffer misfortune of various kinds. A vivid picture is conjured up by the sad story of Richard, the eight-year-old son of John le Mazon, who was walking back to school after he had been home to dinner, across London Bridge. Playing with his fellows, probably 'dared' by them to attempt the feat, he hung dangling from a beam projecting from the side of the bridge, over the water swirling through the narrow arches. Richard's hands were not strong enough, or the beam was slippery, at all events, 'his hands giving way' before his friends could help him, he fell into the river and was drowned. This was in 1301;[1] no doubt other boys before and after this date played in the same way without troubling the coroner.

So little is known about London schools in medieval times that doubt has been cast upon their existence, but the very fact that there were boys like Richard who habitually walked across London Bridge between home and school shows that schools of some kind were certainly functioning at this time. Curiously enough, far more is known of schools founded in provincial towns, very often by Londoners—for instance, Sir Edmund Shaa the Goldsmith provided a school at Stockport and paid the master a salary of ten pounds a year.[2] The *Rolls of Parliament* (vol. iii) complain of a dearth of London schools in 1447[3] and this was remedied to some extent by the creation of new schools by various benefactors designed for the children of citizens and tradesmen.

By the end of this century and the beginning of the sixteenth the position of the London schools—apart from those belonging to gilds and chantries, which corresponded more nearly to the 'song schools' described by Dr. Leach[4]—had become easier to define. The two chief schools when young Thomas More was a schoolboy were St. Anthony's in Threadneedle Street, which More attended, and that of St. Thomas of Acre. The latter was protected and encouraged by the Mercers' Company, and had a long and distinguished history behind it, as had also St. Anthony's. In More's day St. Anthony's was the leading school

[1] *Calendar of Coroners' Rolls of the City of London*, 1300–78. Ed. R. R. Sharpe. London, 1913, p. 25.
[2] A. Abram: *Social England in the Fifteenth Century*. London, 1909, p. 181.
[3] Quoted *ibid.*, p. 182.
[4] A. F. Leach; *The Schools of Medieval England*. London, 1915.

and in the disputations between scholars from a number of grammar schools held in the churchyard of St. Bartholomew's, Smithfield, boys from St. Anthony's generally carried off the prize.[1]

They still did so in the time of John Stow the antiquary,[2] but by his day St. Paul's had been founded by Dean Colet and was well on the road to fame. Colet did not encourage these disputations, he had other (and revolutionary) views on education, but he was unable to prevent his boys from fighting the 'Antony pigs' and banging them with satchels stuffed with books. St. Anthony's boys gave as good as they got, and fought gamely with the 'Paul's pigeons'. At last, however, this school declined and faded into insignificance, leaving St. Paul's to go from strength to strength.

Before the invention of printing had brought down the prices of books, these were very scarce and possessed only by the master. Early title-pages show scholars sitting cross-legged on the floor—or occasionally on forms—learning their lessons by heart from the master's instruction.[3] It was a tedious business, the nimbler-witted boys found it boring and the duller ones could not take in the master's words without frequent repetition. Few had so over-powering a desire to learn that they studied willingly; generally speaking, they mastered their lessons because they knew they would be beaten if they did not.

Colet's foundation of St. Paul's school in 1510, with the image of the child Jesus in the schoolroom, and its 153 pupils in tradi-tional commemoration of the miraculous draught of fishes, was a curious mixture of the old and the new. Its place in the develop-ment of the new learning, and under the enlightened guidance of the school's first high master, William Lily, has perhaps over-shadowed the solid grammatical foundations on which it was built. The importance of St. Paul's and its great tradition, which survived the removal to Hammersmith in modern times,[4] have often been described and need not be recapitulated. Nor can the foundation of Alleyn's, Dulwich, nor the venerable history of

---

[1] R. W. Chambers: *Thomas More*, pp. 56–7.
[2] Who published the first edition of his *Survey of London* in 1603.
[3] P. S. Allen: *The Age of Erasmus*. Oxford, 1914, pp. 35–6, 42.
[4] In 1884. See F. Seebohm: *The Oxford Reformers*, revised edn. London, 1867, chapter vi.

Westminster School, be included in this slight sketch of London schools, since they lay outside the City boundaries.

There were undoubtedly private schools run by individual masters, as well as ancient endowments for education of London boys (and girls), of which no traces remain. Occasionally some illuminating entry is found in official records, as the mention of John Barkeley, 'teacher of grammar in the schools within the hospital of St. Bartholomew Smithfield', in 1476,[1] but they are few and scattered. More is known of foundations such as 'Carpenter's children' that have developed into modern schools carefully guarding their old traditions. The Town Clerk, John Carpenter, contemporary of Whittington, had bequeathed land and tenements in 1442 for the education of four boys 'for ever'; after two hundred years this bequest for his 'children' was converted into an annual money grant which helped to build the City of London School in 1834. Within three years of the original foundation four hundred boys were being educated there, and the shade of Carpenter —who was a scholarly and enlightened man as well as a generous one—must have been gratified when science, French, and English literature were added to the ordinary classical curriculum.

In Elizabethan London, Huguenot refugees might find a living by teaching French to the children of well-to-do tradesmen. One of them opened a school in Lewisham which he afterwards (in about the year 1576) moved to St. Paul's churchyard, and the dialogues he wrote for his boys give an excellent picture of his own schoolroom and the manners and customs of his pupils.[2] This Frenchman, Claudius Hollyband, clearly understood the management of boys, and it would seem that the characters in his dialogues were drawn from life. No school would be complete without 'John Nothingworth' or William who spoke English instead of French, spat on his neighbour's book, and trod underfoot the hat of Nicholas the sneak.[3] Schoolboys, it appears, had changed little in the hundred and fifty years since Lydgate described his own schooldays when he was 'void of reason' and 'given to wilfulness', failed to wash his hands for dinner, stole apples and grapes, was late for school, and 'lyke a yong colt that

---

[1] *Calendar of Close Rolls*, 1476–85. London, 1954, p. 28.
[2] *The Elizabethan Home Discovered in Two Dialogues, etc.*, Ed. M. St. C. Byrne. London, 1930, reprinted 1949.
[3] *Ibid.*, p. 6.

ran without brydell'.[1] Nor would there be fundamental differences between Hollyband's day and the doleful schooldays of Charles Lamb, or between town and country schoolboys. Unless, perhaps, the London boys were a little sharper in seizing an advantage, as the Christ's Hospital scholars who ran rapidly round the corner—like the Keystone Cops of early films—to meet for a second time the old gentleman who used, in memory of Lamb, to distribute shillings to any Bluecoat boy he happened to meet.

[1] *Minor Poems by John Lydgate*. E.E.T.S., London, 1910, p. 351.

Chapter Five

THE GRESHAMS' LONDON

1. THE ROYAL EXCHANGE

> *. . . when you went*
> *To the Indies, there was some shape and proportion*
> *Of a merchant's house in our family; but since*
> *My master, to gain precedency for my mistress*
> *Above some elder merchant's wives, was knighted*
> *'Tis grown a little court in bravery . . .*
>
> MASSINGER: *The City Madam*,[1] 1658.

Just as the City Livery Companies, with their exaggerated dignity, grew out of the earlier gilds and reached an eminence of power and prosperity unimagined by the tradesmen and craftsmen who had laid their foundations, so did the merchants of the Greshams' London develop beyond those of Dick Whittington's day.

From an earlier time than is commonly supposed, great nobles, prelates, and the King himself, had joined in mercantile enterprises, owning ships and cargoes and putting up the money for semi-piratical as well as lawful expeditions in search of trade. With the discovery of new routes and new markets, and the general increase of wealth and expansion of industry that came with the Tudor dynasty, London became more important than ever, both as a port and as the financial capital where many of these expeditions were planned. The rise of a highly educated and intelligent type of merchant, the reasons for the development of this class and the formation of joint-stock companies to exploit its interests, are, however, larger questions. London is part, and part only, of the national pattern of trade.

The three Greshams, Sir John, Sir Richard, and Sir Thomas, were Mercers, and they show three successive stages of progression to the rank of Massinger's hero in *The City Madam*. First came Sir

---

[1] Act I, sc. i. *Massinger's Plays*. Mermaid edn., vol. i, p. 402.

John, who was Sheriff in 1537 when his brother was Lord Mayor, and himself became Mayor ten years later. He was prosperous, hard-working, and respected; he also had the imagination to become one of the founders of the Russia Company and was ready to risk his whole fortune in their hazardous enterprise. Sir John's courage was rewarded, and when he died in 1556 his position was established and secure.

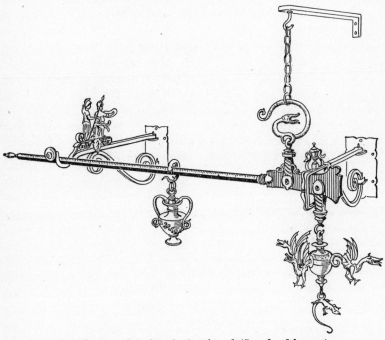

Sir Thomas Gresham's Steelyard (*London Museum*)

Sir John's brother, who may have been older, for he died seven years earlier, at the age of sixty-four, reached greater eminence and was no less successful in his business. This Sir Richard—he was knighted in 1537—was gentleman-usher extraordinary to Henry VIII and lent money to the King and to some of the nobility. There was nothing new in this; we have seen how financially dependent earlier sovereigns had been upon the London trades-men, but it was symptomatic of the new point of view that

Gresham mixed in court circles on terms of easy equality, and his younger son became an intimate friend of Cecil and acted as ambassador in the Netherlands. Sir Richard was rewarded by grants of monastic lands, and he bought Fountains Abbey, perhaps with the intention of retiring there to found a county family. This he did not do, for he died while still at the height of his powers, while he was actually at work upon the design for the Royal Exchange that his son eventually carried out.[1]

The third Gresham, Sir Thomas, was Sir Richard's second son, but he had learned the Mercers' business from his uncle since his father was much occupied with public affairs. He kept a firm grasp upon the family business, but he too entered public life and showed himself a master of statecraft as well as an expert in the buying and selling of mercery. He it was who built at his own expense the Royal Exchange, which immediately became the symbol of London's supremacy. Sir Thomas's shrewdness as a business man is nowhere better shown than in Stow's account of the means he took to expedite the building of the Exchange on the site put into his hands

> thervpon to build a Bursse, or place for marchants to assemble in, at his owne proper charges: and hee on the seventh of June 1567 laying the first stone of the foundation, being Bricke, accompanied with some Aldermen, euery of them laid a piece of Golde, which the workemen tooke up, and forthwith followed vpon the same with such diligence, that by the moneth of November . . . the same was covered with slate, and shortly after fully finished.[2]

Immediately upon its completion, the Royal Exchange became one of the regular 'sights of London' to be shown with pride to foreign visitors. It was a long building, with an open courtyard where the merchants could meet and discuss their business, after the fashion of the Bourse at Antwerp. On the first floor were the shops, let out at a good rental, and Greshams' connection with the building was emphasized by grasshoppers (his emblem) carved in stone. When Gresham's Exchange was burned down in the Great Fire it was rebuilt with all possible speed[3] on a design by Edward

---

[1] See the articles in the *Dictionary of National Biography* for details of the careers of these three men.

[2] John Stow: *Survey of London*. Ed. C. L. Kingsford. London, 1908, vol. i, p. 193.

[3] In 1670.

Jerman, the City surveyor, and this building remained until it, too, was destroyed by fire in 1838.

It was not Gresham's but Jerman's building that made so great an impression upon Colsoni, author of the *Guide de Londres* published in 1693. Colsoni was particularly impressed by 'plusieurs grands Magazins à poivre qui appartiennent à la Compagnie des Indes'.[1] By this time the East India Company (not yet reconstituted, as it would be in 1720) had grown in scope and power, largely owing to the foresight of the London merchants—'men with Long Heads and Deep Purses'[2]—who had successfully attracted investors like the Duke of Bedford into taking up shares in the Company's ships.[3] Some of them saw in the Company's schemes an excellent chance of importing goods for their own needs—Chinese wallpapers and porcelain, chests of tea, and pepper and spices for their households.

Another project of Sir Thomas Gresham, for which he left provision in his will, was the foundation of Gresham College where free lectures were to be provided on seven days a week and the lecturers paid from the rents of the shops in the Royal Exchange. For this purpose he bequeathed his own house in Bishopsgate Street, after the death of his wife; this did in fact become Gresham House where lectures were given according to his plan until 1768. Thereafter the plans had to be modified as the shop rentals no longer sufficed to support the College, but it still exists at the corner of Gresham Street and the lecture rooms are still full of students who owe their presence there to this great and generous man.

It would not, however, give a fair picture of the London merchants of this time to consider only the three Greshams. Some merchants found life harder, as did Richard Chambers, who was fined £2,000 and imprisoned for his disagreeable and ungrateful words in alleging at the Council Board that the merchants were 'in noe parts of the world soe scrud and wronged as in England, and that in Turkie they have more encouragement'.[4]

There were plenty of complaints of unethical behaviour on the

---

[1] Ed. Walter H. Godfrey, for the London Topographical Society. Cambridge, 1951, p. 2.
[2] *The London Spy*, November 1698, p. 11.
[3] G. Scott Thomson: *Life in a Noble Household*. London, 1937, p. 393.
[4] *Historical MSS. Commission*, vol. xi, part 7 (Bridgewater MSS.), 1888, p. 162.

part of some traders, as well as actual instances of fraud. In the mercery trade alone we find three cases in the Court of Star Chamber in one year, when mercers were fined for 'false and corrupt' dyeing of silk.[1] There is no reason to suppose that merchants were either more or less prone to error (or fond of sharp practice) in the sixteenth century than at any other time, but the intention has been to show that they did then have exceptional opportunities to expand their businesses. It seems, too, that the age bred men like the three Greshams who were quick to seize their opportunities and yet were able to keep their integrity.

11. A CITIZEN'S HOME

The wyffe(s) . . . bonettes.
Item, a bonnette of blak vellvet garnyched w(ith) damaske
gulde. xxvj s. viij d.
Item, a nolde bonett of blake velvet, worne sore, pryse
iiij s.
Item, olde ffrontlettes of dyuers Collors, of velvett,
pryse viij s.

Inventory of the Contents of John Porth's House, 1531.[2]

The merchants' houses in Dick Whittington's day showed a degree of elegance and comfort that was remarkable when compared with the bleakness of earlier homes, and probably nowhere else in the country—not even in noblemen's houses or royal palaces—could more agreeable living conditions be found than in those of the richer London tradesmen. A hundred years later, however, their standard had risen to a still higher level; humble kitchen gear is now of the finest brass, elegant furniture is made by craftsmen, plate appears in quantity where a single mazer was once a treasure, and furs and jewels are commonplaces in the wardrobes of many prominent citizens.

By a fortunate chance the inventory of the goods of the Londoner John Porth has been preserved. He died in 1525, but his property was not sold till six years later, at the expiration of the lease of his house in Billingsgate, when all the proceeds were handed over to the churchwardens of St. Mary at Hill as directed in his will. His wife had died the year before. The inventory is

[1] *Historical MSS. Commission*, vol. xi, part 7 (Bridgewater MSS.), 1888, p. 162.
[2] *The Medieval Records of a London City Church*. Ed. H. Littlehales. E.E.T.S., 1904, p. 44.

complete and very detailed, taking the furniture of each room exactly as it stood at John Porth's death, so that a faithful picture is given of all parts of the interior of the house. In form and general plan it was very like the house in Thames Street belonging to Porth's friend and neighbour Andrew Evyngar,[1] a salter living over his business premises, with a fishmonger on the east side and a merchant haberdasher on the other. He, too, had hall and parlour, various chambers, a kitchen or buttery, a counting house adjoining the shop, and useful garrets for storing extra furniture and lumber, 'with all maner tymbre werk, iron werk, lede werk and stoen werk conuenient and necessary'.[2]

The hall of John Porth's house must have been of considerable dimensions for it contained 'turned' chairs, benches, and cupboards in profusion as well as a table with a pair of folding trestles and a 'counter' or sideboard. This was covered with damask, and the hangings—excluding the window curtains—measured fifty yards. There were two carpets and fourteen cushions, elaborate fire-irons, and a latten chandelier with four lights. One of the chairs was 'of Spaynysche makyng'. The parlour was hung with thirty-six yards of green say,[3] and here were six or seven pictures, carpets, cushions 'of nannat makynt' (embroidery from Nantes?) priced 6d. apiece, four old books valued at a penny each, two round tables, one made of cypress and the other 'old' but still worth 1s. 6d. against the other's price of 2s. There was also a pair of 'playng tabolles' for backgammon.

In the bedrooms were found a variety of chests and stools, bedsteads with green curtains, featherbeds, bolsters and blankets, and in Porth's own room an altar with a crucifix and image of Our Lady. The chests were full of rich materials; in the 'longe' chest were eighteen items, ranging from 'a payr of slevys of crimsyng velvet In-broderet with damaske golde' to 'iij lytyll schredes of clothe a sylver' valued at 1s. 4d. The estimated worth of such fragments seems surprisingly high until it is remembered how long might be the life of a pair of sleeves and how often the satins

[1] Evyngar also was a benefactor of St. Mary at Hill, where he was churchwarden for many years. He deposited a pledge with John Porth consisting of a diamond ring, a standing cup, and a gilt salt. *Ibid.*, p. 49. See also Churchwardens' Accounts and Memoranda, 1495-1531. *Ibid.*, pp. 217-358.
[2] *Ibid.*, p. 23.
[3] Thought to be woollen cloth.

and velvets were unpicked and refashioned.[1] Black, crimson, violet, and tawny were the hues chosen by John Porth and his wife for their best clothes; two of mistress Porth's gowns were of 'vyolett', one furred with squirrel and the other with mink, but she had also three black gowns, all fur-trimmed, and two more were embellished with black velvet. In all, she had eleven gowns and five kirtles, of which one was 'broken', and miscellaneous pieces of fur and woven material. It is interesting to note that a yard of crimson cloth, although 'mothe eiten' was still worth two shillings. John Porth's wardrobe was more extensive, for it included buckram tunics or 'coats' to be worn under armour, and such items as 'a nolde grene . . . Rydyng cotte' in addition to his jackets, doublets and gowns.

Supplies of linen and kitchen gear were abundant and well-ordered, with diaper tablecloths seven yards long, and fifteen brass pots 'grett and small', candlesticks, frying pans, toasting-fork, trivets, and knives. In the garrets were old hangings, extra down pillows—eight of them—and superfluous bedsteads and bedding of various kinds. In the counting-house Porth kept a number of his smaller treasures, a Primer printed on parchment with silver clasps, and another written by hand, 'lymmed with gold and imagery', worth more than double.[2] The really impressive possessions of John Porth, were, however, his plate and jewels, and these formed the major part of his estate. The list of goblets, standing cups, mazers, salts and spoons, some chased with designs of roses and garlands, some enriched with diamonds, reveals a love of beauty as well as the ordinary human desire for display. As for personal adornments, the rings, pendants, buckles and girdles amount to a smaller value but give a strong idea of John Porth's personal tastes; he seems to have been a simple person, satisfied with 'a lyttell shelde of golde Innamyled with whyt and grene and with . . . iij perlls, weyng a qwarter of a nounce, prasyd at viij s.'[3] His plate, on the other hand, represented the investment of his fortune.

[1] There is much interesting information concerning dress and household goods at this time to be found in Barbara Winchester's book, *Tudor Family Portrait*, London, 1955 (especially chapters v and vi), based on a series of merchant's letters in the P.R.O.
[2] It was valued at 8s. 4d., the printed one at 4s. *Medieval Records of a London City Church*, p. 45.
[3] *Ibid.*, p. 48.

This delight in simple and inexpensive jewellery was very characteristic of London merchants of John Porth's class and age. Of this there is striking proof in the charming little chains that were beginning to come into fashion again after a long eclipse. As the century unfolded, these 'carcanets' became lighter and more

Necklets from the 'Cheapside Hoard' (*London Museum*)

delicate; they might be of precious or semi-precious stones linked together with gold, or simply of enamel work. One gold chain that is now in the London Museum[1] has a design of alternate roses and leaves, enamelled white and green, that is very English in conception, and wholly charming. This is one of a considerable number that were found by a workman digging in Cheapside in 1912, and constitutes part of the famous 'Cheapside Hoard'.[2] This is a collection of jewellery, gems, and cameos that were contained in a wooden box buried beneath the floor. It may have belonged to a jeweller, or possibly to a moneylender; in either case it is a very clear illustration of current taste and fashion. The date has been put at about the year 1600, but some of the items may be earlier; certainly the existence of so many similar carcanets shows that they were established in public favour well before this time.

Other, far more valuable, pieces of jewellery were found in the same hoard, a precious watch set in a hexagonal emerald,[3] two

[1] Exhibit A.14073.
[2] *London Mus. Cat.*, no. 2. London, 1928.   [3] A.14162.

gold rings set with antique gems,[1] and a miscellaneous collection of bracelets, pendants, and hair ornaments. Some of the unset gems or intaglios seem to be copies of antique models[2] and show that an interest in neo-classicism existed not only in Court or Academic circles but also among ordinary middle-class Londoners of the age of the Greshams. But it is in the simpler rings, the ornaments of amethyst and crystal, the enamel carcanets with their roses and daisies, that the tastes of London businessmen were most clearly shown. These were the presents that they gave their wives and mistresses; not for them the exotic emeralds and rubies: if they had so much money they preferred to convert it into gold plate to deck their buffets and to prove to all the world how substantial was a London merchant.

Seventy years after John Porth died an inventory was made of the 'goodes and chattels, howshold stuffe and debtes' of a London citizen and draper named Thomas Bulmar.[3] He too was a business man of some standing, richer than John Porth and with interests in house property and a considerable stock in trade in his own shop, but his personal effects were chosen with less discrimination. It is clear from the drapery in his possession at the time of the inventory in 1594 that Bulmar was a shrewd buyer; all his goods are very saleable and are in reasonable quantities, ranging from $4\frac{1}{2}$ yards of 'tawny cotton' to 444 yards of 'colloured cottons' at 13*s.* 6*d.* a yard. There are no remnants or useless short pieces and this suggests that he may have been a wholesale dealer rather than a retailer.

It is interesting to notice that the cottons, of which Bulmar had a large stock, both white and in 'sundry colours', are very highly priced—generally 13*s.* to 13*s* 6*d.* a yard—whereas it was possible to buy at his counter '$27\frac{3}{4}$ yards of russet broad silk' for as little as 8*s.* 6*d.* a yard. The Devon frieze in which he specialized, particularly in black or violet, and country-woven russet cloths of various kinds, were all very much cheaper even than this. The frieze was between 3*s.* 4*d.* a yard and 4*s.* 4*d.* according (it seems) to texture and colour. Such expensive cottons must have been brought from a considerable distance—from the Levant, or

---

[1] A.14241 and A.14242.
[2] *London Mus. Cat.*, no. 2, pp. 27–8.
[3] British Museum, Add. MS.28714. The authors hope, in due course, to publish a short study of Thomas Bulmar and his inventory.

possibly from India. European fustians were imported in considerable quantities from Germany and Italy, but if these had formed Bulmar's stock they would surely have been called 'fustian' or 'bombazine' rather than 'cotton'.[1] There is no mention of such materials in his inventory.

The imported cottons mark Bulmar as a man of enterprise and wide connections, but the household effects, which are listed in some detail, do not give the idea of a man who has furnished his house with care and affection. There is furniture in quantity; it may be guessed that he had a large family, for there was a children's chamber full of 'furniture', clothes, and lumber. There was much lumber, too, in his garret, with a variety of old bedsteads, flock beds, a 'Pilo', and an unwanted wainscot press and a wooden table. Another chamber had an old table, miscellaneous furniture and a 'Trondle Bed'; the new chamber however was supplied with a new bedstead and lavish bedding, with bolster and blankets, and hangings of 'paynted clothes' so that the value of the contents of this room was reckoned at the high figure of £8.

The vellum roll on which the inventory is written is much mutilated, so that it is difficult and sometimes impossible to read the details of Bulmar's kitchen gear and the furniture in the great chamber, but the list of his linen is very impressive, beginning with 8½ dozen napkins and eight diaper tablecloths and ending with pillows and pillowberes. Finally, there is a casual mention of a hundred and fifty three items of gilt plate: these are all taken together and valued at £42 1s. 1d. It seems as though Bulmar set little store by craftsmanship, for the gilt 'items' must have been very ordinary or in poor condition to have so low a value. His clothes, too, were very different from the elegant wardrobe of John Porth. He had four doublets, valued at 30s., a 'mantell' and 'an old coat and three pairs of hose,' but little else worth mentioning. There is no jewellery recorded for either himself or his wife, no standing cups 'chased with roses and garlands', no rings with popular mottoes or 'posies', and not a single book. It is only in his choice of materials and the stocking of his shop that Thomas Bulmar shows any real personality, and it must be supposed that here lay his chief interest. His large house, full of stools, cupboards and cushions as it was, seems to have been merely a

[1] From information kindly supplied by Miss Julia Mann.

place to eat and sleep in; it was not for him to exhibit his wealth by translating it into terms of gold plate encrusted with diamonds, or to deck his wife and children in expensive clothes and furs: anyone could see from his shop and its contents that he was an important man of business.

Times had changed, and with them the type of city merchant. Not every successful draper in Elizabeth's reign was so careless of appearances as Thomas Bulmar, nor had every rich citizen of the 1530's the delicate taste of John Porth. Nevertheless, each was partly the product of his age; the more leisurely days of Henry VIII had given place to the fevered activity of the last years of Elizabeth's reign, and the solid conventional virtues in business were superseded by enterprise, foresight and acumen. The battle was now to the swift rather than to the strong.

III. JUSTICE AND MERCY

The Discouerie of the blacke Art

The Black Art is picking of Locks, and to this busie trade two persons are required, the Charme and the Stand: the Charm is he that doth the feat, and the Stand is he that watcheth: there be more that do belong to the burglary for conuaiing away the goods, but only two are imploid about the locke: the charme hath many keies and wrests, which they call picklocks, and for euery sundry fashion they have a sundry terme.

ROBERT GREENE: *The Second Part of Conny-Catching,* 1592.[1]

It is a curious thing that at a time when an educated man was expected to be able to turn his hand to any art—warfare, state-craft, poetry, music, conversation, and all forms of athletics—the activities of rogues and swindlers should have been so sharply specialized. The 'priggers of prancers' worked exclusively as horse-stealers, and a thief who had been trained to be a 'hooker' or 'angler'—that is, to steal by lifting things through windows with the help of a crooked stick—would never practise the black art of lock picking as described by Robert Greene in his notable pamphlet.

The 'conny-catchers' lay in wait for unwary countrymen, who would be persuaded to play with cards and dice by these unscru-pulous professionals. Generally speaking the visitors to London had to go home richer in experience but with empty pockets, but

[1] Ed. G. B. Harrison. London, 1923 (Bodley Head Quartos, no. 1), p. 54.

now and again the seemingly stupid country bumpkin turned the tables on too-confident card-sharpers. If they met with resistance the rogues were liable to retreat at high speed, like the coal merchant who ran all the way from Billingsgate to Wapping, leaving the five bushels of coals he had tried to sell as eight, and the sacks that held them, without waiting for any money, when an irate housewife turned upon him and threatened to take him 'before my Lord Maior'.[1]

In practice, remarkably light penalties were imposed upon cheats—at worst a man who secured a horse by 'cosenayge' would have to stand in the pillory and pay a 40*s*. fine—whereas theft was punishable by death. Cheating, whether at cards or in ordinary buying and selling, does not seem to have been thought reprehensible, and the successful cheat was looked on as a fine fellow and his victim as a fool. Cutpurses could be executed without the right to claim benefit of clergy, and the very fact that sentences were so severe made these thieves look upon themselves as men of high courage. It is significant that a large proportion of the highwaymen convicted in Middlesex during the sixteenth century described themselves as 'gentlemen'.[2]

The customary punishments, the whippings and brandings, the pillory and the stocks, did not differ in London from the barbarous exhibitions to be seen all over England. Only the London executions were more frequent and more sensational. This subject is more fully treated in a later chapter;[3] for although by Tudor times the hanging, disembowelling and quartering of traitors, and the burning of heretics at the stake, had become one of the main sights to be enjoyed by Londoners and foreigners alike, it was in the eighteenth century that hangings for theft and petty crimes became a commonplace. The same crowd of onlookers that applauded the horrors of *The Spanish Tragedie* and *Titus Andronicus* laughed and joked while they watched the agonies of dying men. Only the criminals' friends, we are told, went and pulled the feet of hanging men 'that they might die more quickly'.[4]

[1] Robert Greene: *A Notable Discovery of Coosnage*, 1591. *Ibid.*, p. 58. This tract, and others by Greene, Dekker, Harman, etc., have been reprinted by A. V. Judges in his book *The Elizabethan Underworld*, London, 1930.
[2] F. Aydelotte: *Elizabethan Rogues and Vagabonds*. Oxford, 1913, p. 99.
[3] Chapter Eleven, § ii.
[4] *Thomas Platter's Travels in England, 1599*. Trans. C. Williams. London, 1937, p. 174.

7

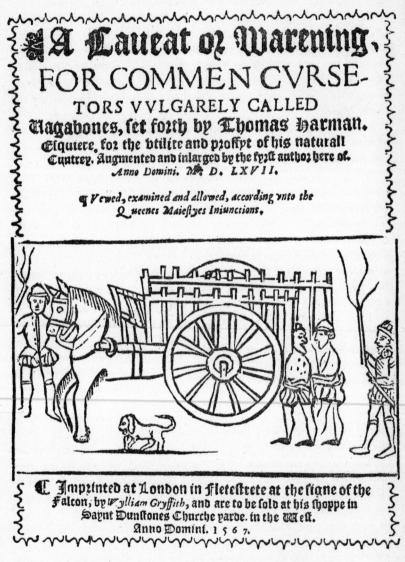

𝕬 **Caueat oʒ Warening,**

FOR COMMEN CVRSE-
TORS VVLGARELY CALLED
Uagabones, set forth by Thomas harman.
Esquiere, for the vtilite and proffyt of his naturall
Cuntrey. Augmented and inlarged by the fyrst author here of.
Anno Domini. M. D. LXVII.

¶ *Vewed, examined and allowed, according vnto the
Queenes Maiestyes Iniunctions,*

❧ **Imprinted at London in Fletestrete at the signe of the**
Falcon, by *Wylliam Gryffith*, and are to be sold at his shoppe in
Saynt Dunstones Churche yarde. in the West.
Anno Domini. 1 5 6 7.

Whipping at the Cart Tail (*Harman's Caveat*, 1567)

Compassionate almsgiving was still practised by individuals, and private acts of unselfishness and generosity can be found to balance the harsh severities of the new legal system. The very officers who chased the sick and the poor across the parish boundary were sometimes those who contributed to collectors' funds when a church brief gave some authenticity to cases of distress. Many who found themselves destitute through misfortune or ill-treatment, or had lost their homes from fire or flood, found relief in this way, though many more did not. The fact that the almsgiving was sporadic and uncertain, and in practice totally inadequate, does not detract from the charitable intention.

As early as 1517 the Privy Council ordered a census to be made of all the London beggars, together with the poor for whom the City was responsible. The number worked out at over a thousand. Tin badges were given to them, and four 'surveyors' were put in charge of these badged beggars.[1] The Records of the London Court of Aldermen, 28 November 1568, show that a licence was issued to Thomas Moone of London and his wife, whose house had been burnt,[2] and when large numbers were made homeless in the Great Fire, collections were made for them all over the country. Others had licences to beg for help in ransoming prisoners captured on the high seas: Lucas Argenter in 1581 was given one for the benefit of his wife and children in Turkey.[3]

Not all the licences to beg, or to collect for persons in distress, were genuine, for they were easily forged and a plausible rogue could make an excellent living by collecting alms that were never delivered. If anyone were discovered begging without a licence properly issued, he was set in the pillory forthwith; Henry Machyn the undertaker recorded in 1562[4] that a man was pilloried for 'counterfeyting a false wrytyng to bege in dyuers places in London, and puttyng in mony honest men(s) ha(nds) to gyff ym lysens to bege, but yt was false': evidently he practised his forgery on a large scale.

Although there were disastrous fires in several other English cities, the fire of 1666 captured the imagination even of those who had never set foot in London. They subscribed to relieve the

[1] Aydelotte: *op. cit.*, p. 61.   [2] *Ibid.*, p. 24.
[3] *Ibid.*, p. 23.
[4] *The Diary of Henry Machyn*, 1553–63. Ed. J. G. Nichols. Camden Society, 1848, p. 292.

homeless not only once, but repeatedly. The Earl of Bedford was, of course, a part-time Londoner, and it is not surprising that he should have given five or ten pounds for several years in succession,[1] but this goodwill and practical help is found in all ranks and in all places. One of the most striking examples that can still be traced is that of a Lancashire apprentice named Roger Lowe who canvassed a large part of his native village and made a list of those willing to help 'the needie persons', within a few weeks of the disaster.[2] He was probably one of many: we know of his activities only because he mentioned them in his diary and this happens to have been preserved.

Many sixteenth- and seventeenth-century wills mention bequests to the poor of specified parishes and to the prisoners in the main London prisons. Typical of his times was a London grocer named Richard Hale, who died in 1617, leaving his house in Mincing Lane to his son and his personal belongings to the rest of his family, but the remainder of his property to the school he had founded and endowed, and to poor scholars at Oxford and Cambridge. He also bequeathed substantial sums to patients in St. Bartholomew's and Bedlam. Other Londoners benefited too; twenty poor maidens at their marriage were to have 6s. 8d. apiece, and on the day of his burial Hale's fellow Grocers were promised a feast costing £25 at the testator's expense.[3]

Hale left bequests too for the prisoners in Bridewell, Ludgate, Newgate and King's Bench. Ordinary prisoners lived on starvation diet in misery and filth, and more would have died of want than actually did perish had it not been for benefactions from compassionate citizens, sickened at heart by the violence and cruelty they were obliged to witness. Yet those who could afford to do so lived well in gaol. Prisoners could go abroad with a keeper at a stated price per day or half-day, and it sometimes paid 'theeves and strumpets' to give as much as fourpence a night to the gaoler to secure a place in gaol when searches were being made. If they could pay enough there was no limit to the food and drink that could be procured for them. By the time of James I the London gaols were well on the way to becoming expensive lodging-houses.[4]

[1] G. Scott Thomson: *Life in a Noble Household*. London, 1937, p. 361.
[2] In October 1666. *The Diary of Roger Lowe*. Ed. W. L. Sachse. London, 1938, p. 108.
[3] P.C.C. Dale 20. From the MS. collections made by F. J. Mitchell in 1893.
[4] Aydelotte: *op. cit.*, pp. 83, 84.

IV. THE PLAGUES OF LONDON

CIVIS: Good wife, the daily jangling and ringing of the bells,
the coming in of the Minister to every house in ministring
the communion, in reading the homily of death, the digging
up of graves, the sparring in of windows, and the blazing
forth of the blue cross, do make my heart tremble and
quake. Alas, what shall I do to save my life?

UXOR: Sir, we are but young, and have but a time in this
world, what doth it profit us to gather riches together, and
can not enjoy them? Why tarry we here so long? I do think
every hour a year until we be gone . . . seeing that we have
sent our children forth three weeks past into a good air
and a sweet country, let us follow them . . . Let us take
leave of our neighbours, and return merely home again when
the plague is past, and the dog days ended.

WILLIAM BULLEIN: *A Dialogue against the*
Pestilence, 1564.

Many people, asked to give an account of plague in London, would respond with a graphic description of the outbreak of 1665, the details drawn from Defoe's *Journal of the Plague Year* (written many years later, Defoe himself being only five years old at this time). Others would recall the incidence of the Black Death in 1348–9, and perhaps the 'sweating sickness' of Tudor times, but comparatively few people realize that these were but the high peaks in the frequent epidemics bred of overcrowded and insaniraty conditions, of neglect of personal hygiene and of ill-balanced diet. London rats were not more destructive of food and goods than those of other cities, and their fleas carried bubonic plague to provincials as well as to Londoners, but in the congested City they were able to flourish and multiply in what were to them ideal surroundings of decay and filth.

'The Pestilence' was a term loosely used to cover various diseases. Sometimes these were traceable to some special cause, as the 1603 outbreak of plague, the extent of which seems to have been due to the influx of people into a London already grossly over-populated, at the time of the coronation of James I and VI. 'This great mortalitie', as Lady Hoby called it,[1] began in London but was soon dispersed 'thorow all the Realme of England', and other waves of disease followed the same pattern or else were

---

[1] *Diary of Lady Hoby*. Ed. D. M. Meads. London, 1930, p. 205.

introduced into the city by visitors from affected areas: whichever
way the infection spread, it was the outcome of London's over-
powering social and economic position:[1] people came, and people
went, and no advice or threats would stop them.

We find that Parliament was adjourned several times in the
course of the fifteenth century[2] and sometimes the justices also
had to postpone their business,[3] but on the whole every effort was
made to keep life moving as normally as possible. It was a constant and difficult problem to know when it was worth a man's
while to shut up his shop, risk losing his business, and take refuge
in the country with his wife and family. William Bullein, in the
heading of this section, puts the matter clearly, but not as suc-
cinctly as did Defoe. 'I had two important things before me: the
one was the carrying on my business and shop . . . in which was
embarked all my effects in the world; and the other was the
preservation of my life.'[4]

Many of the richer citizens betook themselves to houses on the
higher ground near London where the air was better and congestion less. Highgate Hill and Hounslow Heath were favoured by
some families, and even Chiswick, although at river level, was
thought to be much healthier than London. It was here that the
master of Westminster School and his forty King's scholars were
accustomed to migrate, to the prebendal mansion house on Chiswick Mall,[5] described by John Norden as 'a fair house, whereunto
(in time of any common plague or sickness) as also to take the
aire, he [the Dean] withdraweth the schollers of the colledge of
Westminster'.[6]

Reports are constantly being sent home by those who have
business in London, to the effect that sickness is rife there, and
we find an anxious family asking for their boy to be sent home
forthwith as 'the[y] dy fast att londone'.[7] A few years before the
disastrous plague of 1665 a mother wrote to her law-student son
about his health; she was full of foreboding because London was

[1] Dr. C. Creighton: *History of Epidemics in Britain*. London, 1891, vol. i, p. 233.
[2] From the *Rolls of Parliament*, e.g. in 1433 (vol. iv, 420); 1449 (vol. v, 143);
1467–8 (vol. v, 618) and 1474 (vol. vi, 99.)
[3] A. Abram: *Social England in the Fifteenth Century*. London, 1909, p. 165.
[4] *Journal of the Plague Year*. Ed. J. C. Dent. London, n.d., p. 15.
[5] Warwick H. Draper: *Chiswick*. London, 1923, p. 49 ff.
[6] *Speculum Britanniae*, 1593, p. 17.
[7] L. Lyell: *A Medieval Postbag*. London 1934, p. 296.

'so sikeley a place'[1] and urged him to lead a regular and well-
ordered life. She followed up her advice with the practical present
of two pairs of riding stockings to keep his feet dry, and a box of
pies, cheeses, and 'biskates' to comfort his stomach.

Londoners born and bred made little of the dangers to which
they had for generations been accustomed. The panic that struck
the city on the outbreak of the Black Death was succeeded by
apathy, and although the municipal authorities did what they
could to keep the streets and ditches clean and to induce people to
take precautions, especially during the summer months, individuals
continued to practise their careless habits. In 1349 the mortality
had been very severe, and eight years later the city was still
reported to be one-third empty, but it is impossible to guess at the
number or even at the proportion of the population who died at
this time. We know certain facts, as, for instance, that the Abbot
of Westminster and twenty-six monks were victims,[2] but there is
no accurate computation possible in these days before parish
registers existed. There were at least six further outbreaks of this
particular pestilence in the course of the fourteenth century, and a
final one in 1407, but none approached the first in severity. Like
scarlet fever in our own day, the incidence and deadliness of this
disease seems to have come to a peak and then receded, to be
supplanted by other epidemics still unknown in the fourteenth
century.

To balance this, however, there came a decline in the incidence
of leprosy, and during the middle years of the fifteenth century,
when London made a really determined effort to stamp it out by
forcing sufferers into isolation hospitals and burning and fumi-
gating their old quarters ruthlessly, it ceased to be an urgent
problem. Stow records a hospital in Holborn, St. Giles's, that had
been founded early in the twelfth century for forty lepers, and in
1208 we hear of Geoffrey FitzPeter, Earl of Essex, making a yearly
payment of sixty shillings to these lepers of St. Giles.[3] In 1354,
however, it was made dependent upon Burton Lazars in Leicester-
shire and used thereafter for the poor. In 1535 it housed fourteen

[1] *Letters of Lady Brilliana Harley.* Ed. T. T. Lewis. Camden Society, London,
1854, pp. 126, 147.
[2] Abbot Byrcheston. A. P. Stanley: *Historical Memorials of Westminster Abbey.*
London, 1868, p. 353.
[3] T. D. Hardy: *Syllabus of Rymer's Foedera.* London, 1885, p. 15.

paupers. The 'ancient lazar house' in Knightsbridge recorded in 1485 was closed altogether in 1629, and the one that had existed in Southwark was absorbed in St. Bartholomew's. Practically speaking, there were no leper hospitals in London;[1] sufferers had to be sent to Burton Lazars or other avowed lazar houses. Isolated cases still occurred, but London was a long way ahead of the rest of the kingdom, where the disease lingered on for another century or more. As late as 1569 a provincial mayor gave a leper the large sum of four shillings as a bribe to go elsewhere,[2] and this irresponsible attitude was very general.

The mysterious fever that swept through London, and thence into the provinces, in early Tudor days, was known as the sweating sickness. It returned in 1551 but was not then so virulent, nor was London so much affected as the rest of the country by this second outbreak. In its first onset this malady was sudden and violent, it was said to be most often fatal in cases where the victim was a man between thirty and forty years old. Polydore Vergil calls it 'a baleful affliction' and describes the symptoms very candidly.[3] There was a high fever, with head and stomach pains and violent sweating for twenty-four hours—if the victim survived so long. Even when the sweating ceased, there were continual relapses.

Edward Plumpton wrote to his master on 28 June 1490, 'Sir, they begine to die in London',[4] and as the summer progressed the cases multiplied. Polydore Vergil, however, gives an account of the sensible treatment—lying still in bed, well covered up, and taking plenty of warm drink[5]—that was found by experience to be the best, and after a time the number of deaths greatly diminished.

It was the sudden and unheralded onslaught of the disease that added so greatly to its terror; as during the outbreak of bubonic plague in 1665, a man might be working or playing, apparently in perfect health, and a few hours later he would be dead. There was however, this difference, that the sweating sickness—as did small-pox at a later date—tended to attack the well-nourished and the

[1] M. D. Knowles: *Medieval Religious Houses*. London, 1953, vol. i, p. 278.
[2] The Mayor's Accounts. The Borough Records of Lyme Regis.
[3] *Anglica Historia*. Ed. Denys Hay. Camden Society, London, 1950, pp. 7-9. The disease is still found occasionally in Eastern Europe.
[4] *Plumpton Correspondence*. Ed. T. Stapleton. Camden Society, London, 1839, p. 98.
[5] *Anglica Historia*, p. 9.

well-to-do,[1] whereas the plague victims were more often the poor dwellers in rat-infested tenements. Plague flourished in the lanes and alleys and the hovels on the waterfront, in dark attics and overcrowded cellars: its allies were dirt and ignorance and squalor.

The pest-houses were soon full, they were far too few to deal with even a mild epidemic. The next step was to try to isolate the houses where there were known cases of plague; doors were barred and a watchman set to prevent the other inmates from leaving the house, but as the watchmen were obliged to leave their posts to buy food for the family or go on errands, and in any case could not watch the back of the house at the same time as the front, this seclusion was not really practical. Nor were the regulations concerning infected clothing much more effective. Clothes and bedding were supposed to be burnt or fumigated with great thoroughness, but too often were merely thrown away and used as rags, or even sold or stolen for further use. Defoe tells us that people did try to take precautions against contagion. 'When any one bought a joint of meat in the market they would not take it off the butcher's hand, but took it off the hooks themselves. On the other hand, the butcher would not touch the money but [had] it put into a pot full of vinegar . . . They carried bottles of scents and perfumes in their hands, and all the means that could be used were used; but then the poor could not do even these things, and they went at all hazards.'[2]

Defoe also gives ghastly details of the hasty burials in plague-pits, of naked bodies tipped from carts into roughly dug trenches, but it must be remembered that he was a first-class journalist, and was not himself an observer of the scenes he so graphically describes. His *Journal* is given verisimilitude by his apparently correct and sober use of parish registers and mortality bills, but its real value lies in the powerful picture he paints of the terror and consternation of the times. Nor was this terror confined to London and its environs. As far away as Blandford in Dorset, London carriers were not allowed to lodge in the town for fear of the infection,[3] and an inn-keeper from the village of Pimperne, close

---

[1] F. P. Wilson: *The Plague in Shakespeare's London.* London, 1927, pp. 92–3.
[2] *Journal of the Plague Year,* p. 34.
[3] George Roberts: *Social History of the Southern Counties.* London, 1856, p. 290.

by, was committed to gaol because he entertained the luckless carriers in his inn.

Following the normal course of such outbreaks, deaths from plague grew fewer as colder weather came, and there were, too, more recoveries. If the hard swellings characteristic of the disease could be induced to break and discharge, the patient might get well, but too often the swellings were internal and sufferers were mortally ill before they were aware of any infection. Yet, the horror and dread of plague among all classes must not be exaggerated. John Evelyn, who was one of the Commissioners for the Sick and Wounded, felt it his duty to stay on in London and made no particular merit of doing so, although he had been careful to leave his London house when Civil War broke out lest he might be obliged to carry arms. Pepys, too, perhaps a bolder man but probably less sensitive, stayed at home as a matter of course. These two diarists remained in London to chronicle the second great calamity of these years, the Great Fire that roared through the plague-ridden quarters of the city and cleansed it of infection for a time.

Thus ended this particular plague of London, but others were to follow. As 'the pestilence' subsided, smallpox began to increase so that by 1688 it was 'very rife and mortall',[1] and in due course there came the scourge of cholera. These were problems that vexed the whole nation; in London attention was focused upon them because the city was so vulnerable, and it was in London that the solution had to be found. Smallpox was duly vanquished by medical science, but the defeat of cholera was associated with public works of engineering, with water-supply, bureaucracy, and the single-minded efforts of one great man: Edwin Chadwick, to whom London owes a debt that has never been sufficiently acknowledged.[2]

---

[1] *The Portledge Papers*. Ed. R. J. Kerr and I. C. Duncan. London, 1928, p. 30.
[2] For Edwin Chadwick's reforms, see *infra*, Chapter Thirteen.

Chapter Six

BEN JONSON'S LONDON

I. THEATRE

Today I go to the Blackfriars play-house,
Sit in the view, salute all my acquaintance,
Rise up between the acts, let fall my cloke,
Publish a handsome man, and a rich suit,
As that's a special end why we go thither,
All that pretend to stand for't on the stage:
The ladies ask, who's that? for they do come
To see us, love, as we do them.

BEN JONSON: The Devil is an Ass.[1]

THE audiences who flocked to the theatres in the last years of the sixteenth century were quite certain what they wanted to see and hear, and they voiced their opinions without equivocation. The difficulty was not to tempt the public to attend them, but to build the playhouses quickly enough and to supply enough new plays to satisfy the appreciative—though highly critical—London playgoers. Before 1575–6 plays had been performed in the innyards of the City, but at this time 'two public-houses for the acting and shew of comedies, tragedies and histories, for recreation',[2] were set up. This was the beginning of London's theatreland, although for various reasons it was sited at first across the river, in Southwark—to the chagrin of the City authorities, who could not control it, and to the delight of the London watermen[3] who ferried the audiences to and fro.

The English traveller, Thomas Coryat, in his 'hastily gobbledup' *Crudities*—first published in 1611—draws a very interesting comparison between performances in the early English playhouses and a comedy he saw acted in Venice. He found that the Venetian

---

[1] Act I, sc. iii. Everyman edn., vol. ii, p. 275.
[2] John Stow: *Survey of London*. C. L. Kingsford. London, 1908, vol. ii, p. 369.
[3] See *infra*, Chapter Seven. Topography and technical questions concerning the design of the early theatres and their functions are outside the scope of this book: a brief account is given in the authors' earlier work, *A History of the English People*, London, 1950, pp. 297–302.

actors could not compare with the English 'for apparel, shews and music' and thought their theatre 'very beggarly' compared with 'our stately play-houses in England'. Coryat's remarks are to some extent supported by the evidence of a German traveller to England, who was impressed also by the variety in price of the different seats. Prices of admission were low; you could stand for a penny but would have to pay extra for a seat, and still more for a cushion to lay upon it.[1] A further payment entitled onlookers to sit in one of the boxes, or even to take a stool and sit upon the stage.

When a play was on, a flag was flown and trumpets announced that it would soon begin, so that the audience could hurry to secure good seats, for these were seldom, if ever, reserved. Indeed, some licences prohibited reservation at any time.[2] The money was collected by 'gatherers' and immediately put into locked boxes—hence the term 'box-office'.[3] From about the year 1564 play-bills were shown, so that the audience would know what sort of a programme to expect, but extra turns—songs, dances, and acrobatics—were often introduced between the acts. These were impromptu, as were the interpolations sometimes made by members of the audience, those sitting on the stage occasionally taking an unrehearsed and not always welcome part in the play.

Since the plays were generally in the afternoon—'being the idlest time of the day, wherein men that are their own masters . . . do wholly bestow themselves upon pleasure'[4]—they were performed by daylight, but if darkness fell they would be continued by the light of torches or baskets of burning tarred rope. Accidents caused either by the flimsy character of the wooden construction, or more commonly from fire, were fairly frequent. As a rule, a fire was quickly detected and the audience would be able to escape without hurt, but the 'wood and straw' theatres were utterly destroyed. In 1613 at the burning of the Globe, the theatre where Shakespeare had acted at an earlier date, the only casualty beyond 'a few forsaken cloaks' was a man who had his breeches set on fire, but he 'by the benefit of a provident wit' put out the fire with bottled ale.[5]

[1] *Thomas Platter's Travels in England.* Trans. C. Williams. London, 1937, p. 167.
[2] Sir E. K. Chambers: *The Elizabethan Stage,* 4 vols., vol. ii, p. 547.
[3] *Ibid.,* vol. ii, p. 538.
[4] Thomas Nashe: *Pierce Penilesse,* 1592.
[5] Letter from Sir Henry Wotton to his nephew. Quoted Chambers: *op. cit.,* vol. i p. 419.

Our concern is rather with actors and playgoers than with the mechanics of production, questions of technique, scenery and so on. In the lower grades actors ranked as journeymen or 'hirelings', engaged and paid by the week, and the boys who played women's parts were probably apprenticed to the leading players. There does not appear to be any evidence that the boys were pushed into any particular prominence or exceptional esteem. Young Salathiel Pavey, who died at the age of thirteen after a most successful career of three years, was described by Ben Jonson (who wrote his epitaph) as 'the stage's jewel', but contemporary praise was normally all for mature actors like Burbage and Alleyn.[1]

The more prominent actors were 'sharers' in the permanent companies and took their percentage of the profits: the manager was salaried but almost certainly one of the main sharers. As for the owner of the theatre, he was allotted a fixed proportion of the takings as rent.[2] It can be seen that a sharer in a successful company might make a large income; Richard Burbage, on his death in 1619, was said to be worth £300 a year, and Alleyn was able to retire before he reached the age of forty and to buy the manor of Dulwich for no less than £10,000. Among other assets an actor included 'playing apparel': in the *Groatsworth of Wit*[3] Robert Greene claimed that his wardrobe was worth more than £200. After 1597, when actors were officially recognized as craftsmen, their position was better defined and more secure, so that the stage became a better profession for the ordinary competent performer as distinct from the 'star'.

Some actors—Shakespeare is the supreme example—were playwrights as well, and adapters of other men's work to suit the needs of their own company. A few topical allusions could bring an outmoded play again into favour: 'They are as crafty with an old play', wrote Donald Lupton in 1632,[4] 'as bawds with old faces; the one puts on a new fresh colour, the other a new face and name'. It is notable that many of the most eminent of the dramatists writing for the Bankside theatres were not London-born at all. Only Ben Jonson was a true Londoner, the others came from Warwickshire (Shakespeare), Sussex (Fletcher), Kent (Marlowe),

[1] Ivor Brown: *Shakespeare*. London, 1949, pp. 246–7.
[2] Chambers: *op. cit.*, vol. i, pp. 352–62.
[3] Written in 1592. Reprinted 1923, p. 33.
[4] *London and the Countrey Carbonadoed and quartered into seuerall characters.*

Hertfordshire (Chapman) and some from even further afield—
Massinger was bred in Wiltshire and John Ford was a Devon
man.[1]

The audiences behaved with the greatest freedom. Since, as
Dekker pointed out, 'your carman and tinker claim as strong a
voice in their suffrage, and sit to give judgment on the play's life
and death, as well as the proudest Momus among the tribe of
critic',[2] it could be claimed that these Elizabethans were truly
democratic. Some ate pasties and pies, others played cards, all
talked of their own affairs, and shouted their opinions. Booksellers
took the chance of selling pamphlets, men filled their pipes[3] and
puffed tobacco smoke until a blue haze obscured the stage. King
James said that even people who did not care for it smoked, 'as
men eat garlic', out of self-protection,[4] for the custom was very
general and a common ground for the Puritans' condemnation of
theatre-going.

As early as 1564 an attempt was made to suppress the London
theatres, the excuse being that the concourse of people was liable
to spread plague. Again in 1573 the City of London asked for
their suppression, so that, when in the following year City
regulations made the Lord Mayor and aldermen censors of both
plays and playhouses, players found it convenient to erect their
theatres outside the City boundaries. The chief Puritan arguments
were that plays were a waste of time, that they gave every opportunity for immoral behaviour at the time of performance and for
improper assignations thereafter, and that for boys to dress as
women was reprehensible. In a sermon at Paul's Cross, a preacher
asked, 'Will not a filthy play, with the blast of a trumpet, sooner
call thither a thousand, than an hour's tolling of a bell bring to the
sermon a hundred?'[5] Most eloquent of all the objectors was Philip
Stubbes, who in his *Anatomie of Abuses* in 1583, in the midst of
long academic arguments, complained of the 'winking and glan-
cing of wanton eyes'. In 1642 the Puritans, through Parliament,

---

[1] Ivor Brown: *Winter in London.* London, 1952, p. 104.
[2] *The Gull's Hornbook*, 1609. In the later edition of this book—*Vincent's Young
Gallants' Academy*, 1674, this chapter is greatly modified.
[3] Orazio Busino (*Cal. Ven. State Papers*, 1617–19) says that London gentlewomen
also smoked, 'but only as a medicine and in private'.
[4] *A Counter-blast to Tobacco*; written in 1604 but not published till 1672.
[5] In 1597. Quoted by J. Dover Wilson: *Life in Shakespeare's England.* Cambridge,
1915, p. 177.

succeeded in imposing their restrictions and, at any rate officially, the theatres were closed until the Restoration in 1660. During this break ordinary Londoners lost the habit of attending plays and thereafter audiences became more aristocratic and far less lively.

Even before the Restoration there had been performances of a high degree of skill but with far less popular appeal—the masques or revels designed to enliven Court banquets and receptions. These were elaborate and highly specialized, devised for a small sophisticated audience and intended to appeal to the eye as much as to the ear and mind. Although they were often acted by amateurs, the audience at these masques were onlookers only; there was never any question of spectators being swept into the play or of their helping to remove the corpses in the last act. Violence was replaced by elegance, just as flaring torchlight or crude daylight gave place to the gentle glow of candles. Deep harmony between words, music, and setting, was an essential quality of the masque, and the most successful of all partnerships was that of Ben Jonson and Inigo Jones. Their first work together was the *Masque of Blackness*, which was performed on Twelfth Night at Whitehall, in the winter of 1604–5. The sensitive imagination of Jones and the poetic genius and erudition of Ben Jonson were here perfectly combined in the setting of an 'artificial sea' with the masquers in a great ornamental shell. If only their dispositions had been as harmonious as were their talents the partnership might have continued for many years, but jealous quarrels broke up this artistic association, and although—like Gilbert and Sullivan at a later date—each attempted to work with other partners, neither artist could reach his full stature without the other.

Perhaps, of the two, Inigo Jones was the more original. This London-born Welsh boy, son of a poor cloth-worker in West Smithfield, had studied long and carefully, mostly in Italy, and his fastidious taste was matched by his ingenuity. Jones would have done better with a good agent to protect his interests, for he and Ben Jonson were each paid £40 for their 'invention' of a Christmas masque in 1610, but the dancing master who trained the performers was awarded £50: perhaps the latter was a better businessman, or the performers may have been very slow to learn, but it does seem that the poet and the designer were comparatively underpaid.

These masques and interludes at their best were not much more
than elegant and witty trifles: they dated very easily and at their
worst they might be tedious and inept. They were, indeed, a
backwater of the strongly flowing dramatic stream, now checked,
now diverted, which by the end of the seventeenth century was
again flowing with a steady current.

II. BARTHOLOMEW FAIR

Now the Fair's a filling!
  O, for a tune to startle
The birds o' the booths here billing,
    Yearly with old St. Bartle! . . .
Buy any ballads, new ballads?

BEN JONSON: *Bartholomew Fair,*[1] *c.* 1610.

There are cozeners abroad, therefore it behoves men to be wary.

SHAKESPEARE: *The Winter's Tale.*[2]

Thomas Fuller, in contrasting Shakespeare and Ben Jonson, said
that they reminded him of an English man-of-war and 'a Spanish
great galleon'. He claimed that Jonson, like the latter, 'was built
higher in learning; solid but slow, in his performances', but that
Shakespeare could tack and turn and 'take advantage of all winds'.[3]
To represent Jonson as so massive a poet is perhaps a due tribute to the depth and solidity of his mind, but if Fuller had been
thinking of him only as the author of *Bartholomew Fair* he must
surely have described him as some more sprightly vessel. The
whole merry, bawdy spirit of the fair-ground is in this play, and
the traditional sport and frolic of all Londoners.

Ever since Henry I gave a charter to hold a fair to the Augustinian Prior of St. Bartholomew's, Prior Rayer, commonly known
as Rahere, there had been frequent quarrels between the monastery
and the City authorities. Rahere had once been the king's jester,
and tradition has it that he used to attend his own fair and give
exhibitions of skilful juggling there. From the proceeds of the
fair he endowed his Priory and his hospital, and as Bartholomew
Fair grew in popularity and wide renown, so did its revenues
tempt the City to claim a share in the tolls levied on goods carried
to and from the fair-ground. In the mid-fifteenth century the

[1] Act II, sc. i. Everyman edn., vol. ii, p. 197.
[2] Act IV, sc. iii.   [3] *English Worthies*. London, 1662.

City's right to tolls and rents of the Fair on ground outside the Priory's property was grudgingly admitted,[1] and when at the Dissolution the Priory's rights were allotted to Sir John Rich, the Attorney-General, the City attempted to buy them from him and afterwards from his family, but the owners would not agree until nearly three hundred years later, when in 1830 the City bought these long-coveted rights.

By this time, much of its glory had faded, but in Ben Jonson's day the Fair was at the height of its fame. Of all the London fairs this was the one that attracted the largest crowds, and even the business of buying and selling goods was subordinated to the raffish enjoyment of the multitude. When the German merchant J. E. Zetzner visited London in 1700 he was told that it was (with May Fair) one of 'the chiefest nurseries of vice',[2] and even a hundred years earlier it seems to have attracted the maximum number of rogues and swindlers. These cajoled the wide-eyed public into parting with their money in exchange for worthless trifles, quack medicines, and tawdry finery.

It was at Bartholomew Fair in 1642, when Signor Lupino presented *Bel and the Dragon*, that a famous theatrical family first appeared, and the history of the Lupinos can be traced on the stage or in the circus ring right up to modern times.[3] In the same way, tricks and 'gags' that are familiar in radio or television studios today can be traced back to the London fair-grounds. Even here they were not new, but can be found in medieval sermons and miracle plays: sufficiently careful research might identify them with the jests of Noah and his sons when they were building the ark.

The crowds that jostled and pushed one another, thronging the stalls and sideshows and visiting exhibitions of freaks and monsters of all kinds, were greatly to the advantage of cutpurse and pickpocket. They tended also to spread the infection of plague and other, lesser, epidemics, and it was for this reason that the City authorities insisted in 1593 that the Fair must be cancelled for that year, despite a tremendous outcry from stall-holders and all other interested parties, as well as from the general public.

[1] Thomas Frost: *The Old Showman and the Old London Fairs*. London, 1874, p. 9.
[2] Quoted by M. Letts: *As the Foreigner Saw Us*. London, 1935, p. 139.
[3] Ivor Brown: *Winter in London*, London, 1952, p. 133.

8

Ballad-mongers and taverners formed a large class who made money indirectly from the fair. The former, by 1682,[1] were obliged to have licences for singing or selling their ballads, as did mountebanks before they were able to perform; these were issued by the Revels Office in Whitehall, and the mountebanks had the extra distinction that their licences had to be printed in black and red. Typical of many innkeepers' advertisements is that of Thomas Dale, who was ordinarily a drawer at the Crown tavern in Aldgate, but at the time of Bartholomew Fair kept the Turk's Head Musick Booth in Smithfield. Here, he said, 'is a Glass of good Wine, Mum, Syder, Beer, Ale, and all other Sorts of Liquors to be Sold; and where you will likewise be entertained with good Musick, Singing and Dancing'. Dale's dancers included as an extra attraction a young woman who performed prodigies of dexterity with fourteen wine glasses, turning all the time 'above a Hundred Times as fast as a Windmill'.[2]

Some of these music booths were innocent enough, but others had so bad a name that all were prohibited by the Lord Mayor in 1700. By this time there were fewer aristocratic and fashionable fair-goers, and within fifty years even superior shopkeepers and their families were beginning to find Bartholomew Fair beneath their notice. They could find tinsel trifles to buy in such bazaars as the Pantheon in Oxford Street, or the Lowther Arcade, and preferred watching plays and pantomimes in comfort to craning their necks and tiring their feet while contending with a rough and jostling crowd. The Fair declined, and changed its character. Noisy as it had always been, in its last years it became increasingly strident. The entertainment had often been crude, now it became grossly vulgar. Even the pickpockets were dissatisfied, for they had to work harder for less return. As a means of trade and exchange the Fair had outlived its usefulness, its entertainment value had sunk very low, and Ben Jonson's balladmongers were no longer to be seen or heard. By the nineteenth century Bartholomew Fair was dead. The last Fair was held in 1855, but for years before this its vitality had drained away.

[1] Frost: *op. cit.*, p. 50.
[2] Quoted *ibid.*, p. 64.

III. BULLS AND BEARS

28 October 1561. . . . was at Whyt-hall grett baytyng of the
bull and bere for the in-bassadurs of Franse . . . the wyche the
Quee's grace was ther, and her counsell and mony nobull men.

The Diary of Henry Machyn,[1] 1550–63.

Those who flocked to the bull- and bear-baitings at Paris Garden
in Southwark, or in the grander surroundings of Whitehall on
state occasions, were very much the same kind of people as the
play-goers and those who attended executions and mutilations.
Fine ladies and men of elegance and taste witnessed these exhibitions with perfect composure, while the lesser citizens encouraged their champions with hoarse cries.

The banquet and entertainment given by James I to the Constable of Castile at Whitehall Palace on Sunday, 18 August 1604,[2]
was gracefully devised and served by gentlemen of high rank, and
was followed by instrumental music and dancing in which Prince
Henry performed a galliard 'with much sprightliness and modesty':
all was in exquisite taste. Yet as soon as the ball was over 'all took
their places at the windows of the room that looked out upon a
square, where a platform was raised, and a vast crowd had
assembled to see the king's bears fight with greyhounds. This
afforded great amusement.' Later, there was a bull-baiting by
fierce dogs, the bull being tethered by the head on a long rope.
This, too, was well received, and the entertainment was concluded
by an exhibition of rope-dancing and tumbling. The Constable
enjoyed all the entertainment provided without reservation or
discrimination between the items.

It has been pointed out that 'the Londoners who attend nowadays a prize-fight at Harringay arena are most unlikely next night
to be found at a Symphony Concert or a production of Hamlet'[3]
and this underlines the essential difference between audiences in
the reigns of the first Elizabeth and the second. Indeed, Shakespeare's heroes at the Globe had their rivals next door, at Paris
Garden, in 'Harry Hunks' the famous champion bear and another
named 'Sackerson' who is mentioned by Master Slender in *The*

[1] Ed. J. G. Nichols. Camden Society, London, 1848, p, 270.
[2] Described in a rare Spanish contemporary tract, printed by W. B. Rye: *England
as seen by Foreigners in the days of Elizabeth and James I.* London, 1865, pp. 118–24.
[3] Ivor Brown: *Shakespeare.* London, 1949, p. 113.

Merry Wives of Windsor. The groundlings who could appreciate
the beauties and subtleties of *As You Like It* or *The Tempest* were
equally at home with the technicalities of snapping bandogs[1] or
worrying mastiffs, and until this fact is fully realized it is impossible
to appreciate the character of a London audience in either setting.

Generally the bears were set upon by several dogs at once, and
they were further handicapped by having their teeth ground
down so that they were dependent entirely upon their powerful
forepaws. Bulls were generally matched with one highly trained
dog at a time. The German Thomas Platter describes a fight he
saw where a great white bull tossed dog after dog, attendants
catching them on sticks to break their fall so that they would not
be killed but could be nursed back to health for further fighting.[2]
It is reminiscent of the remark of a master of staghounds who is
reported to have said, 'I would not tolerate any cruelty . . . the
same stag is never hunted more than three times in one season'.[3]

Sometimes fights were staged between men instead of animals.
In one of these gladiatorial shows Jorevin de Rocheford saw one
combatant with his wrist nearly severed and the other with his
ear cut off. 'For my part', he said, 'I think there is an inhumanity,
a barbarity and cruelty, in permitting men to kill each other for
diversion.'[4] At much the same date John Evelyn went, after an
absence of twenty years, to the Bear-garden to see 'cock-fighting,
dog-fighting, beare and bull baiting, it being a famous day for all
these butcherly sports'. He added that he, for one, was 'heartily
weary of the rude and dirty pastime'.[5] There were few who
thought as he did, and fewer still who would admit their disgust.
Bear-baiting did, however, begin to die out towards the end of
the seventeenth century, and by the time of Queen Anne the
three bear gardens that still existed were ill-attended.[6] It was not
made illegal, however, until 1835. Cock-fighting continued to be
popular for many years, though it was practised more frequently
outside than inside London's boundaries.

[1] Chained dogs, generally mastiffs or bloodhounds.
[2] *Travels in England, 1599*, p. 169.   [3] *The Times*, January 1956.
[4] Description of England, etc. (Paris, 1672). Trans. Rye: *op. cit.*, p. 571.
[5] 16 June 1670. In this book references to Evelyn's *Diary* are given by date only
because the definitive six-volume edition, ed. E. S. de Beer, Oxford, 1955, is not likely
to be accessible outside the larger libraries. There are earlier editions that can well
be used by the general reader.
[6] John Ashton: *Social Life in the Reign of Queen Anne*. London, 1888, vol. i, p. 296.

If the general public continued to approve these blood sports, the Puritans certainly did not, but their condemnation was less on the grounds of cruelty to the animals and the degradation of the spectators than because such shows were thought to foster vice. When the gallery of the Paris Garden collapsed in 1583, when several spectators were killed and five or six hundred injured, this happening was claimed to be 'an extraordinary judgement of God' and the fruit of 'jolity' upon a Sunday. Even before this date the sternly Puritan Archdeacon of Hereford had written:[1]

> What follye is thys to kepe wyth daunger,
> A greate mastyfe dogge and a foule ouglye bear?
> And to thys onelye ende, to se them two fyght
> Wyth terrible teaarynge, a full ouglye syght.

Every Sunday at Paris Garden, Crowley said, the bear-warden used to collect a halfpenny apiece from two or three hundred spectators, and at special gala performances the number must have been far higher and the entrance fee greater. It is unlikely, however, that anything approaching such large sums—after making full allowance for changed values—were demanded or paid as for ringside seats at boxing contests today.

IV. PAUL'S WALK

Paul's Walk is the land's epitome . . . It is the general mint of all famous lies, which are here, like the legends of popery, first coined and stamped in the church. All inventions are emptied here, and not a few pockets . . . the principal inhabitants and possessors are stale knights, and captains out of service, men of long rapiers and breeches, which after all turn merchants here, and traffic for news.

JOHN EARLE: *Microcosmographie*, 1628.[2]

At some time before the end of the middle ages it had become common practice to treat the great and noble church of St. Paul's as a thoroughfare for citizens, and even as a market place. The great throng of pilgrims, who came to venerate the relics and to visit the shrine of St. Eorcenwald, bought badges and souvenirs from the stalls which were set up in the body of the church instead of in the porch as elsewhere. The Dean and Chapter allowed this

---

[1] *Select Works of Robert Crowley*. Ed. J. M. Cooper. E.E.T.S., London, 1872, p. 16.
[2] Ed. E. Arber. London, 1868, p. 52.

commercialism and also issued licences to the twelve scribes who
sat every weekday at tables in the west end. These were professional letter-writers for the illiterate laity, and helped to draw up
legal documents; from this concession it was a short step to the
allotting of piers in the nave to lawyers beside which they could
receive their clients as in an office.

Very soon, all sorts of business were transacted in St. Paul's,
and the protests of the Dean, and of the Bishop himself, seemed
powerless to control the secular uses. Bishop Braybrook in 1385
forbade 'the playing of ball' within the Cathedral, but to no effect;
and in 1554 the Common Council of London had to step in and
forbid—among many other abuses—the leading of horses and
mules through the sacred building. It seems that the Commonwealth soldiers who stabled 800 horses there (in 1657–8) had some
sort of precedent, as had those who annoyed the inhabitants of
St. Paul's Churchyard by their brawling and incessant playing of
ninepins, but people who had been strangely blind to the dese-
cration of St. Paul's by traffic and trade were deeply shocked when
their church was robbed of its treasures and its statues broken[1]
by zealous Puritans and opportunist looters.

By the late sixteenth century the central aisle of the nave of
old St. Paul's—Paul's Walk—had become the greatest promenade
in London: indeed, in the whole kingdom. Here the news of the
day was whispered, or spoken aloud, here assignations were made
and kept, and it was said that more business deals were carried
out in Paul's Walk than in the whole of the Royal Exchange.

Dekker, in his *Gull's Hornbook*,[2] gives very full instructions to
his young gallant how he can make best use of this fashionable
concourse. He must choose his time carefully, 'when the main
shoal of islanders are swimming up and down', and he must be
wary lest he stand by the wrong pillar, where serving-men's
advertisements are pasted up, for he might be mistaken for such a
one in search of employment. Dekker also warns his gallant that if
he enters the Cathedral wearing spurs, the choirboys will swarm
about him 'like so many white butterflies' and will demand the
fee traditionally theirs—the 'spur-money' that had to be paid
even by the King himself. If he likes, he can pick his teeth with a

---

[1] G. H. Cook: *Old St. Paul's Cathedral*. London, 1955, p. 11.
[2] Written 1609. Ed. R. B. McKerrow. London, 1905, p. 40 ff.

quill or silver toothpick; and this is a good place to display his new clothes or to take careful note of fashion so that he can give due instructions to his tailor. Or the tailor might attend in Paul's Walk in person, and there take the gallant's measurements. If he has a taffeta lining to his cloak, Dekker tells his gull that a little practice will enable him to twitch it carelessly over his shoulder in a manner that will flash the coloured silk before the eyes of all his fellows.

Here, too, the gull can flourish his watch, if he has one, by pretending to set 'the wheels to the time of Paul's', and when he has exhausted all his conversation and absorbed all the news and witnessed all the fashionable notions, then is the time to climb to the leads, draw his knife and carve his name there. 'The top of Paul's', says Dekker, 'contains more names than Stow's Chronicle'.[1] These records were lost when the lead roof of St. Paul's melted in the Great Fire and Paul's Walk was reduced to a sodden mass of ashes, but unfortunately the custom of name-carving survived, as the defacement of many of our monuments can show.

Occasionally an argument might lead to a quarrel, and a scuffle to an affray: in November 1561—a few months after the fire that burned Paul's Steeple—someone 'may da fray in Powlles Chyrche', and a pillory was set up for him in the churchyard, where his ear was nailed to the post and afterwards cut off.[2]

At the north door of St. Paul's you could buy every sort of ballad or broadside, whether a ballad 'very true, and but a month old' as Autolycus claimed,[3] or an account of 'the death of a great man or the burning of a house', either of which, according to Earle, could furnish the ballad-writer with an 'argument'.[4] Booksellers had their shops, too, in and around St. Paul's Churchyard, although not all of them were as slothful as the stall-holder satirized by Thomas Nashe, who was too lazy even to nod his head in answer to a query, but could only point to his boy-assistant with his little finger,[5] and the customer had then to help the boy to rummage for the wanted book. This trade was continued long after Paul's Walk had ceased to be; printers and booksellers

[1] *Gull's Hornbook*, p. 46.
[2] *The Diary of Henry Machyn*, 1550–63. Ed. J. G. Nichols. Camden Society, London, 1848, p. 273.
[3] Shakespeare: *The Winter's Tale*, Act. IV, sc. iii.
[4] *Microcosmographie*, 1628.   [5] *Pierce Penilesse*, 1592.

were still grouped in this vicinity when other great fires a few years ago reduced their stock to ashes and their premises to rubble; but the newsmongers and spreaders of gossip had found another field. They had moved into the new coffee-houses, and that is where they must be sought hereafter.[1]

v. THE MILITIA

The citie hath many courts du guard, with new barrocaded posts, and they strongly girded with great chaines of yron . . . the daily musters and showes of all sorts of Londoners here were wondrous commendable.

WILLIAM LITHGOW: *The Present Surveigh of London*, 1643.[2]

Like other cities, London had its own militia or trainbands and London's only singularity is that the gilds played an even more prominent part in their organization than they did elsewhere. Their young men practised shooting in Moorfields, as they had throughout the middle ages, and competed for prizes, or the price of the party's supper, or simply for the pleasure of winning. The competitions might be between gild and gild, or for bowmen within a gild, or among members of a single parish. Henry Machyn records in his *Diary* for 1562 two summer shooting matches, the one between members of the company of barber-surgeons (with six drums and a flute playing as accompaniment) for 'a gret soper at ther owne hall'[3] and the other, three or four weeks later, between the two sections of St. Gregory's parish. Here the contestants were distinguished by red or yellow scarves and their musical supporters ran to six drums and four flutes: like the barber-surgeons' match it was followed by a festive supper.[4] In September of the same year, the Lord Mayor called out all the Crafts to bring their men 'in harnes to Leydenhall with pykes and gones and bowes and bylles, in bluw clokes garded with red' and paraded his militia in Moorfields the following day, a gay sight to see and a holiday for the militiamen.[5]

Other favourite training grounds were at Islington and Finsbury; indeed, wherever there was an open space butts would be

---

[1] Chapter Nine, § iv, *infra*.
[2] Printed in *Somers Tracts*, vol. iv (2nd edn.), 1810, pp. 537–8.
[3] *The Diary of Henry Machyn*, p. 286.
[4] *Ibid.*, pp. 287–8. This was on 14 July 1562.   [5] *Ibid.*, pp. 292–3.

set up and the arrows would fly thick and fast. When the Venetian
Ambassador's secretary was staying with his master in Sir Paul
Pindar's house, in Bishopsgate Street, he complained that the trainbands made so much noise and disturbance that he could not eat
his dinner in peace. All round the house the fields were being used
not only for shooting but for all sorts of manoeuvres and mock
sieges, and the noise at times was, he said, unendurable.[1]

The trainbands, like the modern Home Guard, often had a
stiffening of old soldiers. The Muster Acts, though they could
fairly easily be evaded, swept young men away for a term of
military service, from which they returned to civilian occupations
toughened and seasoned by their experience. Ben Jonson left his
bricklaying to serve in the Netherlands as a soldier, whether as a
conscript or as a volunteer is not certainly established.[2] Those
who did volunteer for service sometimes returned greatly dis-
illusioned. A friend of the sardonic letter-writer James Howell
returned from the wars with an injured arm and a fixed determination to fight no more, and Howell says: '. . . he confesseth
himself to be an egregious fool to leave his mercership and go to
be a musketeer;'[3] but there were others who came home riper
in experience and with tales to tell to all that they could persuade
to listen.

The fortification of London in 1643 was carried out by the
trainbands with much amateur help. Willing helpers threw aside
tools of their trade and rushed out into the fields in a holiday
spirit to help the soldiers. William Lithgow, in his *Surveigh of
London*, printed in 1643, describes their efforts. All sorts of shopkeepers and merchants, 'with great alacritie', marched to the out-
works carrying on their shoulders iron mattocks and wooden
shovels, to the sound of 'roaring drummes', with flying colours
and girded swords to show their rank. Most of the companies had
with them a number of camp-followers—'ladies, women, and
girls'—marching two and two, and carrying baskets to help with
the work. Lithgow says that all the trades took part in raising the
fortifications, and gives numbers that are almost certainly too

---

[1] Orazio Busino. Quoted by M. Letts: *As the Foreigner Saw Us*, p. 15.
[2] Miss Marchette Chute in *Ben Jonson of Westminster*, London, 1954, thinks he was
conscripted, but see the review of this book in the *Times Literary Supplement*,
31 December 1954.
[3] *Familiar Letters*. London, 1903, vol. ii, p. 238.

round and too high, ending his list with the remark that 'a thousand oyster wives advanced from Billingsgate'.[1]

Londoners could combine for a common purpose, although normally each individual trade or class was more likely to follow its own interests exclusively; in the next chapter there is a detailed study of the position and qualities of the London watermen which bears out this statement and underlines their independence and intransigence. A national emergency was needed to weld together divergent interests; even a calamity like the Great Fire could not do it: the four days' terror is a pitiful tale of non-cooperation.

In 1745 the Volunteer Corps was formed. It was on much the same lines as the old trainbands, which were absorbed in the Militia in 1794. With the threat of the French invasion, Londoners flocked to join the Volunteers, just as in a more recent crisis they joined the Territorial Army—descendants of the casual sport-loving and high-spirited young archers who made such a noise in Bishopsgate.

[1] *Somers Tracts*, vol. iv, p. 538.

Chapter Seven

JOHN TAYLOR'S LONDON

1. THE LONDON WATERMEN

All sorts of men work all the means they can
To make a 'Thief' of every Waterman:
And as it were in one consent they join
To trot by land i' th' dirt, and save their coin.
. . . Against the ground, we stand and knock our heels
Whilst all our profit runs away on wheels.

JOHN TAYLOR: *An Arrant Thief*, 1623.

LIKE Dick Whittington, John Taylor came to London from Gloucestershire[1] to be apprenticed to a London tradesman, but he sprang from humbler stock and never reached high office in the City. His only connection with the Lord Mayor of London was the 'triumph' he composed for more than one mayoral pageant, and the peak of his career was reached in 1613 when he arranged the water pageant at the marriage of the Princess Elizabeth. John Taylor's real claim to fame, however, lies in his championship of the London watermen; he was their spokesman and a very vociferous one. His poetry is of a much higher order than has generally been allowed, and there is a racy topicality about his work that puts him not far below Defoe. Above all, Taylor gives us a vivid picture of the watermen's lives, profits, dangers, and interests—not with the objective view of an observer, but as a frank self-portrait.

London watermen were operating in medieval times but no Act regulating their conduct is found before 1514.[2] By John Taylor's day the watermen were well established; they had become a Company and had their own hall in the City.[3] In organization they conformed to the general pattern and apprentices served

---

[1] He was born in Gloucester, 24 August 1580. See the introduction to the *Works of John Taylor the Water Poet*. Ed. C. Hindley. London, 1872.
[2] H. Humpherus: *History of the Origin and Progress of the Company of Watermen and Lightermen of the River Thames, 1514–1859*. London, 1874–86, vol. i, p. 70.
[3] It was burned down in the Great Fire and rebuilt four years later.

under the usual conditions. The only extraneous circumstance was the hazard of being pressed in time of war: watermen's apprentices were excellent material for the Navy, and were very often seized by the Press-gang. John Taylor himself was pressed; he had been bound to a waterman of Whitehall Stairs at the usual age of fourteen, and within two years had been pressed although eighteen was supposed to be the minimum age. When he was still only sixteen Taylor had seen service at the siege of Cadiz in 1596; soon after this he was wounded and allowed to return to the Thames and his old master.

The pressing of watermen was always a grievance and a danger hanging over the heads of all the younger men; only Trinity House servants were immune. There was, however, another side to the matter. Some masters accepted far more boys than they needed or could maintain, yet would not turn them over to trade rivals who had means to feed and train them. One boy for nearly two years served a master who did not even have a boat, and earned a very meagre living doing odd jobs for a local brew-house.[1] Such masters often persuaded the Press-gang to take their apprentices for the Navy, because they were legally entitled to any prize money the boys might earn if they could lay hands on it.[2]

Those who had served in the Navy were not entitled to any pension, but in the middle years of the sixteenth century some provision had been made for aged watermen who had been in the Navy or who had worked as collectors of wool duties in the Staple offices, when Henry VIII had some almshouses built in New Palace Yard;[3] but there was room here for only seven men and one woman. This provision cannot have done much to solve the problems of those who had grown old in their country's service and could no longer earn their living. Even the chance of winning prize money could not reconcile the watermen to the system of the Press-gang, and they continued to evade the officers by any means they could.

Wild estimates of the number of watermen have been given from time to time; Taylor claimed that there were 40,000 'water-

[1] M. D. George: *London Life in the Eighteenth Century*. London, 1930, p. 383.
[2] *Ibid.*, p. 234.
[3] Humpherus: *op. cit.*, vol. i, p. 89.

men and those that lived and were maintained by them', but this statement is certainly exaggerated.[1] It was difficult to reach an accurate figure because so many grades and types were included, from the regular bargemen to the dare-devil 'bridge-shooters'[2] who specialized in the dangerous art of taking their craft under London Bridge.

It is possible that the fishermen, who were really quite distinct, were included among the watermen in these estimates. The term 'fishermen' was used to cover several different types, from the rough individuals living at Barking or Bankside, or farther west at Hammersmith, each with his own boat and one apprentice, to the capitalist who owned several fishing vessels and imported salmon from Berwick-on-Tweed. In the following century, in 1758, one of these princely fishmongers claimed that for six months in the year he employed between 1,300 and 1,500 men.[3] The apprentices of the poorer types of fishermen certainly had a very hard time. Besides having to sleep in the boat to protect it from being stolen during the night, the boys had to share all the uncertainties of their masters' trade. They were generally cold and often hungry, though not all were as unfortunate as the eleven-year-old apprentice of John Bennett of Hammersmith, who died from cold and hunger and wounds inflicted by his master.[4]

By the eighteenth century the Billingsgate salesmen, who took the Thames fish and sold it on commission to the City fishmongers and the hawkers, or 'basket-people', had become highly organized and the actual catchers of fish were correspondingly depressed— a process that was accelerated by the beginning of the nineteenth century so that Francis Place could write in 1824: 'These people are by no means so well off as they were thirty or forty years ago. Fishing in the river ... [is not] so good a trade as it was even ten years ago'.[5] In John Taylor's London, however, the fishermen were vigorous and flourishing and, on the whole, in better heart than were the watermen. They still caught fish for food and did not then, as was alleged at a later date, destroy the brood or fry to

---

[1] John Norden had made a similar statement in 1594, but he included stevedores, porters, boat-builders, etc. Even so, his estimate was manifestly too high.
[2] Humpherus: *op. cit.*, vol. i, p. 81.
[3] M. D. George: *op. cit.*, p. 162.
[4] Who was found guilty of manslaughter. *Ibid.*, pp. 231–2. This was in 1733.
[5] Quoted *Ibid.*, p. 104.

make an artificial scarcity, or take the fish 'merely for their Scales which they sell to make Beads on'.[1]

The watermen were less antagonistic to the fishermen, who kept to their own business, than to the lightermen who seemed to encroach upon their affairs and sometimes carried passengers as well as goods in defiance of regulations forbidding them to do so. For the most part, watermen took their passengers across the river in six or eight-oared wherries. Technically, there was little to distinguish a barge from a wherry, though the latter was smaller and handier and therefore better for short journeys. Some had an awning for protection against rain or sun, and were furnished with cushions for the comfort of their passengers. Most rich Londoners had their own craft, as did the Earl of Bedford, but, like others, he often found it more convenient to hire one of the watermen's boats. It used to cost him 6*d*. to get from his home in the Strand to Westminster, and half-a-crown for the return fare when he went to Chiswick; the charge was always higher when the journey was made against the tide.[2] In the early nineteenth century it was still possible to persuade 'a jolly young waterman' to row 'folks from Wapping to Rotherhithe for a penny a head', according to 'Ben the Boatswain' in the play of that name.[3]

The smallest craft of the Thames—other than the fishermen's coracles—which were generally employed for very short journeys, were either hoys or the double 'skullers' known as 'oars'. A Frenchman who heard the cry 'Oars! Oars!' was shocked by what he imagined to be the crudity of the English in thus inviting him not to the river, but to a brothel.[4] Zacharias Conrad von Uffenbach, on the other hand, was delighted by the Thames shipping; like an earlier visitor[5] he 'found much to censure' in England, but here he is all praise, and gives a most spirited version of his experiences in shooting London Bridge. 'We got into our boat', he writes, 'and were rowed Londonwards with the tide; and we risked passing right through the centre of the bridge, where the eddy and the waves were so violent that, when we were under the

[1] Roger Griffiths: *A Description of the River Thames, etc.* London, 1746.
[2] G. Scott Thomson: *Life in a Noble Household.* London, 1937, p. 56.
[3] By T. E. Wilkes. First produced in 1839.
[4] M. Letts: *As the Foreigner Saw Us.* London, 1935, p. 71.
[5] Poggio Bracciolini, the Florentine humanist.

arch, the water was piled up . . . on either side of us to a much
greater height than we in our little ship.'[1]

A tilt-boat—an early version of the water-bus—ran between
Gravesend and London, carrying passengers from East Kent who
preferred this means of travel to the approach by road. The service
at first was casual and informal, but in 1736–7 an Act of Parliament
was passed for its improvement,[2] and it became more regular and
frequent.

Less a boat than a jest was the home-made contraption in
which John Taylor, with a vintner named Roger Bird, undertook
for a bet to row from London to Queenborough. This was in
1620. The 'boat' was of brown paper, stretched on a frame made
of cane, and the two 'oars' were sticks with a stockfish tied to the
end. They took with them eight bladders filled with air so that
when the boat fell to pieces, as it did within half an hour, the
oarsmen were able to keep afloat. They also saved the skeleton of
the boat and gave it to the Mayor of Queenborough to hang up
'for a monument', but it was broken up and carried off by sou-
venir-hunters. Taylor and his friend had their frolic, and copy for a
poem, so all ended in good humour although, as Taylor wrote:

> The tossing billows made our boat to caper,
> Our paper form scarce being form of paper.[3]

Much of Taylor's literary output was directed against the
builders and users of the coaches that he declared were taking
away the watermen's living, although he artlessly admits that
when driven in a private coach from Whitehall to the Tower,
'before I had been twenty yards, such a timpany of pride puffed
me up that I was ready to burst with the wind colic of vain glory'.[4]
His loyalty to his fellow watermen was, however, unfailing, and
he wrote a most impassioned account of their virtues (though he
admitted that there were 'many rude uncivil fellows in our company') and contrasted them with

> our fur-gowned money-mongers. A waterman cannot be false to his
> trade for he has no weights or measures to falsify, nor can he curtail a
> man's passage: his worst fault is, that like a lawyer he will take more

---

[1] Trans. and ed. W. H. Quarrel and M. Mare, under the title *London in 1710*.
London, 1934, p. 26.
[2] Roger Griffiths: *op. cit.*, p. 48.
[3] *Works*, p. xii.   [4] *Ibid.*, p. xix.

than his fee . . . very thankfully, his bare fare he will take willingly
(upon necessity) but less than his fare, or many times nothing, me
thinks goes against the stomach.[1]

The watermen felt even stronger hostility towards the players
than the hackney-coachmen, for they attributed much of their
distress and unemployment to the re-siting of the theatres. In the
time of Elizabeth I the opening of the theatres on Bankside had
led to a great demand for boats and the watermen had increased in
number and taken on many more apprentices, but by 1613, when
Taylor was selected to draw up and present the watermen's
petition, theatre-goers were making far less use of the river and
the watermen waited in vain for fares. *The Waterman's Suit concerning Players* was, however, less vituperative than much of
Taylor's work, and the old alliance between Thames and theatre
never wholly lapsed.

When the Hanoverian George I came to the throne the patriotic
manager of Drury Lane had the happy idea of linking his enthusiasm for the new dynasty with the affection he felt for London's
watermen. This Thomas Doggett died in 1721, and by his will bequeathed a sum to provide for all time Doggett's Coat and Badge
as a prize to be rowed for annually by 'Six Young Watermen'.[2]
The badge, of silver, was the prancing Horse of Hanover, and the
livery coat was of orange cloth. The old course, 4½ miles long,
from London Bridge to Chelsea, is still maintained and professional watermen still compete for the Coat and Badge, though few
people remember in whose honour the race was instituted.

Their serious anxiety about the decay of trade and the lying idle
of the ships is shown by the watermen's petition to Parliament in
1641, to which many thousand subscribers set their names. This
petition was strongly Protestant in character, and blame for the
fact that many seamen were going abroad to seek employment
was laid on the 'stout, strong, and insolent' Papists. Whatever the
rights of this charge, it is quite clear that the watermen were very
apprehensive about their position and determined to state their
case as loudly as possible.[3] Their truculence was not wholly

---

[1] 'The Waterman's Suit concerning Players', *Works*, p. 12.
[2] See T. A. Cook and G. O. Nickalls: *Thomas Doggett, deceased*. London, 1908, for
details of this ancient river race.
[3] *Somers Tracts*, vol. iv (2nd. edn.), 1810, p. 354.

OLD LONDON BRIDGE

THE FROZEN THAMES

Robert Adam

Christopher Wren

Henry Holland

John Nash

LONDON ARCHITECTS

bluster, and now that they had a spokesman the watermen were ready to take full advantage of his eloquence.

That they were a formidable body is shown also by their petition to the House of Lords in 1648, for peace between the King and Parliament. Taylor himself was in Oxford throughout the Civil War, and when he returned to London he kept a public-house called the Crown, in Phoenix Alley off Long Acre. After the execution of Charles I he rather daringly changed his inn's name to the Mourning Crown, but his friends persuaded him this was too risky, and so he hung up his own portrait as a sign and called the inn the Poet's Head. Here he died in 1653, an amusing person, a voluminous poet, and a great champion of the London watermen.

11. LONDON BRIDGE AND LONDON RIVER

I find . . . London to be a Town so nobly Situated, and upon such a River, as Europe certainly shows not a more usefull and agreeable.

> JOHN EVELYN: *A Character of England*, 1659.[1]

The bridge at London is worthily to be numbered among the miracles of the world.

> FYNES MORYSON: *Itinerary*, 1617.

[The Thames] . . . is the privileged place for fish and ships, the glory and wealth of the city, the highway to the sea, the bringer-in of wealth and strangers, and his business is all for water, yet he deals much with the land too: he is a little sea, and a great river.

> DONALD LUPTON: *London and the Country Carbonadoed*, 1632.

It is hard for a Londoner of today, however deep an affection he may feel for 'Sweet Thames', to imagine its banks between the City and Westminster lined on both sides with 'pleasant green meadows, like so many gardens', as Henry Belasyze described them in 1657.[2] A friend of Samuel Pepys, in the closing years of the seventeenth century, tried to cross the river to the pier confusingly named 'Westminster Bridge'[3] but lost his way owing to thick mist and 'discovered a shore with flags and reeds' within a bow-shot of the place whence he had launched his boat.[4] The

---

[1] *Miscellaneous Writings*. London, 1825, pp. 141–67.
[2] 'An English Traveller's First Curiosity', *Hist. MSS. Commission: Various Collections*, vol. ii, pp. 201–2.
[3] See *infra*, p. 131.
[4] Dr. John Wallis, F.R.S., writing from Oxford 24 October 1699: *Private Corr. and Misc. Papers of Samuel Pepys*. Ed. J. R. Tanner. London, 1926, vol. i, pp. 210–11.

loosestrife and the yellow flags, the reeds and sedges, the marshy foreground dotted with trim gardens, were as much a feature of the landscape as the river itself and the crowded ships that made Belasyze think of a forest of old trees.

The very beauty of these banks, however, showed how real was the danger of flooding. When the forces of tide and wind coincide the Thames can even now rise very quickly above its normal level; when there were no embankments to contain the flow, flooding might be sudden and violent. The plans drawn up by Wren and Evelyn for the rebuilding of London after the Great Fire each included an embankment, but none was made until the Victoria was begun in 1864. The Albert Embankment was constructed on the south side and opened in 1869, and a further embankment at Chelsea was completed in 1874. At this date the newly-formed Thames Conservancy that had been founded seventeen years earlier, was made responsible for everything to do with such matters as navigation, sources of pollution, fishing, and so on; for although embanking the river had made its behaviour more predictable and solved certain problems, in practice it had created others, until at last it became necessary to set up a special body to deal with them. This was the Port of London Authority, which in 1909 took over the responsibilities, dangers, and difficulties that were the inheritance of any body that tried to control the Thames.

In addition to its constant use as a waterway and for pleasure trips of all descriptions—as any reader of Pepys' *Diary* well knows —the river made a wonderful setting for pageants and spectacles. The part played by the river in the pageants of the Lord Mayor's Show has already been noted, and it was the inspiration of Handel's *Water Music* with which, in 1715, he won back the capricious favour of George I.

Sparkling in the sunshine or from the glow of fireworks and reflected lights, the Thames looked beautiful and wholesome, but on dull days or in cold daylight it could be seen that the water was brown and murky. It could be nothing else, for was not the river host to all kinds of refuse and sewage? The Venetian Orazio Busino, a contemporary of John Taylor, should have known something of 'turbid and stinking waters'; these are the epithets he applied to the Thames, adding that 'the odour remains even in clean linen'.[1] An earlier German traveller had also complained that clothes washed in Thames water never lost the smell of mud and slime.[2]

Under these circumstances one would not have thought that bathing in the river would have been attractive, but that London boys did swim in the Thames during early Stuart days is established by evidence given by an old man before Judge Jeffreys in 1684:[3] 'When I was a boy', he said, 'we used to swim in that place that was near Shadwell.' However, the feat of the Duchesse de Chevreuse in swimming across the Thames in the days of Charles I [4] was more in the nature of a stunt than typical of courtly pleasures. It was in the tradition of Kemp's dance from London to Norwich or Taylor's voyage in his paper boat, for many unlikely activities were undertaken at this period, mostly in answer to wagers.

The 'lost' or hidden rivers of London were in these days still fairly apparent. The Fleet was the most important, and from medieval times until it was finally covered in 1765 it figured strongly in London records. It was constantly becoming choked with mud and filth, and became better known as the Fleet Ditch. Pope in his *Dunciad* (1728) paints an unattractive picture:

> . . . Fleet Ditch, with disemboguing streams
> Rolls the large tribute of dead dogs to Thames,
> The king of dykes! than whom no sluice of mud
> With deeper sable blots the silver flood.

The 'silver flood' was interrupted in its flow only by London Bridge until mid-way through the eighteenth century, although the term 'bridge' was sometimes applied to a pier or landing-stage.

London Bridge was only less venerable than the river that it spanned. There had probably been several versions before the wooden structure that was destroyed in 1014, and it is uncertain how complete were the rebuildings that preceded the solid bridge of nineteen arches that was erected in the time of King John. As was common, a chapel was built on it where travellers could say a

[1] *Calendar of State Papers (Venetian)* 1617–19.
[2] Paul Hentzner: 'Travels in England, 1598'. Printed by W. B. Rye: *England as seen by Foreigners, etc.* London, 1865.
[3] Quoted in *Englishmen at Rest and Play (1558–1714)*. Ed. R. W. Lennard. Oxford, 1931, p. 72.
[4] Described in the *Musarum Deliciae: or The Muse's Recreation*, published in 1665.

prayer in passing and leave an offering for the upkeep of the bridge. On either side were built houses and shops; by the middle of the fourteenth century no fewer than a hundred and thirty-eight tenants were paying rent to the bridge-master.[1] Sometimes tenants failed to pay; one John atte Halle was committed by the Sheriff's court to Newgate in 1315 for arrears that amounted to the huge sum (for those days) of £250. Other properties also paid rent to the bridge-master, and from this income together with tolls

Waterworks by London Bridge (*Universal Magazine*, 1749)

and donations he was expected to meet all the expenses for repairs and maintenance. These were, at times, very heavy, especially for mending the wooden 'starlings', or platforms, built to protect the piers of the arches. It was the rush of water between these star-lings that made shooting the bridge such a perilous enterprise.

There were, as might be expected, many accidents. Arches were carried away by floating blocks of ice; there were fires in the shops and houses; barges overturned and people were swept into the river. London Bridge, however, continued to be the admiration of

---

[1] See the article by William Kent in his *Encyclopaedia of London* (new edn.). London, 1951, p. 56 ff.

all visitors and the pride of Londoners. Even the grim spectacle of traitors' heads exposed on the Bridge was regarded as one of the sights that no visitor should miss. The noise of the rushing water was increased by the forciers, or water-mills, erected to raise water for London's needs by the enterprise of a Dutch engineer in the reign of Elizabeth I, which added volume to the clamour of the traders and stall-holders. About one-third of the bridge buildings were swept away in the Great Fire, and some ninety years later an Act of Parliament ordered that all the houses should be removed. In place of them alcoves, or embrasures, were made at intervals, and in *Oliver Twist* Dickens describes Noah Claypole hiding in one of these and leaning over the parapet to avoid recognition. The bridge was again rebuilt in 1831 and the last traits of its old character were removed.

In the meantime, after much discussion and controversy, other bridges had been made across the river, to the distress and fury of the watermen who opposed each project with great bitterness. Westminster (1739–50), Blackfriars and Southwark Bridges appeared in fairly quick succession, and then came Rennie's graceful and beautiful Waterloo Bridge, which was erected between 1811 and 1817 and quickly won some measure of the admiration that old London Bridge had enjoyed for so many centuries.

The notable recovery of English shipping after the doldrums of the seventeenth century and the very great expansion during the next hundred and fifty years, when tonnage increased almost fourfold, resulted in the crowding of the port of London with valuable ships and cargoes. The magistrate, Patrick Colquhoun, estimated that £75,000,000 of floating property lay in the Thames in the course of a single year, and added that it was 'all of it, more or less, subject to acts of *peculation, fraud, embezzlement, pillage* and *depredation*, through the medium of the various and numerous classes of depraved characters who are upon the River, seeking for opportunities to acquire plunder'.[1] Thus a new and urgent problem was added to the perplexities of those who hoped to bring order and coherence into London life.

It was clear to Colquhoun that Sir John Fielding's efforts in this direction,[2] admirable as they were, were not enough, and

[1] *A Treatise on the Commerce and Police of the River Thames, etc.* London, 1800, p. 24.
[2] See *infra*, Chapter Eleven.

must be reinforced by the introduction of special river police. He
saw, too, that theft on the river was closely connected with smug-
gling, and that both legal and practical reform was imperative.
An Act of 1762 had spoken in its preamble of the bumboats,
plying between ships at anchor and the shore, which encouraged
sailors to steal ropes, buoys and stores, but not for another fourteen years were its provisions put into force. By these the bumboats had to be numbered, marked and licensed by Trinity House,
and justices of the peace were given power to issue search warrants when theft was suspected. The penalties were severe—
merely cutting ropes and cables with intent to steal might mean
seven years' transportation—and there were in fact many prosecu-
ions. Trouble from this source was, in time, greatly reduced, but
as the bumboats gradually came under the control of authority,
the watermen, benefiting from the lack of competition, found
their opportunity and became increasingly daring in acts of river
piracy.

Ships were not safe even in daylight; an American and a Guern-
sey boat were attacked the same day by the watermen who cut
their cables and stole the anchors, wishing a polite 'good morning' to the two masters who raged impotently upon deck.[1]
Lighters might be cut adrift and plundered when they reached the
shore. The watchmen who should have protected the ships at
night were often in league with the watermen and sometimes
helped them dispose of stolen property. Owners or shipmasters
had to bear these losses, for they were often not discovered until
much later: absence of goods might have been due to some error
in shipping the cargo. Casks could be, and often were, reheaded by
confederate coopers after their contents had been plundered. In
a case at the Old Bailey in 1797 it was shown that 30 hogsheads
of sugar had been stolen from three ships, and that one sugar
warehouse near the river had been wholly, and another partly,
supplied by theft. The night plunderers were known as 'Light
Horsemen', the daylight workers as 'Heavy Horsemen'.[2]

There were many classes of thieves, each with its own name
and particular technique: their activities were as specialized as
those of the 'conny-catching' rogues in Elizabethan times. There
were 'scuffle-hunters' who hid goods under their long aprons,

[1] Colquhoun: *op. cit.*, p. 51.   [2] *Ibid.*, pp. 60, 62.

THE BELMAN
OF LONDON.

Bringing to light the most notorious
villanies that are now practised
in the K I N G D O M E.

Profitable for Gentlemen, Lawyers, Merchants, Citizens, Farmers,
Masters of Housholds, and all sortes of seruants, to marke,
and delightfull for all men to Reade.

Lege, Perlege, Relege.

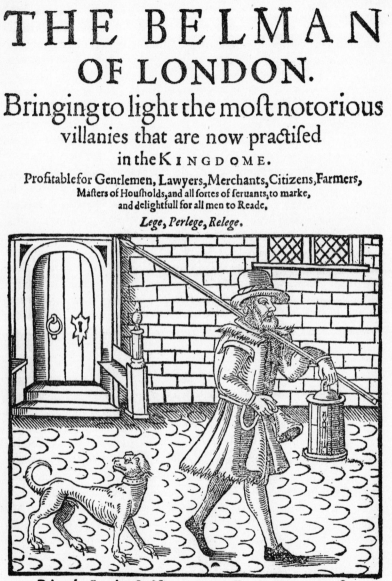

Printed at London for N A T H A N I E L B V T T E R. 1 6 0 8.

The Bellman of London, 1608

smugglers who lived out of the East India trade; even the rat-catchers who were allowed to go on board to set and inspect rat-traps used their chances to pilfer and took live rats they had caught in one ship on board another, so that they could catch the same creatures three or four times over.[1]

In the end it was the West India merchants, stung to action by their huge losses of sugar and rum, who invited Colquhoun to plan for them a Thames police force. These policemen were to supervise the loading and unloading of cargoes, and they would be paid by the owners. The effect was so great that it engendered real enthusiasm for the scheme, and the new force was taken over by the Government. In 1800 a River Police Office was founded, with three justices attached to it, and the old sailors and watermen who made up the ranks of the police force began to build up their great tradition. When the Metropolitan police force was formed in 1829, the river police kept their independence for another ten years; then the two bodies were united. Colquhoun had been dead for nearly twenty years, but he had lived long enough to see the remarkable success of his project: the truculence of the watermen had been turned to keenness and efficiency, corruption all but banished, and London River was more full of shipping than ever before.

III. 'THE WORLD RUNS ON WHEELS'[2]

They keep a vile swaggering in coaches now-a-days; the highways are stopped with them.

MIDDLETON AND DEKKER; *The Roaring Girl*, 1611.

For several centuries the London streets had been uncomfortably narrow for the traffic that surged through them. Space was further reduced by the projecting upper storeys of buildings and the signs hung out from shops and taverns; even the main streets were dark and airless, and their gutters were full of filth. Perhaps because Londoners relied so much upon their river for transport, no one seemed to trouble to repair and maintain the road in front of his house—as he was legally obliged to do—and the highways were disgustingly dirty and in places very dangerous. The narrow lanes and alleys were sometimes entirely obstructed

---

[1] Colquhoun: *op. cit.*, p. 69.
[2] The title of a pamphlet by John Taylor, 1623.

by heaps of garbage and it was a common thing to find the great lumbering waggons from the country hopelessly stuck in the stinking black mud that Orazio Busino said was one of London's special characteristics.[1]

Busino was in England before the Great Fire swept and roared its way through London thoroughfares, and it might be thought that after the rebuilding things would have been greatly improved. There were still, however, complaints of dirt and smell, and the surface of the roads was increasingly being churned up by 'the perpetual Hurry of Carts and Coaches'.[2] The congestion caused by the throngs of coaches, both hackney and private, had begun at the end of the sixteenth century; by the beginning of the eighteenth such deep ruts had been worn in the roadways and the surface was so rough that people complained of being 'so tossed and jumbled about' in their coaches 'that it has been near an Hour e'er they could recover the use of their Limbs'.[3] Indeed, one Member of Parliament on his way to Westminster was overturned in his chariot in King Street; picking himself up he went on foot to the House of Commons and complained 'in very lively terms' of the condition of the roads 'and mov'd for a Bill to be brought in accordingly'. Another M.P. opposed this, giving as one reason that 'as the Publick Companies for raising the *Thames* water were perpetually laying down their *Pipes*, or amending them, such a Bill would prove to little or no purpose'. The first Member 'in great Heat reply'd, Then if the Water companies Pipe, the Members of both Houses must Dance'.[4]

Another grievance of the M.P.s was the cart-stand in the Great Sanctuary at Westminster which, they said, inconvenienced their passage to St. James's Park. The car-men, however, told the churchwardens of St. Margaret's that it had been a 'plying Place for Carts time out of mind'[5] and refused to move elsewhere. A hundred years earlier, at much the same time as the watermen were complaining of the hackney coachmen, the shopkeepers and dwellers in the Strand had protested against 'the multitude of Hackney Coaches that are continually standing in the streets' and

[1] *Calendar of State Papers* (*Venetian*) 1617–19.
[2] Guy Miège: *The New State of England*. London, 1693. Quoted by M. Letts: *As the Foreigner Saw Us*. London, 1935, p. 40.
[3] Anon: *A Trip through London*. Pamphlet published in 1728, p. 4.   [4] *Ibid.*
[5] W. H. Manchée: *The Westminster City Fathers*. London, 1924, p. 71.

had presented a petition on this account to the House of Lords. It would seem, then, that the problem of parking vehicles in London and Westminster has existed—like the car-men's practice—'time out of mind'.

Nor were traffic jams unknown, or even unusual. *The London Spy* for April 1700 gave an account of 'a great stop' in Chancery Lane occasioned by a collision between two coaches that had blocked the road—'the Coachmen all the while saluting each other with such Diabolical Titles, and confounding one another with such bitter Execrations, as if every one was striving which should go to the Devil first'. The coachmen were renowned for their powers of vituperation, not only against one another but also in 'affronting the gentry', as Pepys has it.[1] Pepys himself was affronted when a coachman quarrelled with his fare and tried to induce Pepys (who was sharing the coach with a stranger) to pay extra. The wrangle continued for some time, until Pepys persuaded the coachman 'with fair words' to fulfil his contract.[2] The truculence of the drivers was notorious, as was their language, but in this they had some competition from the curses of passers-by who feared they would be run over.[3]

The number of hackney-coaches—John Taylor's 'caterpillar swarm of hirelings'—was not really very high; under William and Mary the limit had been fixed at 700, and in 1710 this was raised to 800. The coachmen could take out a twenty-one years' licence for the sum of £59 added to which they had to pay an annual tax of £4. They had to face some rivalry from the newly-invented sedan chairs, which were first used in London in 1623 but did not become really fashionable until the time of Queen Anne. Two hundred of these were licensed in 1711 and in the next year a hundred more; their tax was fixed at 10s. a year, and the allotted fare was a shilling a mile.[4] It cost the Earl of Bedford 5s. to hire chairs to carry himself 'and the ladies' the short distance from Bedford House, in the Strand, to church at St. Clement Danes; but perhaps this included a charge for waiting.[5]

[1] *Diary*. Ed. H. B. Wheatley. London, 1923, vol. iii, p. 70.
[2] *Ibid.*, vol. iii, p. 33.
[3] Again Pepys is the authority. *Diary*, vol. iii, p. 167. This was in June 1663.
[4] *Ibid.*, vol. ii, p. 177.
[5] This was in January 1641. G. Scott Thomson: *Life in a Noble Household, 1641–1700*, p. 62.

In addition to the sedan chairs and coaches plying for hire, the streets were full of those that were privately owned. Lord and Lady Dacre used to travel to and fro between London and Hurstmonceux in their own coach-and-six, complete with coachmen and postilions, followed at leisure by their 'sumpters', or packhorses, loaded with luggage.[1] Such journeys were undertaken with astonishing frequency when the state of the roads in most of the London approaches is considered. The agent of the Duke of Newcastle, coming up from Hastings, once had to go round by Canterbury to get to London, and twenty men were needed to lift his coach over ruts and obstructions.[2] It is easy to see why coaches had to be heavily and sturdily constructed.

The anonymous author of *A Discourse on Leather*, printed for the first time in 1629, estimated that at least five thousand 'coaches and caroches' were maintained in London and Westminster. Although his guess must not be taken as authoritative they certainly were numerous and considerably outnumbered the hackney coaches at this time.

There is a delightful tract, published in 1636 under the title *Coach and Sedan pleasantly Disputing for Place and Precedence*, in which the arguments for both types of conveyance are given with great good humour, 'the *Brewers Cart* being Moderator', and it is clear that each served quite a different public. There was, however, a third kind of vehicle that was at one time or another useful to practically everyone who could afford the fare. This was the stage-coach, which carried passengers on regular routes between London and the provinces. Those who wanted cheaper—but much slower—travel would have to make their journeys in waggons or carriers' carts. The industrious John Taylor wrote a most valuable pamphlet called *The Carriers' Cosmography*[3] in which he gave an account of the different types, their routes, starting-points, and frequency.

Most of the *Cosmography* is concerned with the inns and hostelries in London where the 'carriers, waggons, foot-posts and higglers' arrived and set forth; there follows a list, also in alphabetical

---

[1] 'Account book of Hurstmonceux Castle, 1643–49', ed. T. B. Lennard, *Sussex Archaeological Collections*, vol. xlviii (1905), p. 133.

[2] 'Correspondence of John Collier', ed. W. V. Crane, *Ibid*., vol. xlv (1902).

[3] In 1637. Printed by A. Lang in *Social England Illustrated* (a collection of seventeenth-century tracts). London, 1903, p. 357 ff.

order, of the quays on the river where the hoys, tilt-boats, barges and wherries docked when making their regular runs east and west of London. We learn, for instance, that a foot-post, who carried letters only, came from Bury St. Edmunds every Thursday to the *Green Dragon* in Bishopsgate Street, and that many northern carriers from Doncaster and elsewhere lodged at the *Belle Sauvage* outside Ludgate, while those from Staffordshire preferred the *Swan with Two Necks* in Lad Lane. This last inn was also the starting-point of many coaches. The Winchester waggons made for the *Swan* in the Strand, the carriers of Northampton could be found 'almost every day of the week . . . at the *Ram* in Smithfield'.

The Buckingham carriers, who were accustomed to lodge at the *George* near Holborn Bridge (as did those from Brackley and Banbury), had a return service on Wednesdays, Thursdays and Fridays. These were the carriers employed by Mrs. Purefoy of Shalstone in the middle years of the next century, and the *Purefoy Letters*[1] are full of allusions to them. Sometimes glass was broken in transit,[2] sometimes the carrier was delayed on the road and then there was trouble if the goods were perishable. In hot weather fish quickly became stale, and even in January when Mrs. Purefoy received the sturgeon, codling, shrimps, and lemons she had ordered, 'the codling and shrimps stunk . . . we were forced to throw them to the Dunghill'. Once, when her oysters came, 'half of them were black as Ink & the other half was poisoned with the stench, for they were all of a froth . . .'[3] On the whole, however, the carriers' service was good and surprisingly swift.

The wide-wheeled waggons were far slower than the coaches, and were clearly intended for goods rather than passengers. On his annual shopping visit to London, John Hancock of Chastleton used to travel by the Oxford coach, but sent his 'portmantua' by waggon.[4] If he wanted to take a lad with him to look after his horse in London, the boy had to travel in the 'basket' of the coach for this meant a much cheaper fare.

The network of coach-routes, that linked remote districts with each other and with London, was only beginning to be effective in John Taylor's day; it owed its inception to the carriers' organi-

[1] Two vols., 1735–53, Ed. G. Eland. London, 1931.
[2] *Ibid.*, p. 193.
[3] *Ibid.*, p. 62.
[4] M. Dickins: *A History of Chastleton*. Banbury, 1938.

zation that he so lucidly described. In the course of the next century it developed into a nation-wide system that was to be the envy of all foreigners, but London remained, as she had been in the beginning, its central point.

IV. LONDON INNS AND TAVERNS

[The Ale-Wife] Her ale, if new, looks like a misty morning, all thick; well, if her ale be strong, her reckoning right, her house clean, her fire good, her face fair, and the town great or rich, she shall seldom or never sit without chirping birds to bear her company.

DONALD LUPTON: *London and Country Carbonadoed*, 1632.

A tavern is a degree or (if you will) a pair of stairs above an ale-house, . . . it is the busy man's recreation, the idle man's business, the melancholy man's sanctuary, the stranger's welcome, the Inns of Court man's entertainment, the scholar's kindness, and the citizen's courtesy.

JOHN EARLE: *Microcosmographie*, 1628.

Much has been written on the inns, taverns, and eating-houses of the City of London, with many details that are true and more that are apocryphal.[1] The *Mermaid* is as securely entwined in English literature as Chaucer's *Tabard*, and Dr. Johnson is alleged to have frequented far more taverns than a careful reading of Boswell's *Life* can warrant. The *Diary* of Samuel Pepys, on the other hand, can supply an almost complete gazetteer to these establishments.

In the year 1613 Sir Thomas Middleton made a list of all the ale-houses and victualling-houses in the City, and found that he had collected more than a thousand names.[2] Many of these came under the heading of 'ordinaries', or eating-houses, where Henry Peacham says one could find a dinner for threepence, 'in Black Horse Alley, and such places'.[3] By the next century the number of public-houses had enormously increased, so that it was estimated that one house in every six held a licence to sell liquor,[4] but in John Taylor's day London was no more than 'well-supplied' with inns, eating-houses, and beer shops. Peacham says that many taverns were 'very honest and reasonable', but that others might charge

---

[1] William Kent, in his *Encyclopaedia of London* (new edn.), London, 1951, has a good summary of the more famous establishments.
[2] F. Aydelotte: *Elizabethan Rogues and Vagabonds*. Oxford, 1913, p. 74.
[3] *The Worth of a Penny*, 1647. Printed by A. Lang in *Social England Illustrated*. London, 1903.
[4] R. Leslie Melville: *The Life and Work of Sir John Fielding*. London, 1934, p. 95.

three times as much as the food and drink were worth. However, 'the use of them is necessary', he explains, 'for if a man meets with his friend . . . in the street, whither should they go, having no friend's house near to go into, especially in rainy or foul weather, but to a tavern?'[1]

As an example of the sort of fare that could be expected, towards the end of the seventeenth century, we have an entry in the diary of a young North countryman who visited London in August 1695. At the *Eagle and Child* in St. Martin's Lane he supped from 'sack, mutton stakes and pigeons', and next morning he breakfasted on ale and toast. At dinner there more pigeons, also Westphalia ham, chicken, wine, beef and cabbage, and a pudding.[2] He does not tell us the cost, but as he had complained that the inn at Salisbury charged him 1s. for two trout specially cooked for him, which was, he said, 'very dear', we may guess that he demanded value for his money.

A typical London inn, of about the middle of Elizabeth's reign, was the *Tabard*, or *Talbot*, near London Bridge. On the ground floor the 'darke parlour' looked on to the street, and on this floor were also the kitchen, dining-room, hall, and parlour. Three rooms were on the first floor, with garrets over them, and 'Entry chamber', 'Newe chamber', 'Flower de Luce' and 'Mr. Russell's chamber' were on this floor or one above. The warehouse, coalhole, oven-house, stabling and lofts, were tucked away at the back.[3]

It seems to have been unusual for inns to make a settled charge for bedroom and board. In the following century this practice was known, but not yet general, and many visitors preferred to take lodgings with a private family. The German pastor, C. P. Moritz, in 1785 found quarters with a tailor's widow who not only looked after her guests most admirably, but also read Milton aloud to them.[4]

Visitors from the provinces tended to lodge in the inns where they were deposited by their coaches, for the sake of convenience. Parson Woodforde and his niece Nancy stayed at the *Swan with*

[1] *The Worth of a Penny.*
[2] *The Diary and Letter-Book of Thomas Brockbank, 1671–1709.* Ed. R. Trappes-Lomax. Chetham Society, 1930, p. 93.
[3] Hubert Hall: *Society in the Elizabethan Age.* London, 1887, p. 81.
[4] C. P. Moritz: *Travels in England, etc.* Trans. P. E. Matheson. Oxford, 1926, pp. 23, 43.

Two Necks in Lad Lane, whither their coach had brought them in May 1783, but 'we did not like the Inn where the coach put up ... therefore we got into a Hackney Coach and drove to the *Bell Sauvage* on Ludgate Hill and there dined, supped and slept'. Here, the parson 'was bit terribly by Buggs',[1] but remained in these quarters and again stayed at the inn on later visits to London, strongly recommending it to all his friends. In 1786 he suffered so severely from the bugs that he was obliged to sit up all night, but seemed to take even this discomfort as a matter of course.

According to a State Paper of 1619,[2] Southwark's population consisted 'chiefly of inn-keepers', the largest and most famous inn being the *White Hart* that carried the badge of Richard II. This had been Jack Cade's headquarters in 1450, and it will be remembered that Shakespeare makes him say to his 'Rabblement': 'Hath my sword therefore broke through London Gates, that you should leave me at the White Hart in Southwark?'[3] This inn is particularly interesting because its history can be traced from the fourteenth century to modern times. It was burned down in 1669 and again in 1676, but within a few years had recovered its old and pre-eminent position: Dickens gave a famous description of it in the tenth chapter of the *Pickwick Papers*.

The uncertainty of the time the coaches would start, the loading of luggage, and general inquisitiveness led to the assembly of a throng of would-be passengers, ostlers, porters, and onlookers in the inn-yards—a great opportunity for sneak-thieves and pick-pockets. The collusion between highwaymen and inn-keepers may have been exaggerated, but servants and porters who handled elaborate luggage probably did report the matter to professional thieves; much pilfering certainly occurred and was very difficult to check. Sometimes a real connection with a genuine highwayman can be traced; the old Etonian 'Gentleman Harry', is known to have made his headquarters first at the *White Swan* in Whitechapel and later at the *Saracen's Head* in Aldgate,[4] but for the most part these legends have been fostered or invented by modern landlords anxious for notoriety.

[1] *The Diary of a Country Parson.* Ed. J. Beresford. Oxford, 1926, vol. ii, pp. 28–9.
[2] See Philip Norman: *Catalogue of Drawings of Old London.* V. and A. Catalogue, 1913, p. 2.
[3] *Henry VI*, part 2. Act IV, sc. viii.
[4] Hoole Jackson; 'Young Gentleman Harry', *Country Life Annual*, 1954.

Chapter Eight

JOHN EVELYN'S LONDON

1. Frost, Fog and Fire

The Great Frost

*The river . . . is an alley to walk upon without dread . . . The
citizen's wife that looks pale when she sits in a boat for fear of
drowning, thinks that here she treads as safe now as in her
parlour.*

The Great Frost. Cold doings in London, etc., 1608.[1]

THE freezing over of London's river meant the immobility of
all shipping, the loss of perishable cargoes, delay and frus-
tration, a dearth of coal usually brought by water from
Newcastle and, to the watermen, loss of their livelihood. To the
citizens at large, however, it was a time of amusement and delight;
opportunist showmen, pie-men, and enterprising barbers had a
glorious time. Taverns were erected on the ice, so that people could
afterwards claim that they had dined upon the Thames; others
had their hair cut, and some bold spirits played football. The most
famous of all frosts was that of January 1608, but there were other
notable occasions when the Thames was completely frozen over
and people were able to walk from Southwark to London. In
1648–9 John Evelyn described the booths set out in miniature
streets upon the ice, and shops 'full of commodities'; there was
even a printing-press which issued slips on which were people's
names, the year, the date, and the imprint 'The Thames', at
sixpence a time. Evelyn thought that the printer would make £5
a day at this business. He himself, 9 January 1649, walked over
the ice from Westminster to Lambeth to dine with the Archbishop of Canterbury.

The river has frequently been frozen over, but seldom to such
a depth as would allow a coach-and-six to be driven upon it, as
happened in 1698. The last of the traditional frost fairs was held

[1] Printed by Andrew Lang in *Social England Illustrated*, pp. 163–86.

THE PIAZZA AT COVENT GARDEN

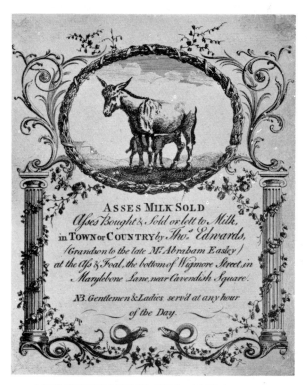

ADVERTISEMENT FOR ASSES' MILK

GIN LANE

THE GORDON RIOTS

in the winter of 1813–14, for some twelve years later old London
Bridge was pulled down and a much freer flow of water resulted.
As late as 1820 the water was frozen to a depth of five feet in
mid-January,[1] and we hear that 'folk were walking on the Thames',
but the great days of the frost fairs were by then only a memory.

The Great Smoke

It is this horrid Smoake which obscures our Churches, and
makes our Palaces look old, which fouls our Clothes, and
corrupts the Waters . . . It is this which scatters and strews
about those black and smutty Atomes upon all things where
it comes, insinuating itself into our very secret Cabinets, and
most precious Repositories.

JOHN EVELYN: *Fumifugium: or the Smoake*
of London Dissipated, 1661.[2]

John Evelyn had no doubt in his mind that the 'impure and thick
mist' which Londoners were obliged to breathe was due to the
burning of sea-coal in London fireplaces, and he said as much to
Charles II.[3] Breathing in this foul mixture of soot and 'poysoned
air' Evelyn found was noxious to human beings and he likened
London to Lake Avernus which was said to suffocate birds
unwise enough to fly across it.

He found, too, that it was impossible to grow anemones in
London without 'extraordinary Artifice'[4] and took that as a sure
sign of the impurity of the air. He had noticed that Whitehall and
Westminster were frequently shrouded in smoke from several
brew-houses nearby, and he had much to say of the 'extraordinary
stench' of the fog that hung habitually over St. Paul's. Evelyn
pointed out that this vaporous, smoke-laden mist was dangerous
not only to the health of those who breathed it into their lungs,
but also to those who tried to make their way through its obscurity, who, hopelessly losing their way, fell an easy prey to robbers.
The fog-bound river was even more dangerous than the streets,
and sometimes it was necessary to beat drums to guide the watermen towards the shore.[5]

From time to time angry citizens have taunted scientists with
their inability to diagnose the causes of the fog or to prescribe its

[1] London in 1820; article in *The Times*, 30 September 1938.
[2] Reprinted Oxford, 1930, p. 20 (Old Ashmolean Reprints, no. vii).
[3] *Diary*, October 1661.
[4] *Fumifugium*, p. 21.   [5] *Diary*, 25 November 1699.

10

cure, and have demanded legislation for smoke abatement. Probably the most prolonged of all visitations was the dense fog that lasted from November 1879 until March of the following year: four whole months of concentrated grime and gloom. Fog in London, swirling through the streets or hanging motionless, seems even in John Evelyn's day to have had its peculiar brown pea-soup quality, but it was the genius of Charles Dickens that in *Bleak House* (published in 1852) gave it its familiar name: 'a London particular'. The trouble has persisted into our own times and many of Evelyn's arguments and recommendations are triumphantly brought out by contemporary reformers as though they were new. The causes and the cure for London's smoke problem are set out clearly enough in Evelyn's pamphlet, but to implement his suggestions is a task that is only now being tackled with any real vigour.

The Great Fire

> *2 Sept. 1666. We . . . saw the fire grow . . . in a most horrid malicious bloody flame, not like the fine flame of an ordinary fire. . . . The churches, houses, and all on fire and flaming at once; and a horrid noise the flames made, and the cracking of houses at their ruine. So home with a sad heart, and there find every body discoursing and lamenting the fire.*
>
> SAMUEL PEPYS: *Diary.*[1]

> *3 Sept. 1666. The conflagration was so universal, and the people so astonished, that, from the beginning, I know not by what despondency, or fate, they hardly stirred to quench it; so that there was nothing heard, or seen, but crying out and lamentation, running about like distracted creatures, without at all attempting to save even their goods, such a strange consternation there was upon them.*
>
> JOHN EVELYN: *Diary.*

It seems that the character of the pair of diarists giving eye-witness accounts of the Great Fire are in these two passages reversed. Generally, it is Pepys who is interested in human beings and their reactions, Evelyn who is the objective recorder of events, but on this occasion Pepys is stunned by the tragedy and it is Evelyn who notices the Londoners' pitiful condition. Both agreed that this was a fire completely out of control, and while it raged there seemed to both of them no reason why any building in the whole city should be spared.

[1] Ed. H. B. Wheatley. London, 1923, vol. v, p. 421.

Earlier London fires had been frequent, and often very damaging; lives had been lost and much property destroyed. St. Paul's had already been burned wholly or in part on at least five occasions, the last of these only just over a century before. This fire was dealt with promptly and wisely by some five hundred volunteers, and 'divers substantial citizens took pains as if they had been labourers', just as the 'diligence of the citizens' had put out the blaze in the time of Henry VI.[1] Had equally strong measures been taken during the first few hours of the Great Fire in 1666 it might have been no more than an insignificant blaze in a side street instead of a catastrophe.

The story of the fire is well-known, how it began in a bakehouse in Pudding Lane, how an easterly wind carried sparks from the burning rafters across the road to an inn-yard opposite where hay was piled, and thence to the warehouses of Thames Street. Only seven years earlier James Howell had written of London's fire defences: 'There's no place . . . better armed against the fury of the fire; for besides the pitched Buckets that hang in the Churches and Halls, there are divers new Engines for that purpose',[2] but the buckets of medieval times and the later hand-squirts were of little use except in the first moments of a small fire; the only effective weapons were the long-handled fire-hooks that could be used to pull down the framework of buildings already alight or in imminent danger. The trouble was that owners of adjacent property might (and did) object to its destruction, and even a strong and authoritative leader had difficulty in imposing his will and making the necessary fire-breaks. The Lord Mayor in 1666 had the authority but he lacked foresight and ruthless determination; he hesitated, daunted by thoughts of the odium and the claims for compensation that such action would cause, and the battle was lost before it was begun.

On the first day, Sunday, September 1st, Pepys after watching the fire from the river went to Whitehall to warn the King, who showed his sagacity in immediately sending orders for demolition. On the following day he put the Duke of York and his soldiers in supreme charge. Charles himself rode through the crowd and set

---

[1] In 1444. See also *The True Report of the Burning of the Steeple and Church of Paul's in London* [1561], repr. in *Tudor Tracts, 1532–88*. Ed. A. F. Pollard. London, 1903.
[2] *Londinopolis*. London, 1657, p. 398.

an example of calmness and efficiency, dismounting from his horse
and handling buckets to the best possible purpose.[1]

Perhaps the resolution of the Londoners was weakened by the
ravages of plague the year before. Panic seized them, and every
man acted for himself and his household, trying desperately to
save his own property, so that the narrow streets were soon
jammed with agitated crowds, weighted down by their belongings,
all intent upon escape, and few making any attempt to beat back
the flames for the common good. The most degraded took this
opportunity to rob and pilfer, and there were some who added
to the confusion by crying out that the fire was the work of the
Dutch, or the French, or the Papists.

The refugees halted outside the city walls and encamped with
their possessions wherever they happened to find themselves,
while a pall of acrid smoke hung above their heads. The terrifying
sounds of fire and destruction rang in their ears. Some of the
homeless took refuge in the fields towards Islington and Highgate,
and there were many more who fled in their panic far beyond the
City boundaries and spread the shocking tale through neighbouring counties. Tents and temporary buildings were put up for
shelter, and people were allowed to store their goods in chapels,
churches, schools and any public buildings that had escaped the
ravages of the four days' fire. In the neighbouring villages and
towns arrangements were made to take in the refugees, and
the King in his wisdom issued proclamations to the effect that
they must be allowed to practise 'their manual trades without
hindrance'.[2]

In the wake of the fire debris blocked and obliterated the
streets, piles of rubbish smouldered for many days and the
air was full of grime and smoke. London was a lamentable
sight, her great buildings reduced to ashes, her cathedral gone,
and some 13,200 houses destroyed, together with eighty-seven
churches.[3] Yet, dismayed and disconsolate as were the citizens,
they did not despair, and with a dogged obstinacy that refused to

---

[1] For an excellent account of the fire see the first chapter in W. F. Reddaway's
The Rebuilding of London after the Great Fire, London 1940. The most ample description is in W. G. Bell's *The Great Fire of London*, London, 1920.
[2] Reddaway: *op. cit.*, p. 27.
[3] *Ibid.*, p. 26. At the rebuilding certain parishes were united, so that the 87 ruined
churches were replaced by 51, all designed and carried out by Wren.

admit defeat, repudiating their former panic, they set about the gigantic task of the reclamation of their city.

II. THE PLANNERS

That this Glorious and Antient City . . . should wrap her stately head in Clowds of Smoake and Sulphur, so full of stink and Darknesse, I deplore with just Indignation. That the Buildings should be composed of such a Congestion of mishapen and extravagant Houses; that the Streets should be so narrow and incommodious in the very Center, and busiest places of Intercourse; That there should be so ill and uneasie a form of Paving under foot, so troublesome and malicious a disposure of the Spouts and Gutters overhead, are particular worthy of Reproof and Reformation; because it is hereby rendered a Labyrinth in its principal passages, and a continual wet day after the storm is over.

JOHN EVELYN: *Fumifugium*, 1661.

25 November 1666 . . . I spoke with Mr. May, who tells me that the design of building the City do go on apace, and by his description it will be mighty handsome, and to the satisfaction of the people; but I pray God it come not out too late.

SAMUEL PEPYS: *Diary*.[1]

Less than a week after the fire had died away, while London dully smouldered and the ground was still hot underfoot, Christopher Wren submitted to the King his plan for the new City. This was on 11 September 1666, and two days later a Royal Proclamation announced that a new plan—not necessarily Wren's nor Evelyn's,[2] but one to be agreed upon—would be adopted as soon as possible, and a committee for rebuilding was appointed forthwith. Three of its members were chosen by the city and three by the King; Wren was one of the King's men, but he had not as yet an official position as surveyor or architect. Even after the passing in 1667 of the Act for the rebuilding of the City of London, Wren's position was still vague, and it was not until three years later, when he was rather unexpectedly appointed Surveyor of Works, that he became the nation's chief architect.[3]

Rebuilding on the old plan was unthinkable, as even the most reactionary citizen saw. For many years it had become increasingly apparent that much would have to be done to find new sites for

[1] Ed. H. B. Wheatley, vol. vi, pp. 78–9.
[2] His plan was produced almost as expeditiously as Wren's.
[3] John Summerson: *Sir Christopher Wren*. London, 1953, p. 76.

the markets that blocked the narrow streets, to improve sanitation
and the water supply, to rebuild in brick or stone the rickety
wooden houses, and to repair the ruinous condition of St. Paul's.
Wren had become interested in the problem while he was acting
as Professor of Astronomy at Gresham College, where the early
meetings of the Royal Society were held.[1] As a friend of Gilbert
Sheldon, who had given Oxford the theatre that bears his name,
and which was built to Wren's design, Wren was the architect to
whom the bishop turned for advice when, on his appointment to
the See of London, he found to what a sad condition St. Paul's
had been reduced. Before long, Sheldon had moved to Canterbury, but Wren for his own satisfaction worked out a complete
set of plans for the rebuilding of St. Paul's, a project in which
John Evelyn also was deeply interested. Both of these men were
members of the Royal Society, and met with some frequency,
renewing their Oxford acquaintanceship. Evelyn felt most strongly the necessity for improving London's street-plan, and these
two amateurs had given deep thought to the matter: so it was that
each of them was able to produce a design for the reconstruction
of the City within a few days of the disaster.

One of the chief difficulties in preparing a plan for the rebuilding
of the three hundred and ninety-five devastated acres was the lack
of any official map to show the extent and exact siting of properties. Title deeds and leases might describe them accurately, but
great numbers of these had themselves been destroyed or lost, and
unscrupulous owners were ready to claim far more ground than
they really held. Even the honest ones were far more interested in
running up some sort of building to house themselves and their
families and to protect their merchandise, than they were in the
widening of streets, improving lay-out, and re-aligning awkwardly
shaped properties. It is easy to say that vested interests made the
adoption of Wren's brilliant and far-sighted plan impossible, but
although there is some truth in this claim, it is necessary to consider also the point of view of the homeless citizens. Many of
them had lost all their possessions, others urgently wanted shelter
for the goods they had salvaged; the great majority were living in
conditions of extreme discomfort and squalor, or were lodged
expensively in the suburbs. Wherever they were, the pattern of

[1] John Summerson: *Sir Christopher Wren*, p. 35.

their lives had been violently disrupted.[1] Time was everything to
them, and it is hard to blame these Londoners for failing to
appreciate Wren's long-term plan, particularly as Wren was at this
time almost unknown as an architect—his only building hitherto
being the Sheldonian Theatre—and his plan must have seemed to
ordinary men both visionary and academic.

Not only had the lines of the streets been obliterated, the whole
area of devastation was piled high with debris. Some witnesses
give the general depth of the rubbish as four feet, and although
this is perhaps an exaggeration, the problem of clearance certainly
was formidable. The levels, too, were very difficult to judge. The
surveyors sent men to stake out the new frontages, but some
owners came by night and altered the position of the stakes to
their own advantage. Those who felt aggrieved or had lost some
of their property by the widening of the streets appealed for compensation to the Fire Court that had been set up to consider such
claims. One man lost a strip seven feet deep on a frontage of sixty
yards and suggested that the staking should be transferred to the
other side of the road. He lost his petition, but others were more
successful. There were those also who resented the widening of
their street—like the inhabitants of Huggen Lane, Wood Street,
who feared that if the Lane were extended in width to the proposed
fourteen feet, it would become a regular route for carts and thus
less safe for those on foot.[2]

In the early days of rebuilding there was general optimism as it
was seen that the new London would be a far better place to live
in, more spacious, and far more healthy. Then came the inevitable
reaction. As Wren's beautiful churches began to take shape, as
the Guildhall was restored and Jerman's new Exchange neared
completion, the City authorities began to realize that it was one
thing to rebuild London and quite another to repopulate it. Something like 80,000 people had fled during the fire, and of these one
in four had not returned six years later.[3] Even before the disaster
there had been a tendency for craftsmen and small shopkeepers to

[1] Reddaway, *op. cit.*, p. 48 ff., where the matter is discussed at length, also the
expedients for raising money to pay the necessary compensation. Under an Act of
1667 a tax had been laid upon coal brought to the Port of London, and three years
later this subsidy was greatly increased.

[2] *Ibid.*, p. 142. E. S. de Beer's edition of John Evelyn's *London Revived*, Oxford,
1938, reproduces three of Evelyn's sketches for the rebuilding.

[3] Reddaway, *op. cit.*, p. 300 ff.

move out into the freedom of the suburbs, away from the con-
gestion, the trade restrictions, and the high taxes of the City. In
Strype's edition of Stow's *Survey of London* we read that the
'Mercers, Silk-men and Lace-men' who had dwelt in Paternoster
Row and attracted to that narrow thoroughfare the coaches of the
'Nobility and Gentry', after the fire settled elsewhere. Some of the
greater merchants set the fashion of moving away to provincial
towns and there restarting their businesses: one of these was
Allan Smith, the 'great sugar baker of London', who went to
Liverpool;[1] and here, too, some of his fellow Londoners settled
and built up a new trade with America. The poor had little choice
in the matter; they could not return to the new brick houses that
had replaced their familiar tenements, for it was quite impossible for
them to pay the new rents. They were glad to find cottage dwellings
outside the City's jurisdiction, or deep in the country.[2] Some even
emigrated to St. Helena, at the invitation of the East India Company.

The census taken in 1673 showed the position very clearly, and
the authorities acted immediately. As a first step, any aldermen
who were living outside the City were recalled at once, and the
next thing was to secure the co-operation of the Companies in
making it easier to become a freeman. At first the Companies were
reluctant to reduce their fees or to forgo any of their privileges,
but in the end the public interest—which included their own—
prevailed. At first grudgingly, then resignedly, the Companies
opened their ranks and lowered their barriers, although some
Courts, still living in the past and blind to the changed conditions,
clung to their rights. The Merchant Taylors continued to make
high—and in the circumstances unreasonable—conditions for
entrance, but in the end they had to conform to the practice of
more enlightened Companies. Already some country craftsmen
had been absorbed—the Plasterers, for instance, admitted an
applicant as early as February 1670—and after the critical year
1673–4 concessions were so freely given that on one day, 5 March
1674, as many as forty-six freedoms[3] were sold.

The new areas that Londoners had made their own outside the
old City walls began to grow and develop a life of their own;

[1] Reddaway: *op. cit.*, p. 245.
[2] *Ibid.*, p. 302.
[3] *Ibid.*, p. 305. This question of country craftsmen in London is more fully treated
in the next chapter, § iii.

Moorfields was soon no longer a great open space, but a patchwork of haphazard new building. Southwark, Whitechapel, Mile End and Spitalfields were all building new houses at speed and there were plans to convert great mansions into tenements to house poor families: both these projects were against City policy and the die-hards there persisted in attempting to prosecute the builders and besought the King to forbid all new buildings in the suburbs.[1] It has been shown that the London watermen were equally reactionary in their violent opposition to the proposed building of a new bridge at Westminster. For a time, progress was halted, but in the end the inevitable compromise was reached: the City remained the hub of the financial system and the new London spread its perimeter to become the largest city in the world, sprawling out into the countryside to become in due course 'the Wen' deplored by Cobbett.

III. FASHION AND MANNERS

. . . how bold, confident, merry, lively, and ever in humour, are Moneyed Men. They go where they list! They wear what they list! They eat and drink what they list! And as their minds, so their bodies are free!

HENRY PEACHAM: *The Worth of a Penny*, 1647.

Puritan London became a strange place to those who had lived there all their lives. 'Who would have thought', wrote one of them, 'to have seen . . . the churches shut and the shops open upon Christmas Day?'[2] The same writer, who was at the time imprisoned in the Fleet for his irrepressible Royalist sympathies, ridiculed the extreme Puritans for their horror of the ordinary courtesies. 'If one passing through a church should put off his hat', he said, 'there is a giddy and malignant race of people . . . who will give out that he is running fast to Rome'.[3] Sabbatarianism, too, at times reached absurd lengths, and many Londoners became restive under Cromwell's rule of austerity, so that they were ready to welcome Charles II at the Restoration in 1660.

Nevertheless, the genuine Puritanism of the City of London remained unshaken by the extravagance and gaiety of the early days of the Restoration. The result was a profound cleavage

---

[1] Reddaway: *op. cit.*, p. 307.
[2] *The Familiar Letters of James Howell*. London, 1903, vol. ii, p. 236.
[3] *Ibid.*, vol. iii, p. 136.

between Court and City that is reflected particularly clearly in the new plays that were acted in the new theatres, the comedies of manners, and the licentious, slanderous, and salacious witticisms that delighted audiences drawn almost exclusively from the Court and its satellites. Drury Lane was built in 1663, and, although it was destroyed in the Great Fire, a new and more famous theatre arose to Wren's design in 1672. Drury Lane rapidly became the most celebrated of London theatres, and the names of all London's leading actors and actresses have been associated with it. Well might Pepys say of the plays he attended here: 'Lord! to see the difference of the times and but two years gone.' Wycherley and Congreve were indeed a change, and their plays exactly fitted the mood of the sophisticated audiences who attended them.

A remark of Pepys underlines one difference between the audiences of Elizabethan and Restoration times: he had taken his wife and her maidservant to the play and was, he said, 'a little shamed' that their clothes were not appropriate—'all the ladies being finer and better dressed in the pitt than they used, I think, to be'.[1] In the old days, the pit would have been full of city men and their wives in their ordinary clothes, bent solely upon enjoyment and caring little how they and their neighbours appeared.

Masks were sometimes worn by both men and women, and ladies continued to wear them on occasion, particularly at the first nights of plays, well into the early years of the eighteenth century.[2] In this, as in other matters, provincial towns followed London fashions: these reached the provinces with a shorter lapse of time than might have been expected, an instance of the close communication between London and other parts of the kingdom at this time. Like other fashionable practices, the wearing of masks descended in the social scale, and by Queen Anne's time they were usually worn only by disreputable people, so that mask-wearers were sometimes excluded from shows where an elegant audience was expected.

The great popularity of all oriental goods, and of Indian stuffs in particular, was a sign of the times, and merchants who specialized in importing and selling them did good business. Another thriving trade was in women's long fine hair that was bought at

[1] *Diary*, ed. H. B. Wheatley, vol. iii, p. 115.
[2] John Ashton: *Social Lifei n the Reizn of Queen Anne*. London, 1882, vol. i, p. 172.

£3 an ounce for making the finest wigs. The *London Spy* reported notices in barbers' shops offering 'money for Live Hair', and since a heavy wig could contain as much as a pound of hair it is not surprising that the most expensive ones were valued at thirty or forty guineas. The prices varied enormously, and so did the cost of the scented powder used with them. Naturally, a great trade was done in second-hand wigs, and also in stolen ones; John Gay refers in his *Trivia*[1] to the ingenious plan of carrying a small child in a basket on a man's shoulder to grab the wigs of passers-by. When a country gentleman wrote to his London agent, in the spring of 1693, with instructions to buy him a periwig but omitting to mention the size, the agent had to make a tour of the shops 'by the old Exchange' and in the Strand before he found one that could be adjusted by a string.[2] At this time the younger men were taking to short periwigs called 'Bobbs' that imitated natural hair, and within a few months these too were seen on the heads of provincial leaders of fashion. Although there were wig-makers in all the large towns, men of taste continued to send to London for their wigs; they were willing to pay the cost of carriage, and a higher charge, in order to be assured that they were wearing the latest fashion.

With this meticulous regard for style in dress and appearance there went great casualness in matters of personal hygiene. Filthy streets and the stench arising therefrom and from the laystalls that surrounded the City were accepted with fatalistic composure. Samuel Pepys, responding to the calls of nature, might make his way to the Harp and Ball tavern in Whitehall or 'a little alehouse at the end of Ratcliffe, and did give a groat for a pot of ale, and there I did . . .',[3] but he was likely to flinch from a cold expedition to the house of office in his cellar and to use instead his bedroom chimney.[4] Nor were ladies much more particular, to judge from the exploits of Mrs. Pepys.

Inadequate provision of 'conveniences' for ladies, or the entire lack of them, continued for many years, so that a day's shopping was a matter of torment even in Victoria's reign. Lady Stanley of Alderley wrote to her daughter-in-law in 1852 concerning the

[1] Published in 1716. Vol. 1, book iii.
[2] *The Portledge Papers*. Ed. R. J. Kerr and I. C. Duncan. London, 1928, p. 162.
[3] *Diary*, vol. i, pp. 38, 278.
[4] *Ibid.*, vol. iv, p. 317.

Duke of Wellington's funeral in St. Paul's: '200 conveniences are provided—how the world improves!'[1]

City records show that ordinances designed to keep the streets clear and to improve public health were constantly flouted or ignored. In Westminster a man who wished to open a dairy kept eight cows in his kitchen 'to the great Annoyance of the Inhabitants and Neighbours near adjoining'; their complaint was based not upon the kitchen-turned-cowshed but upon the danger of fire from the quantity of hay he kept stored in his bedroom.[2] The following year (1613–14) a baker had to be reproved for leaving his dung-pot standing in Palace Yard full of filth on one Sunday in June. Swarms of flies were among the least noxious results of this irresponsibility.

The extreme formalism of Jacobean days, maintained by old-fashioned aristocrats in mid-century, crumbled at the impact of the Restoration. Society lost its rigidity and this offered chances for professional men to rise to considerable heights. The founding of the Royal Society brought several intellectuals into a prominence they might not otherwise have known, and by the time of Queen Anne it did not occasion much comment that the royal oculist, whom the Queen knighted,[3] had started life as a tailor, nor that his chief rival, Roger Grant, was said to have been a tinker.

Descriptions of social occasions, of balls, parties and masquerades abound, and for details of the excursions and junketings of middle-class people the reader is referred to Pepys's *Diary*. But for an account of the completely vapid life led by some London ladies in the seventeenth century there is nothing to compare with the words of George Savile, first Marquess of Halifax, in his celebrated *Advice to his daughter*:[4]

She eats her Breakfast half-an-hour before Dinner, to be at greater liberty to afflict the Company with her Discourse; then calleth for her coach, that she may trouble her acquaintance, who are already cloy'd with her: . . . she setteth out like a ship out of the Harbour, laden with trifles . . . at her return she repeateth to her faithful waiting-woman, the Triumphs of that day's Impertinence; then wrap'd up in Flattery and clean linen, goeth to Bed so satisfied . . .

[1] *The Stanleys of Alderley, 1851–65*. Ed. N. Mitford. London, 1939, p. 63.
[2] W. H. Manchée: *The Westminster City Fathers*. London, 1924, p. 76.
[3] Sir William Read. John Ashton: *Social Life, etc.*, vol. ii, p. 100.
[4] Or 'The Lady's New Year's Gift', *Works*. Oxford, 1912, p. 21.

IV. GARDENS

*[Hog Lane] . . . within these fortie yeares, had on both sides
fayre hedgerowes of Elme trees, with Bridges and easie stiles
to passe ouer into the pleasant fieldes, very commodious for
citizens therein to walke, shoote, and otherwise to recreate and
refresh their dulled spirites in the sweet and wholesome ayre,
which is nowe within a few yeares made a continuall building
throughout, of Garden houses, and small cottages: and the
fields on either side be turned into Garden plottes, teynter yardes,
Bowling Alleys, and such like, from Houndes ditch in the West,
so far as White Chappell, and further towards the East.*

JOHN STOW: *Survey of London*, 1603.[1]

By the time John Stow was writing his *Survey*, many of the former
open fields had been enclosed and made into gardens and bowling
alleys. On one occasion the inhabitants of Hoxton and Shoreditch
became so angry at the enclosure, with hedges and ditches, of the
common lands where they 'were wont to stroll and practise archery',
that they took direct action. Headed by a turner dressed in a fool's
coat, they marched through the City, crying 'Shovels and spades!
Shovels and spades!' and forthwith tore down the hedges and
filled the ditches with the newly turned earth.[2]

The process went on, nevertheless, and little garden houses or
summer houses were erected 'not so much for vse or profite, as
for shewe and pleasure'; these, incidentally, were of great benefit
to dramatists who used them in their plays as places for assignation,
although Stow thought that the citizens could better have 'im-
ployed their wits and spent their wealthes' in building hospitals
and almshouses.[3]

In ordinary London gardens there was no room for 'chinoiserie'
of the style that culminated in the erection of Sir William Chambers' pagoda at Kew; the areas were far too small, and a courtyard
with some tubs of flowers and herbs, with a rose-grown trellis,
was all that most houses could enjoy. The London mansions, of
course, had lawns and 'knots', and ponds of ornamental fish,
perhaps even shrubberies and a wilderness. These grand gardens
attracted the notice and the praise of foreign visitors, but the
humbler town gardens had their attractions too—aromatic shrubs

[1] Ed. C. L. Kingsford, 2 vols. London, 1908, vol. i, p. 149.
[2] *Ibid.*, vol. ii, p. 77.
[3] *Ibid.*, vol. ii, p. 78.

and sweet-scented gaily-coloured flowers, and creepers clinging to the brick and timber of the houses.

As even these small gardens, with their arbours and grass plots and beds of kitchen herbs, needed constant care if they were not to become overgrown with weeds, a man was sometimes given quarters rent free if he would tend the garden regularly, but more often a 'jobbing' gardener was called in to do some particular piece of work. There were several of these professionals dwelling in the City in the fifteenth century; it is impossible to estimate how many for they are only mentioned incidentally in the official records of the time.[1] One such came to tend the grapevine and see to the rosemary, thyme, and eglantine growing in the garden of the Baker's Hall in 1506, and we may suppose that he attended also to the bowling alley with the flagged walk and 'benches for rest' that stood within this walled enclosure.[2] It might be expected that the King would have full-time gardeners for the Royal Palace of Westminster, and no doubt he did; but when Henry III wanted cuttings and young cherry trees planted in the royal garden, he sent for Edward of Westminster, a man known better as painter, goldsmith, and embroiderer.[3]

Towards the end of the reign of Henry VIII, when Hounds-ditch was being enclosed piecemeal by 'brokers' and the sellers of old clothes, a professional gardener named Cawsway secured the rest of the ground and turned it into a garden for growing herbs for the pot and root vegetables, which he supplied to the markets.[4] A large number of these market gardeners existed, but his is the earliest name we have been able to trace; by the seventeenth century however there are references to many seedsmen and nurserymen, and several specimens of their trade cards still exist.

Also in this century we hear of nursery gardens at Brompton, at Brentford—where Francis Ball grew his fruit trees[5]—and at Whitechapel, where the owner[6] specialized in the rarer and choicer varieties of fruit, especially nectarines and peaches, and also the dwarf plums and cherries that were very fashionable at this time.

[1] E.g. *Calendars of Close Rolls*, 1468–76, p. 85; and 1476–85, p. 32.
[2] S. Thrupp: *A Short History of the . . . Bakers of London*. London, 1933, p. 165.
[3] *Calendar of Patent Rolls*, 1232–47, p. 430.
[4] Stow: *Survey, etc.*, vol. ii, p. 77.
[5] G. Scott Thomson: *Life in a Noble Household*, p. 247 ff.
[6] His name was Leonard Gurl, sometimes written Quarle.

Most famous of the Brompton gardens was that of Henry Wise
and George London. Wise eventually became 'Gardener to
Queen Anne'; Evelyn praised him, Vanbrugh consulted him
about the gardens at Blenheim, and he was continually being
asked for advice and 'plant shows' by men of property all over
England. This nursery garden provided the best stock it was
possible to obtain and kept up its standard and good name
throughout the eighteenth century: ultimately it bore other fruit,
for the garden now lies below the foundations of the Victoria and
Albert Museum.[1]

By the end of the eighteenth century, when Sir Frederick Eden
was writing his *State of the Poor*,[2] there were two hundred and fifty
market gardens in the district of Ealing alone, and it was calcu-
lated that a 'garden' (or skilled) labourer could earn 10*s*. a week,
all the year round, or 3*s*. a day if he cared to do piece-work. An
ordinary labourer got about half this piece-rate, and the women
who were employed seasonally, chiefly to pick fruit, were paid
at half the rate of the men. Many of these women were Welsh, and
stayed in the neighbourhood only during the fruit harvest.

Some districts were famous for particular products, Battersea,
for instance, for its asparagus.[3] Here a great many of the gardeners
had their homes, and, indeed, these and their gardens occupied
most of the river bank from Chelsea to Westminster, from which
they supplied 'a great part of the City'. In earlier days Lambeth had
been the great resort for gardeners, and it was said that a boatload
of them could outswear even the watermen from Wandsworth.

Farmers and market gardeners who lived close to the City were
able to use the scavengers' street soil as manure, and of course
horse dung was plentiful and could be had merely for the asking.
It is small wonder that the garden produce was of the highest
quality. The carts full of greenstuff, and the men and women with
laden baskets, making their way to the City in the early hours of
the day, were a familiar sight. Some carts travelled all night to
bring watercress from distant streams, and converged upon the
market that was held outside the garden wall of the Earl of Bedford, in the old convent garden of St. Peter's, Westminster,

[1] David Green: *Gardener to Queen Anne*. London, 1956.
[2] In 1797. Ed. A. G. L. Rogers. London, 1928, pp. 239–40.
[3] Robert Binnell: *A Description of the River Thames*. London, 1758, pp. 38–9.

known from the seventeenth century onwards as Covent Garden. There had been stalls and sheds here for many years,[1] where gardeners had sold any produce that was surplus to their needs, but the idea of growing special crops for marketing did not become general until Elizabethan times. The earliest allusion to 'Covent Garden Market' seems to be that of 1656 when a payment of 20*s*. was made to a craftsman for painting the benches and seats in the market-place.[2] It was not, however, until 1671 that the fourth Earl of Bedford was given a royal patent of licence[3] to hold a market 'within the Piazza at Covent Garden'.

It was possible to buy flowers as well as fruit and vegetables in London—Edward Fuller had a flower and seed shop on the south side of the Strand in the 1690s[4]—but at Covent Garden flowers were still sold chiefly as 'herbs'. Not until many years had passed did the flower trade become really important. The first consignment of narcissi from the Scilly Isles was not sent until 1867, packed in a hatbox, as an experiment, but success was so immediate and progressive that in 1936 a factory at Newquay made a million and a half flower boxes for the trade, and in this year Cornwall and the Scilly Isles alone sent to the market no fewer than a million packages.

Mulberries, figs, and cherries all did well in London soil, but London strawberries grew best of all. Their price varied, then as now, according to the season, and in the year after the Armada ranged from 1*s*. a pint on 23 May to 3*d*. a pint on 7 June. Cream could be bought to go with them at 6*d*. a quart.[5] When Richard Lapthorne wanted strawberries in mid-September he found there were none to be had from the City gardens, and had to send out to Hammersmith for them.[6] He could find 'none neerer': he was lucky to find them there. A young Londoner wrote in his diary in July 1635 that strawberries were 'very cheape'[7] and also that cherries were then at their best, at 2½*d*. a lb. These would not have

[1] Probably as early as the fourteenth century. E. S. Rhode: *Journal of the Royal Horticultural Society*, February 1934, p. 39.
[2] R. Jacobs: *Covent Garden, its Romance and History*. London, 1913, p. 13.
[3] G. Scott Thomson: *Life in a Noble Household*, p. 79.
[4] *Ibid.*, pp. 259–60.
[5] Thes prices all refer to London. See Hubert Hall's *English Society in the Elizabethan Age*. London, 1887, pp. 222, 224, 230.
[6] *The Portledge Papers*, p. 239. This was on 12 September 1696.
[7] E. M. Symonds: 'The Diary of John Greene', *Eng. Hist. Review*, 1928.

suited 'Mistress Minx', the merchant's wife, satirized in Nashe's *Pierce Penilesse* (1592), who would eat no cherries except when they were 20s. a pound.

In the opening years of the eighteenth century the Society of Gardeners was formed; it consisted of twenty working nurserymen, who met at Newhall's coffee-house in Chelsea to discuss specimens and new varieties brought for exhibition by the members who had grown them. One of these, Thomas Fairchild, wrote a delightful and practical book called *The City Gardener*, published in 1722, that is full of information and advice.[1] A tavern yard edged, as he suggested with flowering currants, would certainly attract customers, and a garden planted either for colour or fragrance with the flowers he recommended would have been delightful. The strongly-scented lilies of the valley, sweet peas, and sweet sultan would surely cancel the musty smell of martagon lilies and African marigolds, and the traditional sweet williams, candytuft, and love-in-a-mist would give these city gardens a rustic quality in keeping with London's dual character.

[1] E. S. Rhode: 'Some Early Eighteenth Century Gardening Books', *Country Life*, 20 December 1924.

Chapter Nine

THE RUSSELLS' LONDON

1. HOME AND HOUSEKEEPING

*. . . Although I am in the Country al things are as dere here
As att London, and some derer . . . As for Buchers mett, bread,
bere, and Routs, as turnops, carrots, onions, in fine All Gardinage is derer here A peny in toopence. then for sope, starch,
ote mele, salte, peper, Candels, thread, tape &c Shouse,
Stockins, gloves, Cloath, mending tabs, and A great many more
things to(o) many to trouble you with.*

Esther St. Michel to Samuel Pepys, 24 September 1681.[1]

TYPICAL of many families who owned a country seat, and made use also of their London houses when they wanted to visit the capital for business or for pleasure, were the Russells of Woburn in Bedfordshire and also of Bloomsbury. From this family sprang the Earls, and subsequently the Dukes, of Bedford: the Russells are particularly interesting and hold an important place in London history not because they were so outstandingly rich or supremely fashionable, but because they identified themselves so closely with London life and because they were responsible for so much building and planning in the area to the north of the village of Holborn, and equally because they represented in their own persons so many facets of their times.

The Russells touch the social history of London at many points; they exemplify the problems of housekeeping in both town and country, they were considerable employers of labour, they were enterprising in their adoption of new fashions and new ideas; they were courtiers, patrons of opera and playhouse, and, above all, men and women representative of the well-to-do circles of eighteenth-century London. Nor were they oblivious of the incidence of poverty and want, which were very evident in the regions where the Russells lived.

[1] *The Letters of Samuel Pepys and his Family Circle*. Ed. H. T. Heath. Oxford, 1955, p. 187.

The transition from London to the country meant more than the slamming of the front door and a journey of forty-three miles: much planning and preparation was involved, and provision had to be made for the upkeep and welfare of the deserted house. When the Earl of Bedford left for Woburn, he and the family used to leave behind them a great pile of dirty linen. Professionals came in to deal with it; in July 1675 the soap for 'the great wash when the family left London'[1] cost 4s. 6d. and the washerwomen were paid at the rate of 1s. 6d. a day—half as much again as the cleaners who came to 'scour and wash the rooms'.[2] These cleaners were paid by the housekeeper who was left permanently in charge, and to help her she had a night-watchman living on the premises and also a gardener who looked after the exterior of the house and ordered and supervised any repair work that might be necessary, and employed whatever casual labour he might need to keep the gardens trim and well stocked.

For those who had country estates and, like the Russells, lived for only part of the year in their London houses, the problem of securing fresh fruit, game, and vegetables, was greatly simplified. Hampers well stuffed with produce were sent up to London at regular intervals, and these fortunate families could enjoy fresh eggs, home-fed turkeys, home-grown peaches and asparagus, or whatever happened to be in season. They could shut up their houses at will, leaving a skeleton staff to keep them clean and aired against the family's next coming, and for them problems of supply hardly existed.

It was a different matter for those who had to live all the year in London. Many had gardens where they could grow a few vegetables and perhaps a quince or a mulberry, but not so the dwellers in tenements or, indeed, any of the poorer sort of citizens. These were dependent upon what they could buy in the markets or what was brought by hawkers to their doors. The old-established markets—Billingsgate for fish, Leadenhall for poultry, Smithfield for meat—were reinforced in the seventeenth century by several new ones: Covent Garden had developed from the haphazard stalls grouped round the piazza of Inigo Jones,[3] and

---

[1] G. Scott Thomson: *Life in a Noble Household, 1641–1700*. London, 1937, p. 124.
[2] *Ibid.*, p. 215.
[3] See *supra*, p. 160.

the Spitalfields Market was given a charter (also for the sale of fruit and vegetables) by Charles II.[1] Another market was built by the Earl of Clare in 1657, and called by his name; it was intended for the sale of meat and fish, and was open thrice weekly, but for some reason it did not greatly prosper.

The comparison between London and country prices of goods is interesting. Samuel Pepys's sister, Esther St. Michel, found that it was just as difficult to make ends meet at Brampton (Hunts) as in London, but she was a notoriously bad manager, and would have been in trouble anywhere. Most people found that foodstuffs cost only slightly more in the capital.

In early times much of London's bread came in carts to the city from Stratford-le-Bow, and when there was any shortage people pressed so close to the carts 'that one man was readie to destroy an other, in striuing to be serued for their money'.[2] Of course there were bakehouses in London too; it will be recalled that it was in one of these that the Great Fire started. Each bakehouse had its own seal, which was transferred when it changed hands, and this had to be stamped upon every loaf that issued from the oven. Loaves were of prescribed weight and sold at fixed prices, and a firm distinction was made between the bakers of white bread and of brown.[3] When, at the end of the eighteenth century, the price of bread rose sharply there was panic from fear of a shortage, since the French war had upset shipments of flour from the Continent and no means had yet been found of preventing American flour from deteriorating during the voyage. Parliament authorized the baking of brown loaves from mixed corn, but few cared to eat it—everyone by this time preferred bread from white flour. However, the crisis was partially overcome by a self-denying ordinance: people agreed to cut down their consumption of flour by a third, renounced hair powder, and ate only stale bread.[4]

There were numerous small dairies in or very close to the City, although not every dairyman chose to keep his cows in the kitchen of his house.[5] The village of Hackney had a great name for butter and dairymen here were able to charge nearly double

---

[1] In 1680. For Covent Garden market see *supra*, Chapter Eight, § iv.
[2] John Stow: *Survey of London.* Ed. C. L. Kingsford. London, 1908, vol. i, p. 157.
[3] S. Thrupp: *A Short History of the . . . Bakers of London.* London, 1933, p. 33.
[4] *Ibid.*, pp. 32–3.
[5] See *supra*, p. 156.

the market price; in the Earl of Bedford's accounts for 1654 'the butter from Hackney' was tenpence a pound, whereas 'ordinary butter' cost sixpence or so.[1]

Cream at this time was still threepence a pint, but within a couple of years the price had risen by a penny or two. More frugal households made do with imported Irish butter, bought by the cask: this could be obtained (in 1705) at a certain coffee house.[2]

Milk, on the other hand, was of poor quality and hard to come by. Cow-keepers who fed their lean animals on grass growing in the parks and fields sold it to milk carriers, who stored it in their cellar-dwellings, whence it issued as a bluish fluid, half water, at double the price, in pails that were carried from door to door. 'No delicate person', wrote T. Baird in his *General View of the Agriculture of Middlesex* in 1794, 'could possibly drink the milk were they fully acquainted with the filthy habits of these dealers in it'.[3] At this time, the whole of London was said to be supplied with milk by only thirty-nine cow-keepers.[4] It is small wonder that the wealthy preferred asses' milk at 3*s*. 6*d*. a quart, for the animals were led daily round the streets and milked at the door into the customer's own china bowl.

London was probably better served by fishmongers than were most large towns, particularly those that lay inland, although the problem of keeping the fish in good condition until it reached the table was basically the same. Visitors to London often took the opportunity to send a present of fish to their friends and families, as did John Hancock to his nephew in 1774—he paid the large sum of 14*s*. 7*d*. for a turbot that he sent off to Oxfordshire by the Worcester coach with a letter announcing its despatch: 'hope you received safe and good and picked the bones of it for dinner today.'[5]

Salmon came directly from Scotland—as early as 1434 a safe-conduct was issued to the Master of the *Nicholas* of Aberdeen and the crew of eight to discharge her freight of Scotch salmon in the port of London[6]—and oysters came from Whitstable and other

[1] Scott Thomson: *op cit.*, p. 137.
[2] J. Ashton: *Social Life in the Reign of Queen Anne*. London, 1882, vol. i, p. 194.
[3] M. D. George: *London Life in the Eighteenth Century*. London, 1930, p. 349.
[4] *The Times*, February 1796.
[5] M. Dickins: *A History of Chastleton, Oxfordshire*. Banbury, 1928, p. 52.
[6] *Calendar of Documents relating to Scotland*. Ed. J. Bain. Edinburgh, 1888, vol. iv (1357–1509), p. 222.

beds. The Thames itself yielded a good variety of fish, and from
the earliest times there are constant complaints of the 'weirs' and
illegal traps put in the river by unscrupulous fishermen.

Of the meat and other trades there is not much to be said, for
their technique differed little—if at all—from common practice.
Other towns besides London found occasion to complain of piles
of stinking offal left in the street or thrown into the river, and
also suffered the nuisance of slaughter-houses immediately adjoining their dwellings and churches. At one time, late in the
eighteenth century, bounties were offered for fish to be brought to
London, in the hope of reducing the price of meat,[1] but attempts
to regulate prices in this way were only partly successful. The
price of meat remained high because the demand was steady;
much butcher's meat was eaten at this time, especially roast beef,
in contrast to the woodcock, larks, and capons that had been
popular in the days of Elizabeth I.[2]

The richest men could still import their own wine, despite the
high duties, and lay it down in the cellars beneath their houses.
'Canary' was what the London taverns usually supplied to their
customers, although James Howell thought that only a hundredth
part of what was sold under that name was the true Canary, most
of it being a mixture of sherries and Malagas that satisfied all but
the most critical.[3] Ale and beer remained the ordinary drink, although there was some competition from the new tea, coffee, and
chocolate. These retained their favour throughout the eighteenth
century and beyond; the prices, too, gradually fell so that more
people could afford to drink them. A new tendency is noticeable
before the end of the seventeenth century—a fashion that spread
from London to the provinces. This was the practice, strongly
encouraged by the coffee-houses, of taking 'snacks' between
meals, particularly after attending some exhibition or show. When
Pepys took his wife to see *Bartholomew Fair* played by puppets (in
1661) he accompanied her afterwards to the Greyhound in Fleet
Street 'and there drank some raspberry sack and eat some sasages
and so home very merry'.[4]

While the well-to-do households enjoyed comfort and plenty,

[1] J. Ashton: *Old Times*. London, 1885, p. 137.
[2] S. Thrupp: *op. cit.*, p. 160.
[3] *Familiar Letters*. London, 1903, vol. ii, p. 201.
[4] *Diary*. Ed. H. B. Wheatley, Vol. ii, p. 135.

things were very different for the poor. Since there was practically
no excise duty to pay on English brandy it was extremely cheap,
and when compounded with the essence of juniper berries and
sold as 'geneva'[1] or gin, this fiery, spirituous liquor came within
the reach of almost everyone. Not only was gin sold in the dram
shops, it was stocked by innumerable shopkeepers, from barbers
to grocers, from tobacconists to shoemakers, and was sold also
from barrows in the street. No licence was needed to sell spirits,
and the gin and brandy shops flourished and multiplied. Soon,
many a poor man in London, who could not afford a decent
lodging or food for himself or his family, was either drinking gin
or lying upon straw and sleeping off its effects. Women drank it as
eagerly as men; even babies were given nips of gin to quieten or
stupefy them. The results of this tippling justified everything that
was spoken or written in its disfavour, but once the passion for
spirits had taken hold of the London mob it was very hard to
curb. Something like forty years passed before the evil began to
diminish, and only after the Government had responded to the
stream of petitions that reached the Commons with Act after Act
designed to reduce the consumption of spirits.[2] The appalling,
sub-human conditions to which the great mass of Londoners
were reduced can hardly be imagined. Hogarth's terrible 'Gin
Lane' gives no exaggerated picture. The incidence of disease and
death rose in a steep curve, demoralization increased, and where
one house in four was a gin shop crimes of violence became a
commonplace. The craving was so severe that it seemed there were
no lengths to which addicts would not go to secure their liquor.
Mrs. George quotes the case of a girl who fetched her own child
from a workhouse, strangled it and left it in a ditch at Bethnal
Green, so that she could sell its clothes for 1s. 4d. and spend the
money on gin.[3]

Anyone who is inclined to think of eighteenth-century London
in terms of elegance and refinement should spare some consideration for the wretched conditions that reduced people's resistance
to so low an ebb. Graceful houses backed on to sordid hovels, and

[1] From the French *genièvre* = juniper.
[2] A full analysis of these measures is given by Mrs. M. D. George in her *London Life, etc.*, pp. 29–41. It was not until 1751 that any real headway was made.
[3] *London Life, etc.*, p. 42. See also for this problem Sidney and Beatrice Webb: *The History of Liquor Licensing in England . . . 1700–1830*. London, 1903.

the chandeliers in brilliant drawing-rooms reflected the guttering rush-lights that illuminated a pile of verminous bedding and a huddle of drink-sodden men, women, and puling neglected children crowded in a stinking cellar. The ease with which these people fell victims to gin-drinking was at least partly due to the conditions in which they lived, where spirituous oblivion seemed the greatest good, but it would be wrong to suppose that such misery and ruin were inevitable. People did succeed in leading comparatively decent lives, they bred and brought up their families in conditions made tolerable by their own efforts; this does not contradict the circumstances of Gin Lane but shows the tough fibre and resilience of the human spirit.

II. LONDON FOOTMEN

I once was passing through Palace-Yard, in Parliament Time, when the Master of a little Brandy Shop being at his Door, was ask'd who he had within, the Man very seriously reply'd 'only some few of my Lords the Bishops' . . . I found about a Dozen sturdy Footmen, in Purple colour'd Liveries, waiting the rising of the House of Peers.

[Anon.] *A Trip through London*, 1728.

This identification of footmen with their masters' titles might be, and often was, carried to absurd lengths. The story of the victualler in the Haymarket[1] who lost his trade and was reduced to penury through offending the whole tribe by calling one of them 'Robin' instead of 'my Lord Marquis' is probably apocryphal, but it illustrates the general attitude. Footmen of Members of Parliament went so far as to run their own parliament when waiting for their masters, but, as we have seen, those of the bishops apparently preferred to drink brandy.

Their livery was provided by the masters, and probably other clothing as well, but footmen's wages in the eighteenth century were low indeed; about £6 a year was the average in London. In the country it would be less than that, but there would be more time off and opportunities for sport. In London the footmen's great pastime was theatre-going, and they had a prescriptive right to the Upper Gallery at the play.[2] The hierarchy of menservants in a great house was strict and promotion by seniority very slow; in small households a footman might be called upon to undertake

---

[1] *A Trip through London*, p. 3.   [2] J. Ashton: *Social Life, etc.*, vol. i, p. 78.

very miscellaneous duties, although there would always be maid-servants to do the actual cleaning and housework. According to Addison in the *Spectator*[1] women sometimes employed men as ladies' maids, and conversely Steele speaks in the *Tatler*[2] of his maid coming to light him home at night.

In the Russell household at Bedford House eleven or twelve footmen were employed towards the end of the seventeenth century, and although the higher grades, those who waited personally upon the family, received the usual £6 a year, the lowest had to be satisfied with two.[3] Seventy years later, however, the number of footmen had dropped to seven or eight and their wages had risen to between £14 and £17 a year. This is not indicative of a general rise in wages, but seems to be due to the engagement of a much better and more efficient type of servant.[4] All liveries were ordered and paid for by the Gentleman of the Horse, and it seems that the younger and lower footmen were expected to do some work in the stables. There were, too, young pages, of whom the best were educated and trained for service. These boys had no regular payment, but were fed and clothed and given presents. Sometimes they had pocket-money, and there are details of the arrangements made for cutting their hair and 'scouring' their clothes. One entry in the household accounts is fifty shillings 'For teaching the page on the flageolet',[5] and there are others for such things as 'shoe-buckles, buttons for his cuffs, and a comb'.

Although they were fairly generous to their page-boys, the Russell family were careful managers. Their coachmen, chaisemen, and postilions all wore livery, and in the mid-eighteenth century the bill for it might come to as much as £150 in a single year, but in 1757, when the cost of a postilion's new suit was given as £4 16s. 11½d., the accounts also show 10s. 6d. 'For altering a full livery coat and making them fit for the new coachman'.[6]

The tips or 'vails' given to footmen and pages amounted to large sums where there was much entertaining. Everyone tipped their friends' servants for even the slightest service, and the

---

[1] No. 45.   [2] No. 130.
[3] G. Scott Thomson: *Life in a Noble Household*, pp. 118–19.
[4] G. Scott Thomson: *The Russells in Bloomsbury, 1669–1771*. London, 1940, p. 228.
[5] In 1663–4. Scott Thomson: *Life in a Noble Household*, p. 119.
[6] Scott Thomson: *The Russells in Bloomsbury*, p. 237.

footmen grumbled bitterly when the vails were too small. This was only natural, since these extras were supplementary to their wages and were looked on not only as a perquisite but as a right. Female servants seldom received vails. Up to the end of the seventeenth century no women were employed in the kitchens of Bedford House but throughout the eighteenth the accounts show a number of cooks and kitchenmaids paid at the flat rate of £8 a year. The French chef got £60, but he, like the women, could not expect his wages to be augmented by his master's friends. By 1771 the number of indoor and outdoor servants at Bedford House, excluding the casual workers such as cleaners and chairmen, had risen to forty-two and the cost of their wages to £859 16s. 0d. per annum; this was of course a great establishment, but even in middle-class households the number of servants employed is astonishingly high.

Negro slaves sometimes acted as personal servants, but they were by no means peculiar to London.[1] Two points of interest may be gathered from the advertisements in contemporary London newspapers: the first is the extreme meagreness of the rewards offered for the recapture of runaways. The second point is a negative one. In all the twelve years of Queen Anne's reign the indefatigable John Ashton was able to find only one instance of a slave being sold, which could mean that the families became strongly attached to their 'blackamoors', finding them like Dr. Johnson's 'Francis', faithful and tractable. There is no evidence that negroes were employed in large numbers in London households; they were rare enough to be remarkable right up to the time of their emancipation.

It seems that the general lawlessness and 'insolence' of the times was to some extent affecting the behaviour of London footmen, who were increasingly concerned in tavern brawls, and sometimes in highway robbery. Apprentices also were showing an independent spirit and there are frequent charges of 'saucy' behaviour and an unwillingness to sweep the shop and clean the windows. Some of them refused to attend their masters to church, and desired to wear silver buckles on their shoes.[2]

Even female servants, generally far more docile, sometimes became tired of housework. John Turbervill wrote from his

[1] Mitchell and Leys: *A History of the English People*, London, 1950, pp. 525-6.
[2] *A Trip through London*, p. 51.

house in Clerkenwell that his maid was unsatisfactory: 'To make cleane a house it is too paynfull for her, and to make cleane a shooe she scorns it.' Moreover, she had given notice simply because he called her a 'base slutt'.[1] Pepys called his maids such names, and worse, and beat and kissed them, but they were still treated as part of the family and taken on frolics and expeditions. It was not for another hundred years that servants were treated as of different clay, and it is a guide to etiquette dated 1818[2] which says, while recommending the affluent to bestow tender attention on their deserving fellow-creatures, 'it would be highly improper for young people to associate with their servants, and to converse with them in the same unreserved manner as they would with an equal'.

Masters advertised in the newspapers for servants, and those who wanted places often found them by the same means. A Jeeves among footmen once advertised in a London paper: 'A likely sober Person . . . has a mind to serve a Gentleman as a Valet de Chambre or Buttler . . . he is known to shave well and can make Wigs; he well understands the Practice of Surgery which may be of great Use to a Family in the Country, or elsewhere; he is a Sportsman; he understands Shooting . . . Hunting and Fishing . . .'[3]

III. COUNTRYMEN IN LONDON

*'Tis here the wearied Plowmen find rest, first become Servants,
next Masters, and then Gentlemen: 'Tis here the distress'd
country wench discharges her Burthen, gets into Place, marries
her Master, and becomes an Alderman's Lady.*

[Anon.] *A Trip through London*, 1728.

It is not always realized how close the City was to the countryside in the seventeenth and early eighteenth centuries. We read of countrymen riding daily into London with their fruit and dairy produce, and a foreign visitor noticed that farmers in London were always spurred and booted and clad in riding-coats 'as they will be going home on horseback'.[4] To Londoners these

---

[1] 14 November 1640. Printed in *Somerset and Dorset Notes and Queries*, vol. xix, p. 6.
[2] *The Female Instructor, or Young Woman's Guide to domestic happiness*. London, 1818, pp. 366–7.
[3] Quoted Ashton: *Social Life, etc.*, vol. i, p. 79.
[4] César de Saussure: *A Foreign View of England in the Reign of George I and George II*. Trans. Mme Van Muyden, 1902.

countrymen were so familiar as to attract no notice; it was only when they came to make their homes in London that they invited attention.

It has already been shown how difficult was the lot of the casual stranger seeking to make a living in one of the trades strictly controlled by the gilds. The runaway serf would have little chance, unless he were quite young and possessed some outstanding skill or talent, when it might be to someone's interest to take him as an apprentice without premium. Even then, with his foot on the lowest rung, he might never have a chance of climbing beyond the hireling or journeymen stage, or he might be pushed off the ladder altogether by pressure from above. The newcomer could, however, always find a living, and a fairly good one at that, in rough manual labour and particularly in 'porterage'—fetching and carrying bales of goods for woolmen and wine-merchants, and lifting their heavy casks and packs in and out of storage cellars. In the building trade, too, there were opportunities for unskilled men; they were paid at a low rate, but could generally find continuous employment.

With the Great Fire of London, however, came the country craftsman's opportunity. One of the by-products of the fire was the opening of a number of new brickyards and timber stores for the materials needed. Much of the new timber came from Scandinavia, but the English forests provided some, and the necessary stone—from Kentish chalk to Purbeck marble—came from the English quarries. From Portland Bill[1] to Tadcaster in Yorkshire, from the Cotswolds and from Surrey, came the stone that built the new St. Paul's, and to London came also provincial carpenters and masons.[2] They were attracted by the prospect of steady work as well as by London wages, and came in force to work upon the gaunt and calcined ruins. One carpenter had come from Ireland, and other journeymen had served their apprenticeship in Wales, or Yorkshire, or Cornwall. Master-masons accompanied their stone from Burford in Oxfordshire or from the Isle of Portland.

---

[1] 50,322 tons of stone came from the Portland quarries, and special roads and piers had to be arranged for its transport. See W. F. Reddaway: *The Rebuilding of London after the Great Fire*. London, 1940, p. 124. Some stone also came from Beer in Devon.
[2] Notably the Oxfordshire mason Christopher Kempster. D. Knoop and G. P. Jones: *The London Mason in the Seventeenth Century*. Manchester, 1935, pp. 35, 45.

Londoners in the various building trades complained that foreigners had come from all quarters of the kingdom, and they heard many unfamiliar and uncouth accents as the new London painfully grew, brick by brick and stone by stone. Sometimes the newcomers surprised London workmen by their skill; and, coming as they did from places where they had been accustomed to turn their hands to any job that needed doing, their ideas of specialization were rudimentary. This exasperated the Londoners, who were used to distinguishing between the joiners who made the cupboards and the carpenters who put in the shelves.[1] In normal times there would have been conflict, but so much had to be done, and done so quickly, that for the moment all differences were set aside. A few years later, when the houses were finished, both Londoners and provincial journeymen found themselves in a bad position, for the new buildings needed little repair work, but by then the immigrants had settled with their families and were hardly distinguishable from natives.

By 1673 with many of the new houses standing empty, awaiting tenants who could afford their rents, well-to-do provincials began to come to the capital and to ask for admission to the Companies and freedom of the City so that they could bring their families to live there. Four of these desirable new residents—'a button maker from Gloucester, a merchant tailor from York, an Oxford apothecary, a trader in Indian gowns moving from the suburbs to Ludgate Hill'[2]—were among those accepted by the City with open arms. Indeed, this particular year saw two hundred and ninety houses let to country craftsmen,[3] many of them quite humble workmen, others belonging to the new and rising class of building contractors.

There was always a tendency among Londoners to resent the intrusion of foreigners: we have seen to what lengths they would go in repudiating alien visitors,[4] and in a lesser degree the Scotsmen who accompanied James I and VI on his journey south were unpopular when they settled in London or Westminster. The bakers were angry when they were undersold by Scotsmen cooking oatcakes for the 'Poorer Sort of People', though one Mungo

---

[1] Reddaway: *op. cit.*, p. 119.
[2] *Ibid.*, p. 303.   [3] *Ibid.*, p. 305.
[4] *Supra*, pp. 73–7.

Spotswood claimed that the Scotsmen had thereby 'saved many from Starving'.[1]

Of course, temporary residents were accepted as they always had been: agents, litigants, country Members of Parliament—all these came and went without hindrance. In earlier times it was something of an adventure for these M.P.s to come to Westminster and sit in the Commons, as well as an interference with their private business. The boroughs that sent these often unwilling representatives were obliged to pay their expenses of travel and, at any rate in some cases, the cost of their board and lodging while Parliament was sitting. In 1463 we find the City of York paying two aldermen 'in going, staying, and returning, for 45 days . . . £8 0s. 0d.'[2] The boroughs grumbled at having to pay these expenses, and in one west country town—Chard, in Somerset—the citizens actually forfeited the privilege of Parliamentary representation through their unwillingness to pay their members.[3]

By the eighteenth century the attitude of country M.P.s had greatly changed and the possibilities of profit and pleasure in a parliamentary career were fully realized. Country gentlemen stood for election, prompted by these and by better motives. Thomas Fuller saw this type as 'willing to do his Countrey service. If he is no Rhetorician to raise affections . . . he counts it great wisdome to be the good manager of Yea and Nay'.[4] On the other hand, the antiquary Abraham de la Pryme in 1697 decried all the Commons as 'irreligious wretches'[5] and thought that England would be far happier administered only by the House of Lords. A Swiss visitor who stayed in England in 1782 has left in his memoirs an unforgettable picture of the House of Commons in his day. ' . . . they . . . come into the house in their greatcoats', he wrote, 'and with boots and spurs. It is not at all uncommon to see a member lying stretched out on one of the benches while others are debating. Some crack nuts, others eat oranges . . . There is no end to their

[1] W. N. Manchée: *The Westminster City Fathers.* London, 1924, p. 64.
[2] *Extracts from the Municipal Records of the City of York.* Ed. R. Davin. London, 1843, p. 15.
[3] Chard sent burgesses to Parliament only from 1300 to 1329 and then lost the privilege. See George Roberts: *Social History of the Southern Counties.* London, 1856, p. 469.
[4] *Selections from Thomas Fuller.* Ed. T. Broadus. Oxford, 1928, p. 55.
[5] A. Ponsonby: *English Diaries.* London, 1923, p. 142.

going in and out.'[1] Although many, if not most, of the Members behaved as though Parliament were a not very exclusive club, it was a place where London and the country met, where ideas could be exchanged and points of view adjusted. Londoners were kept in touch with countrymen's interests, just as north and south countrymen learned to know and appreciate one another as they could have done in no other way.

So far, an impression has been given that the traffic was one-way, that countrymen flocked to London and sometimes made their homes in the City. The converse is also true. Many Londoners turned countrymen; not only those who dwelt in the pleasant villages of Highgate and Chiswick, of Islington, Stoke Newington and Hackney, of Clapham and Streatham, and thence travelled to and from their City premises, but others who went further afield. These were not always bent upon setting up as country gentlemen; sometimes they merely wanted a small estate where they could go for weekends and where their families could spend the summer months. William Braund[2] built himself a solid and comfortable house at Hacton in Essex, taking four years over the work, making his own bricks and employing local carpenters to construct the furniture. He was typical of many more.

Another Londoner, a grocer, at a rather earlier date gave up his trade and moved into the country. He also chose Essex, and leased a manor there from a yeoman who had farmed the land successfully. The Londoner, however, could make nothing of it, and after a year the venture failed because—the former owner said—his skill was 'all together unfytt and insufficient'.[3] Others, more adaptable, applied their business acumen with more success, and blended as easily with their new surroundings as the many countrymen who had identified themselves with a London background.

[1] C. P. Moritz: *Travels in England in 1782*. Trans. P. E. Matheson. London, 1924, p. 64. His account of other English institutions is equally vivid.
[2] L. S. Sutherland: *A London Merchant, 1695–1774*. Oxford, 1933, pp. 1–7.
[3] Mildred Campbell: *The English Yeomen under Elizabeth and the Early Stuarts*. Yale, 1942, p. 171.

IV. 'COFFEE-HOUSE TALK'

Although excellent eaters, the English would, I think, go
without breakfast or supper rather than neglect their morning
or evening papers.

J. H. CAMPE: *Reise durch England und*
Frankreich, 1801.[1]

. . . This onely I can tell you, that hee does give out in his
Coffee-house talke, that hee has Eleven Witnesses to bring . . .
against us . . .

Samuel Pepys to B. St. Michel, 8 December 1679.[2]

In one sense the coffee-houses were the inheritors of the news
and gossip disseminated in Paul's Walk; in another they were
forerunners of the London clubs. Club life, with its amenities and
its concentration of people with one over-riding interest within a
single group, was foreshadowed by the coffee-houses that soon
became adopted by a particular sort of customer.

They were a specially 'London' institution: as Macaulay pointed
out in his famous third chapter 'the coffee-house was the Londoner's home, and . . . those who wished to find a gentleman
commonly asked, not whether he lived in Fleet Street or Chancery
Lane, but whether he frequented the *Grecian* or the *Rainbow*'. The
Rainbow was one of the earliest—if not the very first—of London
coffee-houses; it was opened about the year 1656 by James Farr,
a barber. Soon, the neighbours were complaining, and just before
Christmas 1657, Farr was charged with being a nuisance since the
'evill smells' of his drink called coffee offended other dwellers
in the street.[3] Contemporary with the *Rainbow*, but less famous,
was a coffee-house opened in St. Michael's Alley, Cornhill, by
Rosa Pasquee of whom nothing is known except that he was a
'Turkey merchant'.[4]

Within a very few years, every shade of opinion was catered for
by one or other of the coffee-houses: here you would go if you
wanted to consult a medical man, there if you only wanted witty
conversation. At *Hogarth's Coffee House* Latin lessons were given

[1] Brunswick, 1803, vol. ii, p. 64. Trans. M. Letts: *As the Foreigner Saw Us*. London, 1935, p. 137.
[2] *The Letters of Samuel Pepys and his Family Circle*. Ed. H. T. Heath. Oxford, 1955,
p. 140.
[3] John Timbs: *Clubs and Club Life in London*. London, 1872, p. 280.
[4] Ashton: *Social Life, etc.*, vol. i, p. 216.

daily at 4 p.m.—by the master of the house himself if the 'Learned Gentleman' happened to be absent.[1] At *Garraway's* you could also buy tea; at *White's* or the *Cocoa Tree* chocolate was on sale. *Lloyd's* in Lombard Street became a centre for the selling of wines and ships, and John Salter made his house a museum of curiosities which included Robinson Crusoe's and Man Friday's shirts, and the Queen of Sheba's fan and cordial bottle.[2] At *Will's*, which stood at the north-west corner of Russell Street and Bow Street, it was possible to meet all the luminaries of London's literary world. Dryden frequented *Will's*[3] and later Steele, Addison, Swift and the great Dr. Johnson himself.

Stock jobbers and financiers foregathered at *Jonathan's* in Change Alley, and here the talk was all of speculation and visionary projects. At the time of the South Sea Bubble many other strange schemes were launched and some of these had their inception in this house, where fortunes were lost and won by rumour and by credulous cupidity. At nearly all the coffee-houses newspapers and journals were displayed, so that it was possible to go the round of the houses and acquire information of many different kinds. A Swiss traveller[4] in the late seventeenth century was quick to recognize the value of the coffee-houses. 'These houses', he said, 'are extremely convenient. You have all Manner of News there: You have a good Fire which you may sit by as long as you please; you have a Dish of Coffee, you meet your Friends for the Transaction of Business, and all for a Penny, if you don't Care to spend more.' No one has better summarized the advantages; but it may be that he was fortunate, for the rather censorious German, Zacharias Conrad von Uffenbach (who travelled through England in 1710) found only one that he cared for—'the so-called Paris Coffee-House'[5] where the host was a Frenchman and all the customers were Germans. Even here, he said, there was great danger of being cheated, for it was noted as a gaming-house.

Not all the patrons were members of the London intelligentsia; the caustic anonymous observer who made *A Trip through London* in 1728 one day took refuge from a shower of rain in a coffee-house

---

1 Ashton: *Social Life, etc.*, vol. i, p. 16.
2 *Ibid.*, vol. i, p. 229.
3 Will's name was Will Unwin.
4 Misson de Valberg: *Mémoires, etc.* (1698). Trans. H. Ozell. London, 1719.
5 *London in 1710.* Ed. W. H. Quarrel and M. Mare. London, 1934, pp. 27-8.

near Charing Cross 'where I observ'd a good number of thick-leg'd and broad-shouldered Fellows tolerably well dress'd, cursing themselves, and eny Body else, at a most extravagant Rate'.[1] Then there were the politicians. Whigs resorted to the *St. James*, Tories to the *Cocoa Tree*, and there were other houses where both parties met and argued. To country members the coffee-houses were of the highest value, for here they could find the information and exchange of ideas, not to mention the newspapers, that would keep them in touch with the world beyond their own park gates.

Dr. Johnson experienced 'an oblivion of care, and a freedom from solicitude' as soon as he entered a tavern; this comfortable state was common to most coffee-house *habitués*. It was possible, but much less convenient, to read the newspapers elsewhere. There was a 'Three-half-penny Library' in the Strand where people could go to read the papers, and bedridden gentlefolk used to send their servants to borrow them, leaving in each case a deposit to cover the full value of the paper 'as a Hostage for the Safe Return of it'.[2] When, at the end of the eighteenth century, the stamp tax was imposed on newspapers, hiring them out in this way became illegal and keepers of reading rooms who did so—and thus allowed readers to escape payment of the duty—were fined for the offence.[3]

The earliest newspapers were developed from the newsletters written by special agents to particular correspondents, or, at a later stage, by professional journalists. They were passed from hand to hand, and copied, and eagerly discussed. The *London Post*, *London Gazette*, and several more were issued only thrice weekly, and the first daily paper—the *Daily Courant*—did not appear until 1702. Four years earlier what might be claimed as the first evening paper was seen, but this was really no more than a newsletter, issued by a man called Dawks, printed in imitation handwriting and published in the evening. The subscription to it was 30s. a year.[4]

On the whole the newspapers, though concentrating mainly upon foreign news, gave much more reliable information than could be gathered from the reports and rumours that circulated in the coffee-houses and gave rise to what Pepys disparagingly

[1] Pages 4-5.
[2] *A Trip through London*, 1728, p. 7.
[3] John Ashton: *Old Times*. London, 1885, p. 133.
[4] Ashton: *Social Life, etc.*, vol. ii, pp. 64, 69.

called 'coffee-house talk'. The more sensational the rumours the quicker they flew; the chatterers were under an obligation to amuse rather than to inform.

The coffee-houses were, however, a delightful institution and filled a very real need. Good conversationalists could sharpen their wits and speech; those who enjoyed an argument could always find one to their taste; writers found encouragement, politicians enlightenment; the lonely found solace; and everyone enjoyed good company, warmth and comfort, and stimulating refreshment, in the place of his own choice—in short, all the amenities of a London club—without the entrance fee.

Chapter Ten

THE CHIPPENDALES' LONDON

1. TRADESMEN AND CUSTOMERS

*John Speer, Cabinet Maker etc. at Ye Lion and Lamb, the
West side of Fleet Market, sells Leghorn and English Straw,
Chip, Horse-hair and all other sorts of Women's hats, English
and Dutch Matts, Mahogany, Walnut-tree and other Chairs
. . . with all sorts of Turners' Goods—Wholesale and Retail.
Carpenters, Joyners and Cabinet Work Performed in
General.*

Trade Card, *c.* 1730.[1]

THE first impression given by John Speer's advertisement is
that he had a very mixed stock. The term 'Cabinet-Maker'
could certainly be extended to cover a very wide variety of
goods, and the kindred trade of upholsterer (or 'upholder')[2] also
included some unexpected items. A contemporary of Speer, one
Wilson of Aldersgate, who advertised himself as both cabinet-
maker and upholder, issued a trade card that named him also a
'Dealer in Coals' and claimed that he sold 'Organs, Harpsichords,
and Piano Fortes'.[3]

There was no rigid separation of trades at this time, or for many
years to come. Anyone who excelled at making one particular
article was naturally inclined to specialize in this, and he would
supply it either directly to his own customers or to some other
shopkeeper for resale. The processes of separating trade from
trade and retailers from wholesalers were very slow and very
intricate and are not wholly complete even today. Nor is the small
craftsman doing his own work on his own premises, often in the
public view, yet extinct: in country districts working saddlers can
still be seen stitching leather, and in London girls sit in shop-
windows plying their needles and crochet-hooks beneath the
sign 'Invisible Menders'.

[1] Sir Ambrose Heal: *The London Furniture Makers*. London, 1953, p. 164.
[2] A shop in Eton High Street still has 'upholders' on its sign, and the term is still
used by some old-established firms.
[3] Heal: *The London Furniture Makers*, p. 204.

London had almost complete supremacy in matters of taste: this was particularly noticeable in the furniture trade. Good pieces were made in the provinces, often exact reproductions of London-inspired designs, but they could never command London prices. London taste continued to be accepted uncritically throughout the country until it reached its apotheosis in the Great Exhibition of 1851.

There was a general reluctance to trust the craftsmen in local towns not only to create but also to repair valuable property. The squire of Shalstone in Buckinghamshire was not the only one to send his watch to London when it needed mending;[1] it was, as it still is, a common practice. Another country landowner, although he could surely have found a suitable craftsman in Andover close by, sent his silver to London to have the crest removed,[2] and he even packed his harpsichord in a load of hay and sent it up there to be tuned. This last exploit cost him ten guineas: he might as well have paid for a tuner to come to the instrument, since the Bath coach came near enough to his home to bring to his gates parcels of London hats for his son and daughter.[3]

When Mrs. Purefoy of Shalstone wanted a second-hand sedan chair that would be 'strong and tite' she did not look for it in Bicester, or even in Oxford; she sent directly to London, to a chairmaker in Warwick Lane.[4] Normally, however, she wrote instructions to her London agent to buy her what she needed, and her directions were very exact. When ordering satin for a petticoat she would say firmly, 'be sure it be of the colour with ye pattern',[5] although sometimes her man of business might use his discretion: 'They say Sallat Oyll is very cheap in London, if so pray buy mee 2 gallons.' Mrs. Purefoy and her son had varied needs, but practically all of them, they felt, could be satisfied only in London.

The point of view of a London agent who did the shopping for a family living in a remote district is illustrated in the letters written by Richard Lapthorne to his Devonshire employer.[6]

[1] *The Purefoy Letters, 1735-53.* Ed. G. Eland. London, 1931, pp. 193-428.
[2] In consequences of the new tax on armorial bearings.
[3] In 1798. The journal of Henry White, in *Notes on the Parishes of Fyfield, etc.*, by R. H. Clutterbuck. Salisbury, 1898.
[4] *The Purefoy Letters*, p. 108.
[5] *Ibid.*, p. 217.
[6] *The Portledge Papers.* Ed. R. J. Kerr and I. C. Duncan. London, 1928.

Together with the goods he used to send newsletters from London, keeping the family abreast of the times and telling them of changes in taste and fashion. Lapthorne was given no instructions as precise as Mrs. Purefoy's, but did the best he could and, particularly when prices ran high at a book auction, he had to use considerable judgement. The Exeter carriers were constantly conveying boxes of books and periwigs, not to mention a fringed velvet saddle that Lapthorne had found after much search in the shops of 'most eminent sadlers both in the City and the Suburbs',[1] and had finally secured from the Queen's own saddler near Pall Mall.

Both in London and the country, customers were very willing to accept the advice of well-known furniture dealers, and often entrusted them with commissions to supply the whole of the hangings and household gear and wall-papers, as well as the necessary furniture for their homes. One of the most famous and least satisfactory of the Chippendales' clients, the actor David Garrick, commissioned them to supply all that was necessary for his new house in the Adelphi, lately designed by Robert and James Adam. The bill came to £1,000 and Garrick found that he could not pay it; after much dispute it had to be reduced, and the Chippendales were out of pocket and much displeased.[2]

Sometimes customers would consider the charges too high and might refuse to pay in full. Sir Ambrose Heal has in his possession a bill made out by William Linnell of Berkeley Square to Sir Richard Hoare, in which Sir Richard has struck through some of the charges in red ink and written against others 'too much' or 'extravagant charge'.[3] Mrs. Piozzi, too, was dissatisfied with Gillow's bill for furnishing Streatham Park, and, after disputing it, knocked off three hundred pounds.[4] Clients might accept with meekness the dictates of the professionals and write obediently in their journals: 'Received the Gothic paper for the staircase',[5] but they could be difficult and intransigent when it came to payment.

Shopkeepers were accustomed not only to clients who tried to reduce the price, but also to those who were procrastinating payers. Sometimes the goods were sold for a deposit and then payment would be made by instalments: a commonplace today

---

[1] *The Portledge Papers*, pp. 184–5.   [2] Heal: *The London Furniture Makers*, p. x.
[3] *Ibid.*, p. ix.   [4] *Ibid.*, p. 63.
[5] *The Journal of Gideon Mantell*. Ed. E. Cecil Curwen. Oxford, 1940, p. 8.

but it is something of a surprise to find this custom as far back as the early seventeenth century. Dekker in *The Honest Whore* makes Penelope Whorehound say: '. . . God is my judge, sir, I am in for no debts; I paid my tailor for this gown the last five shillings a-week that was behind, yesterday.'[1] It was therefore a startlingly new idea when, about 1750, a Mr. Palmer opened his shop on London Bridge and sold his goods at fixed prices for ready money, and the customers found themselves bound by arbitrary figures on a price-ticket. No time was wasted; if the customer could not make up his mind immediately 'the article asked for was withdrawn . . . and another customer attended to'.[2]

After the first shock of surprise, people flocked to Mr. Palmer's as soon as the shop opened—at eight in the morning—and had to be bundled out at 11 p.m. or they might have stayed until midnight .The turnover was so great and so brisk that prices could be kept very low, and the business was organized into departments to enable customers to find what they wanted without delay. They still continued their practice of tossing and tumbling the goods upon the counters, especially in the haberdashery, so that the unfortunate assistants had to spend hours refolding and rewinding and stowing them away when they could hardly keep their eyes open from fatigue, and 'Frequently at two o'clock after being actively engaged on foot all day from eight o'clock in the morning, I have scarcely been able with the aid of the banisters to go upstairs to bed'.[3]

The writer of these words was Robert Owen, who went to work for Mr. Palmer in 1785 at about the age of fifteen. He already had some experience, and a good recommendation, so his salary was unusually high—£25 a year and his board and lodging, which included a really good dinner on Sundays and rather scrambled meals on weekdays. Palmer seems to have treated his assistants well—there were many of them, and some were quite elderly. Robert Owen made firm friends with the youngest Palmer, and the two boys went for excursions together on Sundays, and when business was slack found time to read and play games together. The tumultuous rush of customers occurred only in the spring; although hours were always extremely long by modern

---

[1] Part 2. Act v, sc. ii. (First printed in 1630.) Mermaid edition, p. 281.
[2] *The Life of Robert Owen, by Himself.* Ed. M. Beer. London, 1920, pp. 25–6.
[3] *Ibid.*, p. 27.

standards, they varied with the season. Robert was happy in his work, and it was with real regret that he felt obliged to leave Palmer's and accept an offer from a Manchester firm who would give him 'board, lodging, and washing, and . . . *forty pounds a year*!'[1]

The interesting point about Palmer's business is his bracing treatment of his customers; he was polite but firm, and although the assistants were made to take great pains with their appearance and manners, they were expected to make rapid sales with no argument. Indeed, as Owen says, 'The favour appeared to be more to the purchaser than to the seller of the articles'.[2] Palmer was a pioneer and his business a forerunner of the departmental store, but his example does not seem to have been widely followed. Most shopkeepers continued to indulge their customers and to conduct their business in a leisured manner, and there were few indeed who improved upon Palmer's treatment of his assistants: generally speaking their conditions of work were far less humane and they might be expected to cringe before the arrogance of tiresome customers.

The appearance of shops at this time is easy to discover from contemporary pictures. Some shop-fronts still survive and are at pains to preserve the reticence of the original shopkeepers who regarded their windows as architectural features, not as a means of cunning display. The art of window-dressing was not studied, simply because it did not exist. If a cap or bonnet was exhibited, it was merely to show the type of merchandise to be found within. In effect, this might be very decorative, and there are modern chemists who have unearthed great pot-bellied jars and filled them with glowing liquids in imitation of their ancestors, but any Rosamund who sought today to buy one of these purple jars would probably receive a dusty answer.[3]

Within, the shops were often cramped, stuffy and ill-lit. There were exceptions; when Sophie von la Roche explored the London shops, she was delighted by the brightly-lit interiors. That she was charmed by Mr. Wedgwood's china and Mr. Vulliamy's clocks is understandable enough, but it is harder to appreciate her pleasure in visiting butchers' shops unless it was due to surprise at

[1] This was the beginning of Owen's highly successful business career.
[2] *Ibid.*, p. 26.
[3] See Maria Edgworth's story of Rosamund and the Purple Jar in *Early Lessons*, 1801.

finding them 'neat and clean'.[1] In most shops there were wooden counters, as today, but not much use was made of glass for the display of goods. These were stacked in boxes behind the counters, often in a pile reaching to the ceiling. If something were needed from a top dark corner the ladder and a lighted candle might be called for, and the single assistant was in no position to keep an eye upon his clients, who might indulge in shop-lifting or take their chance of stealing from a fellow customer. It was the fact that an apothecary in Leadenhall Street was searching in this way for some obscure item that put temptation in Moll Flanders' mind. Defoe describes her standing outside, looking at a bundle that a careless customer had left lying on a stool just before the counter while she watched the shopkeeper at work. Moll Flanders could not resist the opportunity: ''twas like a voice spoken to me over my shoulder, "Take the bundle, be quick; do it this moment"'.[2] There must have been much thieving, either the work of professionals or by victims, like Moll, of sudden temptation; until better designed, better lighted and more adequately staffed shops had been evolved it was a danger very hard to combat.

It is interesting to notice the gradual drift westwards of London's main shopping centre. Whereas in medieval times the fashionable shops had been in Fleet Street and Cheapside, by Jacobean days they were moving to Covent Garden and Leicester Fields. As late as 1614 the Court of Burgesses at Westminster held that Piccadilly was 'no fitt place' for the sale of tobacco[3] and the 'Pickadilly' of James Howell's *Londinopolis* (1657) was 'full of fair houses roundabout'. It may be noted that the name was used vaguely to cover a district rather than a street, and that the road now known as Piccadilly was in the seventeenth century either 'Portugal Street' or 'the way to Reading'.[4]

Pall Mall was noted particularly for the booksellers who offered all the books essential to a gentleman's library, often specially bound and stamped with the purchaser's coat of arms, and also engravings and prints. It was from John Parker's shop in Pall Mall that the first Earl of Bristol bought his copy of Bishop Burnet's *History of his own Times* and it may well have been Parker who

---

[1] In 1786: *Sophie in London*. Trans. and ed. Clare Williams. London, 1933, p. 26.
[2] Daniel Defoe: *Moll Flanders*, 1722. Repr. London, 1947, p. 210.
[3] W. H. Manchée: *The Westminster City Fathers*. London, 1924, p. 66.
[4] C. L. Kingsford: *The Early History of Piccadilly, etc.* Cambridge, 1925, p. 97 ff.

supplied the Earl also with the '144 tomes of ye Classicks' that he gave to his heir at the cost of three score guineas.[1]

New Bond Street, an extension northwards of the original street, was first rated in 1721. Here were sold elegant luxuries of many kinds, and the agent of the Duke of Bedford bought His Grace comfits, limes and pistachio nuts from Richard Robinson the confectioner, and lavender water at 5s. 2d. a pint at the sign of the Civet Cat.[2] The fourth Duke bought his gloves and stockings from a haberdasher in Holborn, and his accounts show that most of the materials used in his wardrobe came from mercers in Covent Garden, where the richest stuffs were to be found. 'Crimson Genoa velvet' at 27s. a yard, and yellow-flowered silk were imported from Italy and France, and some merchants dealt expressly in goods from the Levant or silks and embroideries from China and Japan. As the mercers who stocked these rare stuffs tended to congregate in the same quarter, it was easy to compare qualities and prices, and it became a fashionable pastime to spend the whole morning roving from one shop to another, fingering brocades and satins, comparing and appraising, but seldom making a purchase.

Advertising was an art still in its infancy; notices of sales appeared with some frequency in the early newspapers, but most trades relied upon elegantly designed trade cards that were often used as billheads. From the earliest times tradesmen had advertised their wares and tried to attract customers by hanging out their signs or emblems, just as the heraldic achievements of the royal family, the nobility, and the City companies directed attention to their dwellings. Many shop signs sported the King's arms, so many, indeed, that it is clear this was no more than a protestation of loyalty and did not necessarily imply royal patronage. The tendency was for the signs to be made ever larger and heavier and so to become increasingly obstructive to all traffic. There had been complaints about this from the middle ages onwards, but little had been done to curb the nuisance. In Cornhill, for example, many of the signs projected several feet into the roadway, and grew ever more numerous and more elaborate.

In 1718, however, a huge sign hanging in Bride Lane crashed

[1] In 1723. *The Diary of John Hervey, etc.* Wells, 1894, pp. 93, 96.
[2] G. Scott Thomson: *The Russells in Bloomsbury, 1669–1771.* London, 1940, pp. 254, 277.

to the ground, tearing away the front of the house to which it was fixed, and killing four people.[1] This really did stir public opinion, and agitation against the signs became general, as any reading of the *Tatler* and *Spectator* must show. The suggestion was made that houses in every street should be numbered, a simple idea but one that was new at the time and which would mean that directive signs would become superfluous. In 1762 the removal of all signs within the City of London was ordered by proclamation[2] and the numbering of the streets began.

For some years the shopkeepers retained their old designations on their billheads and trade cards, but in the end the numbers triumphed. No longer would the familiar Highlanders guide customers to the tobacconists, or Indian Queens beckon people to the linen drapers' counters. Gabriel Douce, the mercer of the Lamb and Black Spread Eagle, would no longer have to direct his customers to the house 'next door to the Golden Goate, in New Round Court, in ye Strand': he would have a proprietary interest in his own number. It was a much more convenient system, but with the passing of the London signboards much colour and interest vanished from London life. Only the barbers' poles remained; there were no more curious affiliations, of the Hand, Star, and Lock of Hair, for example, or the Wheatsheaf and Speaking Trumpet,[3] to interest a passer-by and set him musing upon their origin.

11. The Workshop

SIR!

I have received the Desk, but wee can't open the Draw but do suppose it opens in the two slitts down the Legs. I desire you will let mee have a [letter by the] next post how to open and manage it, as also what it comes to that I may order you payment. My mother joins with mee in our compliments to you & Mrs. Belchier, & I am, Sir!...

HENRY PUREFOY.[4]

The next letter from Henry Purefoy shows that the drawer was only 'stuck together thro' damp' and that there was no faulty

[1] Sir Ambrose Heal: *The Signboards of Old London Shops.* London. 1947, p. 2.
[2] In 1763 Westminster followed suit.
[3] These titles were generally the result of the amalgamation of two or more businesses—cf. some odd pairings in tavern signs.
[4] *The Purefoy Letters,* p. 111. "ffor Mr. Belchier at the Sun the South side of St. Pauls in St. Paul's Churchyard London," The desk cost £3 10s. 0d.

workmanship. Mr. Belchier was, indeed, one of the most reliable of cabinet-makers and his workshop had a very high reputation. The London furniture trade included an astonishing number of grades and types of workmen;[1] careless work must occasionally have passed unnoticed, but the employers were very jealous for their good name and watched closely to discover any slovenly or incompetent craftsman who might bring discredit on the firm.

There was an immense gulf between the skilled artisans and the rough labourers—the porters, the chairmen, and the intractable mob. These last belong rather to the London of Hogarth and Sir John Fielding; in the Chippendales' London skilled workmen carried on the old traditions; the journeymen had served their apprenticeship and did not work as a group of unskilled or semi-skilled labourers under a competent foreman, as in some of the newer businesses. In time, economic conditions would favour the latter class, but in the eighteenth century there was still room for the genuine craftsman, with his rigid hierarchy of professionalism, his contempt for mass production, and his jealously guarded trade secrets.

While the furniture trade was setting its standards at so high a level, other London craftsmen were absorbed in their own processes, each contributing a bright strand to the industrial fabric of the time. The makers of exquisite porcelain figures, craftsmen painting roses in the factories of Bow and Chelsea, were creating new and beautiful works of art, not with self-conscious-ness or self-admiration, but simply as their ordinary daily work. Yet their achievements, as those of the furniture makers and Spitalfields silk-weavers and many more anonymous artists, gave a special richness of quality to the times, in strange contrast to the drabness and darkness of other aspects of the age.

The London tradesman producing his own goods on his own premises was the direct descendant of his medieval forebears, although by the eighteenth century he was working on a much larger scale to supply a greatly extended market. Within a very few years of his emergence from apprenticeship and setting up on his own account, a skilled craftsman might own large workshops and be master of eighty or a hundred men. He might have saw-mills and timber yards attached to his premises as well as a show-

[1] M. D. George: *London Life in the Eighteenth Century*. London, 1930, pp. 156-8.

room where he could demonstrate his wares and take orders from his clients. A typical craftsman of this class was George Seddon, who was apprenticed at an early age and at twenty-three (in 1750) set up for himself in the fine premises of London House in Aldersgate Street. Within eighteen years he was employing eighty workers who included upholsterers, carvers, gilders, mirror-makers and ormolu-workers as well as cabinet-makers of supreme skill.[1] London House turned out some of the finest furniture of the day, from the 'capital billiards table' exported to Calcutta for the use of William Hickey[2] to the delicate mirrors and exquisitely made close-stools inspected by Sophie von la Roche in 1786.

It was natural for the tradesman in a small way of business to specialize; he had neither the skilled workmen nor the special materials for carrying out very miscellaneous orders, and it was only sensible to concentrate his efforts on what he did best and most easily. Thus we find small tradesmen making a great name for some special product. For instance, there is the 'Turner and Small Furniture-maker' at the Beehive and Patten who is thought to have been the first maker of cricket bats in London. Others followed his example, and fourteen years later, in 1778, we hear of a fire in the shop of Wilkes in the Strand, who was a 'Turner and Maker of Kentish Cricket bats and balls'.[3] Others, again, found it convenient to specialize in billiard cues and balls, and one inventive carpenter took out a patent for his 'new and peculiarly constructed Venetian blinds' for which he charged 1s. per square foot.[4]

One of the people who made fortunes from anticipating the trend of fashion was Henry Clay, who died in 1795 worth £80,000, said to be entirely the fruits of his output of papier-mâché furniture. This 'japanning' was a special trade, and many of the pieces were made for export. Those destined for Spain and Portugal were in brilliant colours, the groundwork being scarlet or gold, whereas the home market preferred grounds of dull blue, black, or olive green. Some cabinet-makers imported Chinese lacquered furniture for their clients, or supplied them with Chinese porcelain made and painted from European designs and brought to this

---

[1] Heal: *The London Furniture Makers*, pp. viii, 38.
[2] In 1791. See his *Memoirs*, 1749–82. Ed. A. Spencer. London, 1913–18.
[3] Heal: *The London Furniture Makers*, p. 183.
[4] *Ibid.*, p. 203.

country by the East India Company.[1] In this sense they were dealers rather than craftsmen, and they must have possessed a good supply of capital. These leading tradesmen formed a class apart, but they were not necessarily arbiters of taste as were those who issued books of their own designs and became nearly as important in their own days as Palladio had been in his.

The elaborate catalogue published by Thomas Chippendale the elder marks him out as one of these leaders; he and his son typify the best in a great tradition, as far as craftsmanship is concerned, although there were better and more successful men of business. *The Gentleman and Cabinet Maker's Director* has 160 large engraved plates; it must have been extremely expensive to produce and is proof of Chippendale's secure position. The *Director* was published in 1754 and within seven years had gone into three editions; the list of subscribers shows that they were indeed, as the author said, 'patrons and customers in all classes of society'. There was no need to issue a trade card, for the *Director* and further books of designs issued by him and his son spread Chippendale's fame far and wide.

In all of these the elder Chippendale owed much to the skill of his office draughtsmen—who were, in a sense, his partners—but still more to his business manager James Rannie. On Rannie's death in 1766, the young Thomas found it necessary to take Thomas Haig into the firm, for he himself had a poor head for figures, and indeed, when Haig retired in 1796, the firm went bankrupt within eight years and the whole stock had to be sold by auction. Nevertheless, there was no cabinet-maker in London who had a higher reputation for integrity, and the designs of both father and son had enormous influence upon provincial furniture-makers, who carried them out carefully and skilfully although sometimes in cheaper materials than those prescribed.

Not every firm consented, as did the Chippendales, to make ordinary household stuff. The elder Thomas supplied to Sir Rowland Winn[2] for Nostell Priory many fine mahogany pieces that are still there, but we also read in the accounts of a deal stool made for fifteen pence, and a 'Large strong Elm Chopping block for the kitchen' that cost 10*s*. In this they stood midway between

---

[1] M. D. George: *London Life in the Eighteenth Century*. London, 1930, p. 162.
[2] Between 1766 and 1771. See R. W. Symonds in Heal's *London Furniture Makers*, pp. 219, 220.

firms like Vile and Cobb who made exquisite pieces at enormous prices, and incidentally supplied Horace Walpole with some of his best items at Strawberry Hill, and the much humbler joiners who made sea-chests in deal or 'wainscot',[1] shop furniture, bedsteads, and small boxes.

Of Chippendale's famous contemporaries several were also known as designers. George Heppelwhite's *Cabinet Makers' and Upholsterers' Guide* was not published during his lifetime, but by his widow in 1788, two years after his death. It is interesting that of Heppelwhite's and Sheraton's work, although each gave his name to a distinctive style, few if any pieces can be certainly identified.[2] Their influence was felt, however, far beyond the bounds of London through their designs and also through the craftsmen they had trained. This connection between London and the provinces is illustrated also by the interesting experiment of the firm of Gillow. Robert Gillow was the second son of the well-known Gillow of Lancaster, and when he started a branch in London he was setting a precedent later to be followed by Mallet of Bath and many others. Young Gillow set up shop in 1760, and he and his brothers carried on until 1817. Of course the converse —London firms with provincial branches—was later to become a commonplace, but it was still rare in the eighteenth century.

III. THE LONDON FIRE BRIGADE

On Wednesday a fire broke out within a few houses of myne in Hatton Garden but blessed bee God was soon stopt.

Letter from London, 20 October 1694.[3]

The frequent outbreaks of fire that persisted after the rebuilding of the city engendered great nervousness in the minds of Londoners, to whom the events of 1666 were still a childhood memory. In spite of the new precautions these sometimes threatened to repeat the great disaster; we hear of as many as forty dwellings swept away in one single blaze,[4] and there was often considerable destruction and loss of life.

---

[1] Made from oak imported from the Baltic, softer and straighter-grained than the English variety.
[2] See Symonds: *loc. cit.*
[3] *The Portledge Papers*, p. 187.
[4] *Ibid.*, p. 231. This was reported from Wapping in May 1696.

Many of these fires started in cabinet-makers' shops: an over-turned or overheated glue-pot might cause widespread damage, and open fires among inflammable materials—shavings blowing about the floor as soon as a door was opened—were responsible for many accidents. One fire was caused by an upholsterer in the Haymarket who was carrying out an experiment 'to smother bugs',[1] and the smoking-out of vermin was always a dangerous process. Elimination of bugs was a serious problem for cabinet-makers and upholsterers. Heat or smoke, or both, seemed the most effective weapon, although one craftsman advertised that his 'Bedsteads, Sophas, and Chairs' were 'finished so that no vermin of any Denomination can possibly exist in either'.[2]

Some firms lost their premises three or four times in the course of the century. London House in Aldersgate, where the Seddons had their workshops and showrooms, was burnt down in 1768 and immediately rebuilt on an impressive scale; fifteen years later it was again burned to the ground, and again rebuilt.[3] The intro-duction of steam for heating, in place of the traditional open fires, was a sound and practical improvement. A Bond-Street cabinet-maker substituted for his twelve coal fires one small boiler that was found to warm the place quite adequately.[4] The workmen were able to heat their glue by the boiler's pipes, and altogether this proved a much safer system and was commended alike by public opinion and the insurance companies.

It is surprising to find that, up to the middle of the eighteenth century, cabinet-makers' premises were accepted as normal risks. Most of the insurance companies were newly formed and were feeling their way; their great concern was to attract customers and it was not until they were well established, towards the end of the century, that they felt strong enough to increase their rates to cabinet-makers and to list this work among the 'hazardous' trades.[5]

Several companies had been formed within a few years of the Great Fire; the Phoenix was established in 1682 and the Friendly Society began only two years later. By 1710 the Amicable Contri-butors had completed its first fifteen years and secured 13,000 members; at this point it changed its name to the well-known one

1 *The London Gazette,* 17 August 1723.
2 Heal: *The London Furniture Makers,* p. 34.
3 *Ibid.,* p. viii.   4 *The Observer,* 4 December 1808.
5 Heal: *The London Furniture Makers,* p. xv.

A TRADESMAN'S CARD

SIGNBOARDS IN A LONDON STREET

DR. SYNTAX AND THE FOUNDLING

A SERMON IN NEWGATE

of the Hand-in-Hand.[1] Like the other societies it was based on the principle of mutual contributions with the sole object of protection for its members. The Hand-in-Hand took to meeting at Tom's Coffee-house in Westminster and built a strong-room there for its assets, but some of the members objected to meeting in Westminster since it was too far from their business premises, and it was decided to move the headquarters to the City. Others preferred their old meeting-place and seceded from the Hand-in-Hand to form the 'Westminster Fire Office' in the year 1717.[2]

At first the new company, following the usual practice, issued its policies on buildings only and not on their contents, and also made a firm distinction between brick buildings and those that were of timber. Payment of a deposit secured seven years' insurance; at the end of this term it would, after the deduction of office expenses, be returned to the client and an agreed yearly dividend paid. The deposit was reckoned as 12/– for every £100 of the building's value which was assessed by the company's own surveyor. Should anyone wish to insure his property for more than £1,000, a general meeting had to be called and a special resolution passed by all the members.[3] There were a hundred and fifty of them, mostly craftsman and small tradespeople living in Westminster, but also a few who had thrown in their lot with the Hand-in-Hand and, although they owned property in the City, preferred to insure it in Tom's Coffee-House. These were minor gentry and professional men. It is also worth noting that the very first building insured by the Westminster Fire Office, on 24 September 1717, was the Chapel in Conduit Street, not a local property at all.[4]

One of the directors of the company was a coach-painter named Roger Askew, who lived in Long Acre, and he it was who designed the company's fire mark. It was based on the portcullis from the arms of Westminster, and the three feathers surmounting it were set there out of compliment to the Prince of Wales (later George II). This tribute led to the hoped-for royal patronage, and the Prince—through his agent—insured six of his own properties with the Office during its first year of business.

---

[1] John Ashton: *Social Life in the Reign of Queen Anne*. London, 1882, vol. i, p. 66.
[2] E. A. Davies: *The Westminster Fire Office*. London, 1952, pp. 16–17.
[3] *Ibid.*, p. 18.
[4] *Ibid.*, p. 77. See the charming illustrations of this building on p. 76.

13

Askew's design was used by Ince and Mayhew when they made the magnificent set of twenty single and three arm-chairs that are still in use today;[1] the same firm supplied the rest of the office furniture—desks, and an iron chest for use as a safe, down to candlesticks, snuffers, shovels, and a poker.

Each company had its individual mark; these were generally of lead cast in a mould and then painted or gilded. In early times these badges carried the member's own number; the Westminster Fire Office charged each policy-holder 1*s*. 8*d*. for his mark, which he set up on his property in a prominent position. These marks became a familiar sight not only in London but also in the provinces: some are still to be seen in their original position. The practice of numbering them was soon discontinued, and by the beginning of the nineteenth century most of them were no longer made of lead, but of thin copper plate.

The object of displaying these marks was very practical; they were intended to guide the primitive fire engines belonging to the companies to the property insured in their name. To help put out a fire in adjoining premises was unthinkable, even where buildings insured by the company were directly threatened. Rivalry was far too keen for this, and the idea of co-operation simply did not exist. Some technical lessons in fire-fighting had been learned from the bitter experience of the Great Fire, but organization remained extremely rudimentary and casual.

It must be stressed that the insurance was of property only and the companies were not concerned with saving human life. The mortality in these fires was terribly high; if it is mentioned at all in the newspaper reports it is only as an afterthought. Typical of many is the account given in *The Universal Magazine* for April 1770,[2] of a comparatively small outbreak in Holborn. Two houses were destroyed and four people perished in each of them; this excited very little comment and the reporter only says it is 'supposed' that they died as they had not been seen since. Indeed, it was not until the formation of the Society for the Protection of Life from Fire in 1836 that any effective steps were taken to save life as well as property, and mobile fire-escapes began to operate.

[1] Davies: *op. cit.*, p. 30.
[2] Page 222.

Eighty years earlier Sir John Fielding, in a letter to the *Public Advertiser*,[1] had suggested having water-cocks in the streets for the use of fire-engines: hitherto a turncock had had to be found who could insert a plug into the main, and by the time he had been extracted from his bed, or the local tavern, and his tools were found, it might well be too late to save the blazing building. In any case, the pressure was too low and the hoses were too narrow to give more than a feeble jet of water. Once fire had really taken hold of a building, all efforts had to be directed towards containing it, and hope of extinguishing anything but a very small outbreak was tenuous indeed. At a fire in a warehouse, for instance, as late as the year 1803, it was nearly two hours before any water at all could be procured, and the volunteers who 'immediately beat to arms'[2] and came to help the firemen were obliged to stand idly by and watch the blaze.

The early engines were hardly more than small water-tanks on wheels, man-handled and man-propelled. The Westminster Fire Office ordered one 'of middle size' in 1720 and kept it in a watch house near Hanover Square, then being built. The Society had considerable property in and near Conduit Street, so it was convenient to move the 'appliance' there and to build for it (at the cost of £7) a special shed.[3] The leather pipes had to be kept carefully oiled lest they should dry and crack, and it was important too to keep the wheels greased so that the engine could be trundled along at speed.

After a few years, the maker suggested taking the old engine in part exchange and supplying a new model with a copper cistern in place of the wooden one. This was done, and in 1730 the same firm also supplied one of their largest models, with shafts for a horse and a hose of 2-inch bore. A guarantee was given, providing free maintenance for ten years.

Both these engines helped to fight the big fire in Piccadilly when Berkeley House was burned down,[4] and on this occasion some joint effort was seen, for many companies turned out their appliances and others stood by for fear their own property might

[1] R. Leslie-Melville: *The Life and Work of Sir John Fielding*. London, 1934, p. 104.
[2] *The European Magazine and London Review*, December 1803, p. 484. The warehouse was in Soho, between Frith St. and Dean St.
[3] Davies: *op. cit.*, p. 52.
[4] In 1733.

be damaged. By 1780 the Westminster Fire Office had so much to protect that they had in use one small and five large engines, and a regular brigade of thirty-six men trained to operate them.

Like most other fire brigades, the men were recruited from the London watermen. These retained the independence and spirit they had shown in John Taylor's day, and they welcomed the fire service because an Act was passed in 1707 that gave to its members protection from the Press-gang. They were not paid a fixed salary, but twelve of them formed a band under a foreman who gave them regular training, and they were paid at the rate of 6*d.* for a small chimney fire, 1*s.* for a larger one, and as much as 2*s.* 6*d.* for a serious fire that meant some hours of work and danger as well as labour.[1]

Their equipment was all supplied—helmets or caps of iron, hatchets and long hooks called 'preventers' for pulling down dangerous or threatened buildings. Badges distinguished them from their fellow fire-watermen; the Westminster men had the portcullis and feathers in silver. By 1719 they were being equipped with a livery of blue and orange. Even the leather buckets wore badges, and were handsomely designed.

Public opinion, guided by Sir John Fielding, led to a demand that all brigades should be equipped with ladders, not necessarily a fire-escape on wheels, but short ladders carried with the engine, and this became compulsory in 1774.[2] At about the same time Fielding was carrying on a campaign against bonfires in the streets, on the Fifth of November and on many other occasions as well: these were not only smiled on by authority but were laid and lighted at the public expense, yet, said Fielding, 'seldom a bonfire is made but several lives are lost by these means.'[3] Here, however, he was less successful, and the public continued to stoke the fires and to throw squibs and firebrands, to the terror of horses and the danger of all passers-by.

One of the London engine builders in 1755 issued a trade card claiming that his engines could be used either for extinguishing fires or for watering gardens;[4] this is typical not only of the

---

[1] Davies: *op. cit.*, p. 47. When three firemen were killed in 1756 at a fire in Old Palace Yard, the company paid £15 each to their widows. *Ibid.*, p. 52.
[2] Leslie-Melville: *op. cit.*, p. 104.   [3] Quoted *ibid.*, p. 198.
[4] Sir Ambrose Heal: *London Tradesmen's Cards of the Eighteenth Century*. London, 1925, plate xxxi.

inadequacy of the smaller engines at this time, but of the levity of public opinion. Another tradesman, a trunk-maker in Cheapside, advertised leather fire-buckets among his 'Portmantuas' and periwig boxes:[1] these were decoratively painted and would look well standing in the entrance hall, but their usefulness would be very limited. Even the handsquirt, which had to be operated by three men—two to hold and one to squirt—took only two gallons. It should, however, be remembered that there were in these days no great stores of inflammable materials such as paint, rubber, petrol, or celluloid.

The initiative in forming the London Fire Brigade was taken by twelve of the largest insurance companies, and it was established in 1833 when, at long last, the value of coherent organization gained recognition. In other parts of the country brigades had already been formed, and London had to look to Edinburgh for her first Chief Officer. This was James Braidwood, who published a pamphlet on fire-brigades that is still a classic in its kind; he devoted himself to creating a great tradition in fire-fighting and finally gave his own life in the Tooley Street fire of 1861. Four years later, by the Metropolitan Fire Brigade Act, insurance companies handed over the protection of London to the Metropolitan Board of Works, afterwards the London County Council, but from the first fumbling efforts of these companies to prevent and fight the danger grew the calm efficiency that defended London in this century's ordeal by fire and saved St. Paul's from yet another burning.

---

[1] *London Tradesmen's Cards of the Eighteenth Century*, plate xciii.

Chapter Eleven

THE FIELDINGS' LONDON

1. MURDER, ROBBERY AND FRAUD

*Never was there such beare faced outrages committed in and
about London, as of late, not a day or night passes but robberies
if not murders committed, in our very streets as well as by
breaking into our houses.*

RICHARD LAPTHORNE: letter from London, 24 January 1690.[1]

THE crime wave that reached its peak about the middle of the
eighteenth century was due to a variety of causes but above
all to the gin-drinking habits of the poorest and most miserable class of London's population. This factor has already been
discussed,[2] and the dreadful truths need not be repeated here. Nor
is it necessary to dwell upon sordid details of the crimes: what is
important is the attitude of the general public. There was little
that was constructive about this; most people seem to have
accepted the situation as it was, guarded their own property as
well as they could, and felt little if any responsibility for the state
of society that produced the criminals.

There were those persons, living in respectable houses, who
complained that they could not sleep at night for 'the doleful cries
of murther' that came from slums and dark alleys round the
corner.[3] Others took an academic interest in crime and collected
all the pamphlets and broadsheets and other 'murder stories' that
they could find—much as their descendants do today. Many
crowded to the scenes of horrible crimes in the hope, perhaps, of
securing some blood-stained souvenir. Late in the seventeenth
century a dismembered, headless corpse was found in Parker's
Lane, near Little Queen Street, and was exhibited at the Coach
and Horses nearby. Here it was seen by 'above thousands of

[1] *The Portledge Papers*, 1687–97. Ed. R. J. Kerr and D. I. Duncan. London, 1928,
p. 98.
[2] See *supra*, pp. 167, 168.
[3] G. Scott Thomson: *The Russells in Bloomsbury*. London, 1940, p. 355 ff.

Spectators'.[1] Again, some human remains were found in a boat lying at Bull Stairs on Bankside, and we read that 'The Spectators that go to see it are Innumerable'.[2]

This curiosity was akin to that which drew crowds to witness executions and punishments of all kinds, for these spectacles gave excitement to those whose lives were dull and drab. The crowds are generally represented as gloating and exultant, but among them there were some compassionate spirits who went to pray rather than to mock, and it is worth remark that an orange-seller who was knocked down and injured by three footpads and taken to a nearby inn to be nursed, was visited next day by 'some hundreds of people'.[3] Whether this helped the sick man greatly is not known, but he did recover; and at all events it was kindly meant. The rowdy youths, who made nuisances of themselves by their idiotic pranks and at best were noisy hooligans, were sometimes members of noble families: more often they were apprentices or footmen aping the vicious young aristocrats. They called themselves the Mohocks; one of the least tiresome of their habits was to wrench the doorknockers off street doors—about as sensible a pursuit as the collection of policemen's helmets by a later generation. They took advantage of the lawlessness of the times to mock and insult both men and women, but their delinquency was quite futile and not designed for any personal gain.

Robbery of all kinds, from the depredations of house-breakers, through all the varieties of pilfering, to raids by highwaymen practising within the City itself, had become so common that it created a special problem of its own—the disposal of stolen goods, which became so numerous that receivers gave very low prices or even refused to take them at all. Brokers posing as honest men, having studied the advertisements of lost property, would visit the victims and offer to buy the property back on their behalf. As a rule, people were satisfied to recover what they had lost, and very few had enough public spirit to insist on prosecution. This technique was perfected by Jonathan Wild,[4] who was able to

[1] Misc. pamphlets from the Ashmole Collection in the Bodleian Library, Oxford, no. ccxxxi.
[2] *Ibid.*, no. ccxxx.
[3] *Ibid.*, no. ccxxv.
[4] Henry Fielding: *The History of Jonathan Wild the Great*, 1743. This is less a biography than a political satire.

run his agency in Cock Alley, Cripplegate, quite openly. He did
not have to handle the stolen goods, or even see them, he merely
pocketed his commission. Wild had a genius for organization, and
before long he was arranging matters for thieves as well as victims,
both of whom looked upon him as a benefactor. There were those
who suspected Wild's activities, or even knew the extent of his
roguery; these he bribed to silence, and to make himself doubly
secure, Wild himself became a 'thief-taker' working for the
Government and paid by results. This system was an extension
of the Act of 1693 that had offered on the conviction of a highwayman a reward of £40, together with his horse, arms and money.
A regular tariff was fixed for lesser offenders, dropping to an army
deserter who brought the thief-taker only £1 as a reward.[1]

It was inevitable that a thief-taker would make enemies, and
he could not claim police protection because there was, as yet, no
police force. The powerful gangs could defy him, unless he had an
organization like Wild's behind him. In the end, Wild himself
came to the gallows, and although he pleaded that he had brought
seventy-six criminals to justice, he was hanged at Tyburn to the
accompaniment of the cheers and jeers of an excited mob.

11. Punishment and Prisons

> . . . *The Pilory indeed is to punish perjur'd persons, which is a
> greate crime; there is alsoe whipping, some at a cart's taile,
> and for some crimes they are burnt in the hand or cheeke as a
> brand of their evil, and if founde again to transgress, that
> marke serves as a greater witness to their condemnation.*
>
>   *The Journeys of Celia Fiennes, c.* 1703.[2]

In the belief that crime could be halted, or at least diminished, by
increased severity, the eighteenth century saw more and more
capital offences added to the statute book: in a hundred years their
number increased from sixty-seven to one-hundred and fifty-six,
children being liable to the same penalties as adults. In practice,
this severity defeated its own end, for people became as reluctant
to prosecute as juries were to convict, and in cases of theft valua-
tions were made at absurdly low rates to minimize the offender's
crime and keep the assessment below the amount that would mean

---

[1] Patrick Pringle: *Hue and Cry*. London, 1955, p. 35.
[2] Ed. C. Morris, 2nd edn. London, 1948, p. 311.

a capital sentence. Even if a man were brought to trial the odds were against his conviction, for any slight error in drawing up the indictment—such as a wrongly spelled name or some small technicality—could win him acquittal. In the end, only a few of those sentenced to death were hanged; reprieves were frequent, and might be repeated several times until the prisoner was finally pardoned. In 1748 a ten-year-old boy was sentenced for the murder of a girl half his age, but four times his execution was postponed: nine years later he was pardoned and sent off to sea.[1]

It is easy for a later age to point to the barbarity of the penal code in these times, but without a profound knowledge of how matters worked out in practice, and without making full allowance for the extraordinary difficulty of achieving any sort of law and order, comparison with our own day is most unfair. There was a strong tendency to regard the criminals taken to be hanged at Tyburn as leading players in the public show. This attitude is well illustrated in *The Beggar's Opera*. If a condemned man bore himself gallantly or nonchalantly in the face of death he would win warm approval from the crowd and, indeed, was sometimes rescued by them from the hangman's clutches. This nearly happened to Captain Kidd; the rope broke at the executioner's first attempt, and if the pirate captain had not been so drunk he could easily have escaped. As it was, still in his gold-brocaded gown, Kidd was recaptured and strung up a second time.[2] Sometimes the malefactors were bold and truculent, and then the crowd would laugh and cheer. Two robbers, who had already at their trial behaved with great insolence and given the Court 'very reproachful language', when they were brought to Tyburn assaulted the executioner and twice struck him to the ground; calling for wine they drank the health of the Old Pretender, and 'slighted' the exhortations offered them.[3]

It was a three-mile journey from Newgate prison to Tyburn, and crowds lined the route to watch the passage of the condemned man. On 'hanging days' apprentices and workmen of all kinds left their work, to the great annoyance of their employers, and the richer citizens found places in windows and balconies overlooking the scene, or in specially-erected wooden stands. The more

---

[1] Quoted by Pringle: *Hue and Cry*, pp. 49–50.
[2] On 7 June 1701.   [3] *The Portledge Papers*, pp. 84–5.

ghastly penalty of half-hanging a man and then disembowelling him and beheading and quartering the remains, was reserved for traitors, but treason was widely interpreted and could be made to cover the crime of coining.

The lesser punishments, the whippings and the brandings, also took place in public—generally outside the prisons—and these too attracted crowds. The mob could themselves take part in the punishment of the pillory or the stocks, pelting the helpless victim with every sort of filth and, when they felt particular animosity, with stones. People sometimes lost one eye or both, and on occasion died from their injuries: a public brought up on throwing sticks and stones at a living target ('cock-throwing') could easily transfer their aim to their fellow creatures and felt little compunction, if any, in so doing.

Since the prisons were intended less as places of punishment than as temporary lodgement for prisoners, in practice they had become expensive and vicious lodging houses. The prisoners themselves made the rules and bullied and browbeat newcomers into accepting them. In 1699 the Society for the Promotion of Christian Knowledge was founded, and a committee visited both Newgate and Marshalsea in an attempt to secure reform, but in vain. Some abortive attempts were made by Parliament to improve matters, for both Lords and Commons had been made aware of the cruelties that were taking place.[1] In the same year that saw the foundation of the S.P.C.K., a Quaker named John Bellers published a book of *Essays*[2] in which he marshalled his views on the futility of capital punishment and pointed out that 'To make no difference between the Punishment of Theft and Murder, seems a great deficiency to our present Law'. Bellers was an interesting person who, though his ideas had little influence at the time, gave a lead to later social reformers.

[1] Sidney and Beatrice Webb: *English Prisons under Local Government*. London, 1922, p. 24 ff.
[2] Reprinted with a memoir by A. Ruth Fry. London, 1935.

III. 'THE BLIND BEAK'

The English have no word in their language to express 'police';
but it would be a great mistake to suppose that the thing itself
did not exist among them.

J. W. VON ARCHENHOLZ: *England und Italien*, 1780.[1]

Henry Fielding is rightly awarded a high place among English dramatists and novelists, but less than justice has been done to his work as a magistrate. When the Licensing Act put an end to his career as a playwright—for the Lord Chamberlain could not be expected to grant a licence to any of his caustic political satires—Fielding entered the Middle Temple and read for the Bar, intending to practise as a lawyer; but he had no success, and was glad to be appointed in 1748 to the office of Principal Magistrate of Westminster with headquarters at Bow Street. No regular stipend was paid to the magistrates; they were entitled to certain fees and it was supposed that they would help themselves to commissions and accept bribes to make up the balance. When Fielding took office the income was reckoned at about £500 a year; in his *Journal of a Voyage to Lisbon* he called it 'the dirtiest money upon earth' and said he had reduced it to £300—'a considerable portion of which remained with my clerk'. He now knew at first-hand what was meant by a 'trading justice', knowledge that he used to excellent effect in several of his novels. His most recent biographer[2] has been at great pains to uncover Henry Fielding's activities as a magistrate and reports that he has been unable to find 'the slightest evidence that Fielding ever took a bribe or any other illegal payment'.[3] Later on, it seems, the Government did pay salaries of some kind to the magistrates, certainly to Sir John Fielding (Henry's brother), for a letter from him and his colleague Saunders Welch is extant, dated 14 October 1756, asking for payment already overdue.[4] But the amount of their salaries is not known; probably it was very small.

From the first moment of his appointment, Fielding set himself to fight against crime, corruption, and hypocrisy. London was then at its lowest depth of degradation, and nobody saw more

---

[1] An (abridged) Eng. trans., *A Picture of England*, was published in Dublin, 1790, repr. 1797, p. 292.
[2] Pringle: *Hue and Cry*, chapters v and vi.
[3] *Ibid.*, p. 80.   [4] *Ibid.*, p. 81.

clearly than Fielding that much of the trouble came from the
rewards offered to thief-takers who conformed closely to the
pattern laid down by Jonathan Wild. He began his campaign by
inviting the public to bring to his office the best description they
could of those who had robbed them, together with details of the
property lost and exact information as to time and place. When
these advertisements of Fielding's appeared in the press people
acted on them with enthusiasm: to report one's losses officially
was an idea that had the charm of novelty.

There were eight parish constables of Westminster, who were
probably no more corrupt and inefficient than others of their kind,
and Fielding was very fortunate to find as an ally Saunders Welch,
a man as honest, and nearly as able, as himself. Welch had already
trained six constables, who declared themselves ready to stay on
and work for him and Fielding after their tour of duty was finished.[1]
There were no funds from which to pay them, so these men were
dependent upon the rewards they received as thief-takers—and
this is what, to all appearances, they were. But they had their
training behind them, and the acute lawyer, Fielding, to resolve
any legal difficulties, so that they became, in fact if not in name,
the nucleus of London's first police force—'Mr. Fielding's
people'.

In 1751 Fielding dedicated to the Lord Chancellor his *Enquiry
into the Causes of the late Increase of Robberies, etc., with some Proposals
for Remedying this Growing Evil*—the first really constructive exami-
nation of the situation. He appealed to common humanity, 'for
that many cart-loads of our fellow creatures are once in six weeks
carried to slaughter is a dreadful consideration,' he wrote, and
added: 'and this is greatly heightened by reflecting that with
proper care and proper regulations, much the greater part of
these wretches might have been not only happy in themselves but
very useful members of society'.[2] Even Fielding's enemies—
Horace Walpole for one—had to admit the sagacity of this admirable pamphlet. The same year Henry Fielding was joined by his
half-brother John who carried on and extended Henry's work
after the latter's death three years later.

---

[1] A seventh was afterwards added to their number; they were the original Bow
Street Runners, but the name was not commonly used until the next century.
[2] Quoted Pringle: *op. cit.*, p. 97.

John Fielding was fourteen years younger than Henry: he had been blinded at the age of nineteen but with Henry's help had established in the Strand a general agency under the name of the 'Universal Register Office', where he handled miscellaneous business and in his spare time learned law from Henry. John worked with his brother as a magistrate at Bow Street, hence his nickname of 'The Blind Beak'. (The Bow Street Runners were sometimes known as 'beak-runners', for 'beak' was a very old word for a person in authority.) Together, the brothers tackled the insistent problem of breaking up the gangs of street robbers, and planned that the Bow Street house should be open to the public day and night, with two runners always on call, and that there should be co-operation with police magistrates in all parts of London and even beyond. Henry soon started a register of crimes and suspected persons: a Criminal Record Office in embryo. Shortly before his death one of the largest and strongest gangs was broken up, and this put new heart into the magistrates and 'Mr. Fielding's people', while many criminals fled from London in a panic. A famous highwayman was caught, and another gang disbanded: it seemed that the tide was turning, and at last the Government was persuaded to make some financial contribution.

John Fielding was very loyal to his brother's ideas and reaped much of what Henry had sown. The really important part of Henry's work was the three-fold principle that he laid down. He had shown that it was not necessary, or even expedient, to set a thief to catch a thief, and he had demonstrated the ancient constitutional principle that the prevention of crime was the duty of every citizen and that it was every man's business to walk uprightly and with all due vigilance.

Many London magistrates were slow to follow this lead; they continued to dispense justice in their own houses or shops or even taverns, with the usual measure of corruption. Fielding, however, had three of them removed from office for scandalous behaviour —one had already been discharged from the Navy, one convicted of using fraudulent scales, and the third used to borrow money from gaolers and constables, which he failed to repay.[1] This sternness worried the magistrates, and they were startled too when the Blind Beak began admitting journalists to his court. He also

[1] R. Leslie-Melville: *The Life and Work of Sir John Fielding.* London, 1934, p. 144.

kept up the register, and began to exchange information about criminals with county justices; ultimately the War Office decided to send the names of deserters to Bow Street and to pay £20 per annum towards the cost of keeping the records.[1] In his exiguous spare time Fielding wrote, in 1761, a book of *Extracts from the Penal Laws* with comments of his own.

Like his half-brother, John Fielding was kind and compassionate, particularly in dealing with first offenders, and where he could be, he was lenient. In dealing with young offenders he tried to win the co-operation of parents, and made them—when they could be traced—attend his court. Where the boys were homeless —'wretched boys, ragged as colts, abandoned'—Fielding was deeply concerned for them, and, like Captain Coram's, his thought turned to the Navy. He had himself served in the Navy for a short while before his accident and subsequent blindness, and with the help of the philanthropist Jonas Hanway and others, the Marine Society was founded to clothe and equip boys suitable to be trained as officers' servants. Fielding and Hanway were associated also in their work for young girls, and together they helped to found an orphanage for deserted girls and a reformatory for prostitutes, the Magdalen Hospital. Sir John Fielding became a life governor of both these institutions.

Through the pamphlets he wrote, and still more by the example he set of selfless devotion to his work, the Blind Beak succeeded in stirring the public conscience, making it accept the necessity of ameliorating the conditions under which parish apprentices sometimes had to live. Although time passed before all the abuses he had exposed were remedied, it was due to Sir John Fielding's efforts—many of them inspired by Henry's acute perceptions— quite as much as to the more academic exhortations of the philanthropists, that a beginning was made in the great campaign against social irresponsibility, smugness, and apathy.

[1] R. Leslie-Melville: *The Life and Work of Sir John Fielding*, p. 147; Pringle, *op. cit.*, p. 135.

IV. WOMEN AND CHILDREN

When Syntax, all amazement, said,
'Here at my door a child is laid.'
'Well,' the Attorney then replied,
'By no law is it specified,
That you're obliged to take it in.'
'But think,' said Syntax, 'what a sin,
To leave the infant here to lie
Throughout the night—perhaps to die!
It would be murder in my creed,
And my heart shudders at the deed.'
The Lawyer then withdrew the light,
Said, 'Wish you joy, and so goodnight.'

The Third Tour of Dr. Syntax, 1821.[1]

In William Coombe's poem his hero, Dr. Syntax, followed his impulse and did adopt a baby boy left on his doorstep, found a wet nurse for him and arranged for his maintenance. The theme of the foundling is very common in eighteenth-century fiction—it will be recalled that Fielding's *Tom Jones* was one of these unfortunates—and obviously it was a situation very familiar to the reading public. It was still more familiar to the justices and the parish constables who found the abandoned babies, or their corpses, lying in the street. Poverty rather than unnatural feeling occasioned mothers to cast out or murder their unwanted children, but for the suffering children the motive mattered not at all. Sometimes they were left in the Temple, and were taken care of by the Benchers; many of these foundlings were given the name of 'Temple'. In 1777 the sub-treasurer of the Inner Temple was ordered to pay four guineas to a nurse employed to look after the foundlings, 'for her additional care and expence in nursing four of the said children in the small pox'.[2]

Even if this last hazard was avoided, the expectation of life for an illegitimate child born in poor circumstances, if it was allowed to survive at all, was low indeed. The Bills of Mortality show that in the worst years more than 75 per cent of children born in London died before they reached the age of five,[3] and Jonas Hanway reckoned that of 'parish infants' under the age of one year, only one in a hundred would survive.[4] Some of the children were put

[1] By William Coombe: *Doctor Syntax's Three Tours*. London, 1869, p. 331.
[2] Sir D. Plunket Barton, C. Benham, and F. Watt: *The Story of the Inns of Court*. London, n.d., p. 104.
[3] M. D. George: *London Life in the Eighteenth Century*. London, 1930, p. 42.
[4] *Ibid.*, p. 43.

out to nurse by the parish and, poor as were their chances of
reaching maturity, they were the lucky ones, for those sent to the
parish workhouses in London were in the care of demoralized
and gin-sodden nurses with no shred of maternal feeling for the
puny children, disease-ridden from birth, committed to their
care.

It is ironical that Jonas Hanway should be remembered as the
inventor (which he was not[1]) of the umbrella, and seldom acknowledged as the author of the Act of 1769 which made it compulsory
for London parishes to send infants into the country to be nursed.
This enormously increased their chances of survival, and to
Hanway as well as Coram should be given the credit for saving
hundreds of children's lives.

When, after seventeen years' labour on behalf of the helpless
children whose wretched plight filled him with compassion, the
merchant seaman Captain Thomas Coram composed his memorial
to the Government, he drew up a terrible indictment of human
wickedness and barbarity. This succeeded in touching the hearts
of a number of ladies of rank, who willingly signed his memorial,
and subscriptions for building his Foundling Hospital came
trickling in from many sources. In 1739 a charter was granted, and
Captain Coram was able to make a home for his first children.
Three years later the foundation stone of the Foundling Hospital
was laid, and one wing was in working order by 1745. Only a
small number could be taken of the many thousands needing care,
and the hospital was besieged by those who wanted to dispose of
children they were too poor, or unable, or unwilling, to bring up.
The congestion was appalling; children from all over London,
and from the country as well, were dumped on the premises, often
in a dying state, and many succumbed soon after admission. At
last, in 1760, the House of Commons decided that reception of all
comers must be stopped, and although Parliament agreed to
continue making grants for children already there, the character
of the hospital was radically changed. Henceforward it was to be
run as a private charity, and children would be accepted only 'on a
statement of the particular circumstances of each case'.[2]

[1] Mitchell and Leys: *A History of the English People*, p. 272.
[2] This brief summary of the circumstances of the Foundling Hospital is taken from
Mrs. George's account which is itself abridged from the authorities (notably Jonas
Hanway) quoted in note 66 to Chapter I of her *London Life, etc.*

THE MUSIC PARTY

COVENT GARDEN THEATRE

John Fielding

Thomas Coram

Octavia Hill   Edwin Chadwick

REFORMERS

In the early days of the Foundling Hospital only about a third of the children survived to be apprenticed, but after 1760 three-quarters reached this age. By the end of the century only one child in six died before it was ready to be sent out into the world. A beginning had certainly been made in tackling this problem, but there were many other dangers and difficulties in the path of young apprentices, both boys and girls. Being forced into crime, particularly theft, or being framed by thief-takers for offences they had not committed, was common to both sexes, but girls had their special troubles, and those who had been seduced or raped at an early age were compelled to go on the streets for their livelihood or to eke out flagrantly inadequate wages. Many of London's prostitutes were girls barely in their teens: since the age of consent was as low as twelve (it remained so until 1885) it was difficult to secure a conviction for rape.[1] Some were hired into brothels, and when they became disease-ridden were thrown into the streets. Here they were found by constables, arrested, whipped and given short terms of imprisonment, before being cast back into their old life, broken in body and spirit. It is not surprising that what money they could earn by the sale of their bodies was immediately spent on gin that could at least enable them to forget their troubles for a while.

Prisoners of both sexes were herded together, and young females accused of theft welcomed pregnancy as a means of escape—for the time being—from hanging. They were safe until their child was born, when perhaps the reprieve would be repeated and they might ultimately be pardoned—although of this there was no guarantee. The issue of reprieves was, indeed, as capricious as the course of justice itself. In *Moll Flanders* the narrator tells us that her mother, being imprisoned for 'borrowing' three pieces of fine holland from a Cheapside draper was found to be with child, and was respited for seven months. She was then sentenced to transportation and the plight of her six-months-old baby is poignantly described: she had to be left behind and, being born in prison, no parish was responsible for her welfare.[2]

Foreign visitors to London were taken aback by the extreme

---

[1] Pringle: *Hue and Cry*, p. 20.
[2] Daniel Defoe: *The Fortunes and Misfortunes of the Famous Moll Flanders*, 1722, chapter i.

14

youth of the prostitutes who accosted them, and were often aware of the bullies who lurked in the shadows.[1] Fees were low enough; Boswell boasts in his *London Journal*[2] that he never paid more than 6*d*. a time, and although he felt a moment's pity for the 'young Shropshire girl, only seventeen, very well looked', he spares the readers of his *Journal* no detail of his amorous adventures, which are as monotonous as they are sordid. The courtesans with their own special quarters and clientele were in a different class; there was a publication called *Henry's List of Covent Garden Ladies* describing their charms. This quickly went out of date and new editions were called for. It is reported that these were sold out as quickly as they could be printed.[3] No better study of the life and conditions of these professionals can be found than in Hogarth's six pictures of 'The Harlot's Progress'.[4] From her arrival at the *Bell* in Wood Street by the York waggon—a country girl with a brass-nailed trunk and a goose in a basket—Moll Hackabout's career is traced through success to misery, and the last picture shows her pitiful funeral with only her 'bunter' (or servant) as a genuine mourner. Moll Hackabout is as true a portrait as is Defoe's Moll Flanders.

Something has already been said of Sir John Fielding's efforts to reclaim young offenders, and his *Plan for Preserving Deserted Girls* contains good and constructive ideas, but the whole structure of society was against him: London in the first half of the eighteenth century had reached a degree of depravity and misery almost beyond comprehension. Probably even now only half the tale has been told: some of the worst cases of cruelty—particularly towards the parish apprentices who were too terrified to complain and too ignorant to be articulate—have been revealed only by chance. The famous case of Sarah Meteyard and her daughter, who murdered a girl apprentice with fiendish cruelty, would never have come to light if the two women had not fallen out two years later and accused each other of the crime. If this had not been reported to Sir John Fielding, nothing would have been known of the circumstances, for the other apprentices dared

---

[1] M. Letts: *As the Foreigner Saw Us*. London, 1935, p. 145.
[2] Covering the years 1762–3. Published London, 1950.
[3] Letts: *loc. cit.*
[4] For interpretation of this well-known series see Peter Quennell: *Hogarth's Progress*. London, 1955, pp. 91–101.

not speak, and the constable who had found the remains had thought they came from a dissecting room.[1]

Sir John wanted to take deserted girls between the ages of seven and fifteen into a 'preservatory', to train them as domestic servants and put them in good 'situations'. This was not really a very safe plan, for some of the most callous employers were people of comparatively high position: Mrs. Meteyard herself kept a good haberdasher's shop and her apprentices were expected to make nets and mittens; it sounded a most desirable 'place'. For those girls, many of them only twelve, who had already been seduced, Fielding planned a reformatory and suggested they should run a public laundry. He, like Coram, made great efforts to interest fashionable ladies in his projects, and invited them to act as visitors. Had he succeeded in nothing else, the Blind Beak should always be remembered as the man who (in some measure) induced the fortunate and the educated to cease averting their eyes from the spectacle of their depraved brothers and sisters, and even to stretch their hands towards them.

v. THE LONDON MOB

We found enormous crowds on both sides . . . they were all shouting each other down . . . They yelled after us, throwing their caps in the air . . . Since the tumult was so great, and we had been warned beforehand, we remained in the coach; it was lucky we did so, for we should else have been in great danger . . .

A Parliamentary election at Westminster in 1710.[2]

Zacharias von Uffenbach misjudged the situation; he was in no danger and was witnessing the activities of a good-humoured crowd on the occasion of a contest that had been widely canvassed, in which the Whig candidate, General Stanhope, was defeated by a brewer named Cross supported, Uffenbach says disgustedly, 'for the most part by common folk'. The irresponsible, unpredictable London mob was quite different from this; something has already been said of its component parts, but it is well known that a mob, as an angry or frightened crowd, adds up to something much more than the sum of the individuals of which it is composed.

---

[1] Quoted Pringle: *op. cit.*, p. 145. See also George: *London Life, etc.*, p. 231.
[2] Zacharias Conrad von Uffenbach: *London in 1710*. Trans. W. H. Quarrell and M. Mare. London, 1934, p. 146.

In their gin-sodden condition, Londoners of the depressed classes were capable of sporadic violence, utterly reckless of consequences; committing acts of bestial cruelty, but incapable of sustained or reasoned effort to secure their objective. They were not by any means easily quelled, and the authorities were disinclined to call out the soldiers to restore order since this seemed to inflame the mob the more. Magistrates had the power to summon troops to help restore order, but not a shot could be fired before the Riot Act[1] had been read aloud—that is to say, the proclamation it contained. This was of considerable length, and by the time it was finished the mob might have swept on out of earshot and into fresh trouble.

The riots against the Gin Act, which sought to check the sale of spirits, led to the murder of several informers, against whom there was great bitterness, and the people's violence was in this case so continuous that the Act proved unworkable. Another cause of riotous behaviour, which continued for many years, was the Londoners' resentment of the intrusion of the Irishmen who came over to help with the harvest and stayed on as hawkers or unskilled workers at very low wages. The Spitalfields weavers were notoriously ready to flare into passion, and in 1736 they violently attacked the Irishmen whom they supposed to be working 'at an under rate'.[2]

More formidable than these sporadic outbursts against trade conditions were the Gordon Riots of 1780, when for six days and nights it seemed that there might be another fire of London. At this time the London mob was completely out of hand, and men yelled and brandished torches without any firm idea of what they wanted to destroy or why. It was a curious feature that the primary idea of these London rioters was to demolish property, not to secure loot: a strong contrast to the anti-Jewish riots of medieval times.[3] The rioters seldom gained any advantage from their outbreaks, indeed they risked transportation or even hanging, but perhaps they gained some satisfaction from the devouring flames and broken furniture.

How much genuinely anti-Papist spirit entered into the Gordon Riots is a matter for conjecture. It may have had some connection

---

[1] It was passed in 1715.   [2] George: *London Life, etc.*, p. 180.
[3] See *supra*, p. 25.

with the prejudice against Irishmen illustrated by the destruction of a public house in Golden Lane kept by a Papist named Murphy.[1] The extent of the 'No Popery' movement, and its strength, are matters whose causes lay outside London's boundaries, but the riots themselves were certainly London's affair and made a very deep impression on those who witnessed the violence. As usual, the Lord Mayor was very reluctant to call out the troops, and when asked to do so by James Malo, a silk merchant from Cambrai, replied, 'I must be cautious what I do'.[2] The course of the disturbances is well known—how Newgate was burnt and plundered, how Lord Mansfield's precious library was destroyed, and the rioters ranged far and wide, sometimes bought off with beer or money, but more often firing houses and chapels, storming prisons and freeing debtors.

The rioting ceased almost as suddenly as it had begun, less from the efforts of the troops who now numbered more than ten thousand, than from the fact that the leaderless rioters lost heart. It was one thing for Lord George Gordon to incite the mob to action, but quite another matter to direct their fury once it was aroused, and still more difficult to keep their fitful energy at fever pitch. When the smoke had cleared away and the ashes had settled it was seen that the damage was far less than had been thought. A projected raid on the Bank of England proved abortive, but perhaps it is possible to find here one of the real causes of the outbreak. Although it seems true that there was a genuine element of anti-Papist feeling, it can hardly have been strong enough to generate so much fury in so short a time. Were the riots not a symptom of the deep resentment against the solidity and smugness of over-moneyed people, when so many were in want? A Bermondsey barge-builder, when told the householder he wanted to attack was a Protestant, replied: 'Protestant or not, no gentleman need be possessed of more than £1000 a year; that is enough for any gentleman to live upon.' Here, perhaps, we have a key to the strange behaviour of the London mob.

[1] George: *London Life*, etc., p. 119.
[2] Dr. G. Rudé: 'The Gordon Riots', *History Today*, July 1955, p. 431. Cf. also this author's 1955 Alexander Prize Essay: 'The Gordon Riots: a study of the Rioters and their Victims', printed in *Trans. of the R. Hist. Society*, series 5, vol. vi (1956).

Chapter Twelve

ROWLANDSON'S LONDON

1. The Royal Academy

*I have been at the Royale Exhibition which the Conisurs hold
very cheap being one of the worst that they ever saw.*

Letter of John Hancock to Arthur Jones in 1778.[1]

THE violent, satirical, and often grossly unfair caricatures of the
eighteenth-century cartoonists, particularly of Gillray and
Thomas Rowlandson, were mainly political in character.
Many of them were concerned with the physical, moral, and men-
tal shortcomings of the royal family,[2] and the extraordinary thing
is that they aroused so little resentment at the time they were
published. Rowlandson was more mellow than Gillray, and interested less in politics than in social life. Some of his drawings show
the frank crudities of his time, but for every three of Rowlandson's
pictures that seem coarse to modern eyes, there are five more that
appear wholly charming. He could be unkind, but was seldom
cruel, and he was often comic where Gillray would have been
savage. The delicately coloured illustrations that Rowlandson did
for the *Tours of Dr. Syntax* show him at his best as a reporter of
the social scene: his hero is a figure of fun, and absurd within
wide limits, but he is allowed to retain his humanity if not his
dignity.

Thomas Rowlandson was born about 1755,[3] and spent his early
years in Old Jewry where his father traded in silks and woollens.
After some schooling in Soho Square, at the age of fifteen young
Thomas joined the newly-opened Royal Academy Schools, and
from this time until his death in 1827 he turned out quantities of

---

[1] M. Dickins: *A History of Chastleton, Oxfordshire.* Banbury, 1938, p. 55.
[2] G. Paston: *Social Caricature in the Eighteenth Century.* London, 1905, *passim.*
[3] This date seems preferable to the generally accepted 1756. See B. Falk: *Thomas
Rowlandson, His Life and Art.* There is a good summary of Rowlandson's work as an
historian of social life, by Adrian Bury, in *History Today,* July 1956, pp. 466–76.

drawings in pencil or pen and wash—a few portraits or land-scapes, but for the most part representations of scenes and people that caught his fancy. It was no accident that Rowlandson won such sudden fame in 1784 with his drawing of ʻVauxhall Gardensʼ,[1] for when this was published as a coloured print almost everyone could find in it something to his taste. Here was a delightful landscape, thronged with figures both grand and humble but all ineffably gay. Dr. Johnson himself, with Boswell, Mrs. Thrale, and Goldsmith peered out from a ground-floor supper box to the left of the picture, while the Prince of Wales strutted in the foreground; there were artless groups of strollers under the trees, and others spellbound by the singer, Mrs. Weichsel. The grouping and deployment of these figures gave the picture balance and rhythm; it was not a mere panorama, or series of sketch-book impressions, but a genuine work of art, and although Rowlandson sometimes reached these heights again, he never surpassed his ʻVauxhall Gardensʼ. The gaiety and delights of this picture, and of the less well-known ʻSpring Gardensʼ, and of Rowlandsonʼs many other renderings of Londoners bent on pleasure, are in strong contrast to Hogarthʼs representations of vice and squalor, of the boredom and the emptiness of fashionable life. Between them, these two great artists offer posterity an unsurpassable ʻportrait of an ageʼ, as far as London is concerned.

The immediate popularity of these prints with many different types and classes, is indicative of the great change that had come over public taste, and the extension of picture-fancying to a much wider circle than the aristocrats who had been the picture buyers hitherto. In the seventeenth century, Vandyckʼs royal portraits and Lelyʼs series of court beauties had been greatly admired but had had no general appeal. A hundred years later, however, things were very different. The great houses, already adorned by Old Masters—both genuine and spurious, brought home as souvenirs of the Grand Tour—began to find room for pictures of all kinds. Tapestries were taken down, rolled up, and bundled into lumber-rooms, and were replaced not only by portraits but also by pictures of flowers and animals and, after mid-century, by landscapes. As early as the reign of Queen Anne, the Duke of Bedford had sent to Italy for a set of flower pieces to hang in his wifeʼs dressing-room

[1] Sold at Christieʼs on 27 July 1945 for £2,730.

at Bedford House,[1] and the inventory taken there in 1771[2] mentions eight views of Venice by Canaletto that were hung in the large dining-room, and sixteen more in the adjacent small eating-room.

Soon, this fondness for pictures of all kinds had percolated through all classes, and even cottage homes were decorated with prints or pictures in frames of pear-wood and burl elm. Painters found new markets and new patrons, and, particularly in London, many more artists were earning their living by brush and pen than ever before. Several of them opened schools or academies where students could be taught at a high level, but it was not until the Society of Arts was founded in 1754 and prizes offered for promising work that poor students had any hope of securing first-class teaching;[3] their chances were again improved a generation later, when many others besides Rowlandson studied in the newly-opened Royal Academy Schools.

The Royal Academy itself had begun almost fortuitously. In 1759 a Society of Artists had been formed to arrange exhibitions of contemporary art. For the first of these, the new society borrowed the rooms in the Strand belonging to the Society of Arts, and although no charge was made for admission, more than six thousand copies of the catalogue were sold,[4] and it became clear that the London public was deeply interested. From this small beginning there grew the Royal Academy, whose first dinner and exhibition were held in 1770 under the first president, Sir Joshua Reynolds. At first, the exhibitions were held in Somerset Palace, and it was not until a hundred years after its foundation that the academy moved to Burlington House.[5]

Londoners were fortunate in the quality of the paintings shown to them during the first twenty years; all the great painters of the day were represented, and most of them supported the academy with strong enthusiasm. The first idea of the Hanging Committee in these early days was, however, to hang as many pictures as could be crowded on to the walls; a contemporary engraving[6]

[1] G. Scott Thomson: *The Russells in Bloomsbury, 1669–1771*. London, 1940, p. 139.
[2] *Ibid.*, p. 347.
[3] W. R. M. Lamb: *The Royal Academy*. London, 1935, p. 6.
[4] At sixpence a time: Lamb: *loc. cit.*
[5] *Ibid.*, p. 56. [6] By P. Martini after H. Ramberg.

shows the exhibition of 1787 with pictures fitted together like the fragments of a mosaic: the small ones 'skied' at ceiling level must have been scarcely visible. In this representation the visitors —who included many children and three small dogs—show greater interest in each other than in the pictures, but it is a lively scene.

Visitors to the academy were of various kinds. Most of them were genuinely interested in what they saw, and not a few of them planned to buy the pictures they liked and could afford. The 1815 exhibition resulted in sales amounting to £2,255, and although this has since been surpassed it was at the time a very high figure. In this show the choice was wide and some famous pictures made their first public appearance. Raeburn portraits jostled Constable's landscapes, Peter de Wint's 'Cornfield' illumined the water-colour section,[1] Lawrence's portrait of the Prince Regent was there, and two early Turners—'Crossing the Brook' and 'Dido building Carthage'. There was, too, an example of the type of subject-picture that appealed to a wide public and became increasingly popular in Victorian times—Wilkie's 'Distress for Rent'. Such pictures tended to be bought by those who shared the views held in a later day by the Baroness Burdett-Coutts, Dickens' friend and correspondent. 'She cared for Art', wrote her secretary, 'for the sake of its message, rather than from a love of beauty . . . It was the sentiment of a picture, the feelings it touched, that attracted her. The skill of the artist was a matter of secondary consideration.'[2]

The critics might quarrel among themselves, captious countrymen like John Hancock might find little to admire,[3] and Reynolds' didactic dispraise of his own countrymen might carry weight among the connoisseurs, but members of the public bought the pictures they admired and wished to hang upon their walls, and, like all customers who know what they want, they got what treasures they deserved. The country squire who disregarded the Italianate prejudices of Sir Joshua, and commissioned a portrait by George Stubbs, to include his horses and dogs and favourite loader, was matched by the City magnate who insisted on having all three of his wives simultaneously represented in his family group despite the protests of the third wife and of John Singleton

[1] The Society of Painters in Water Colours was founded in 1805.
[2] *Letters of Charles Dickens to the Baroness Burdett Coutts*. Ed. C. Osborne. London 1931, p. 15.
[3] See the heading to this section.

Copley, the dismayed painter. He knew what he wanted, and was prepared to pay for it.[1]

Eighteenth-century Londoners of taste and education might still mourn the dispersal by Cromwell of Charles I's great collection of Old Masters, but there can be no doubt at all that the taste for pictures and prints was spread more widely from late Georgian to early Victorian days than at any previous period.

II. THE SIGHTS OF LONDON

La Quatrième Tour

*Prennez un Hackney-Coach & vous en allez en droiture a
'Whitehall', vous y verrez la statue de Jacques Second . . .
Entrant dans le Jardin, n'oubliez pas d'ajuster votre montre au
quandran Solaire qui y est, car c'est la plus belle pièce que vous
puisses jamais voir en ce genre.*

F. COLSONI; *Le Guide de Londres*, 1693.[2]

On his arrival in London the foreign visitor, as well as the provincial, would naturally feel impelled to seek out certain conventional show places, and then, his moral duties accomplished, he would be free to make such explorations as accorded with his special interests. Tastes differed greatly: two individuals selected from many more must suffice to illustrate this point.

First, Zacharias Conrad von Uffenbach. He was a rich citizen of Frankfurt-am-Main, who had already travelled through much of Europe and who came to England for a five months' stay in 1710[3] with the intention of adding to his already large collection of books and manuscripts. Von Uffenbach was observant and a shrewd scholar, but a disagreeable person; Dr. M. R. James has said that 'his diary is full of girdings and sniffings'.[4] When Von Uffenbach went to St. James's Park—which he was forced to admit struck him as an 'extremely pleasant walk, famed wellnigh throughout the world'—his visit was spoiled for him because most of the people (it was Whit Sunday) were 'of the commoner sort'. One of the few acquaintances he seemed to find really congenial

---

[1] But the patron did dispute the bill for painting out the two earlier wives whom he decided, upon reflection, to be redundant. The picture is now in Boston, Mass. Randall Davies: *English Society in the Eighteenth Century*. London, 1907, pp. 66–7.

[2] Ed. Walter H. Godfrey, for the London Topographical Society. Cambridge, 1951.

[3] *London in 1710*. Trans. and ed. W. H. Quarrell and M. Mare. London, 1934.

[4] *Ibid.*, introduction, p. 8.

was an Italian from Lucca who did 'a lively trade in antiques, and manages to swindle the English shockingly, palming off on them for prodigious sums articles which he gets from France and Italy for nothing'.[1] He went to the theatre only, it seems, to improve his English pronunciation, but there is a very interesting account of his visit to the Tower, where he found four men 'copying the ancient records for Mr. Rymer' and Von Uffenbach is even moved to speak of Rymer's 'magnificent work'.[2] He can also praise St. Paul's, which he found to be one of the finest buildings in the world, being equally impressed by its size, its elegance, and its strength. With German thoroughness, Von Uffenbach not only visited the Exchange, the Tower, the Abbey, London Bridge, Bedlam, and all other familiar landmarks, but found time also to attend book auctions and sessions at the Old Bailey, to explore Chelsea and Hampton Court, and he seems to have failed in only two ambitions—to his great vexation he was unable to secure a couple of lottery tickets, and he also mentions wistfully that he 'would have liked to see the execution of several persons who were to be hanged, but we waited in vain . . .'[3]

No greater contrast to Von Uffenbach could be found than the seventy-six-year-old Mrs. Purefoy, widow of a Buckinghamshire squire. When she came to London with her son at the end of May 1749, undaunted by the fourteen-hour journey she threw herself heart and soul into the business of shopping and sightseeing, determined to make the most of every minute of her stay. In one day, the 6th of June, the Purefoys dealt with a saddler, an upholsterer, and a silversmith before entertaining friends to luncheon; they then visited Wren's church of St. Stephen's (Walbrook), the Bank, the South Sea House, the Guildhall, and Moorfields, before making an expedition to Westminster Abbey. A few days later they undertook a thorough inspection of the Tower, taking special note of the lions, and then boarded a boat for a trip down the river to Greenwich. In her eleven days' visit this indomitable old lady had seen practically all the 'sights' of London and had found time to bargain with at least a dozen shopkeepers, returning home in the best of spirits.[4] Indeed, Mrs. Purefoy can compete

[1] *London in 1710*, pp. 70–1.
[2] The *Foedera*, 30 volumes of documents, published between 1704 and 1735.
[3] *London in 1710*, p. 139.
[4] *Purefoy Letters, 1735–53*: Ed. G. Eland. London, 1931, pp. 359–60.

with that most indefatigable of all female tourists, Miss Weeton, who during her two months' stay in London walked (she says) 538¾ miles and, in addition to the usual round, watched the ascent of a balloon, climbed to the ball of St. Paul's, and attended Byron's funeral.[1]

The ascent to the very top of St. Paul's, whence the view over London was incomparable, was not an uncommon exploit—but few if any emulated the German philosopher, G. C. Lichtenberg, who carried with him a bottle of cherry brandy in order to toast his friends from that vantage point.[2] Already the new St. Paul's was becoming defaced, as the Abbey had been for generations, by visitors' names scratched everywhere upon the leads and on the monuments, as several foreign visitors noted with disfavour.

An Italian language-master who kept a Chocolate House near the Royal Exchange published a London guide-book in 1693 for the convenience of his customers. This man was F. Colsoni, who taught French and English, as well as Italian, and he wrote his *Guide de Londres* in French and sold it in the shop together with his *Ladies' Grammar* and *Anglicum Vade-Mecum*. Colsoni's *Guide* begins with five days of easy outings, so that the reader can get his bearings before venturing further afield, and is very clearly and sensibly arranged. He includes a list of the names and addresses of tradesmen, and tells his Catholic countrymen that they can worship at the chapels of the Royal Ambassadors and Embassies. Colsoni enumerates all the familiar 'sights' and some that were less widely-known, such as Gresham College and the garden of the Drapers' Hall in Throgmorton Street, soon to become 'a fashionable promenade'.[3]

There were other guide-books, mostly repeating one another, just as the pilgrims' *Itineraries* of the middle ages were a medley of plagiarism, but Colsoni's was written for a definite public and is so effectively done that it deserves more attention than it has hitherto received. Perhaps the best single piece of advice Colsoni gives is at the beginning of the fourth tour, where he advises his reader first of all to secure a hackney-coach: few sightseers have the endurance of Miss Weeton.

[1] *Miss Weeton; Journal of a Governess, 1811–25.* Ed. E. Hall, Oxford, 1939.
[2] *Briefe*, quoted by M. Letts: *As the Foreigner Saw Us.* London, 1935, p. 78.
[3] Ned Ward in the *The London Spy*.

III. MUSICAL LONDON

After having talked slightingly of music, he was observed to listen very attentively while Miss Thrale played on the harpsichord.

(In 1775.) Boswell's *Life of Dr. Johnson.*[1]

Dr. Johnson was himself no musician—although he once admitted to being 'affected' by the French horns he heard played at a Freemason's funeral[2]—but he was ready to accept the social implications of a 'musical evening'. Musical parties were given in the eighteenth century at many different levels, not only in London but in the provinces as well, and music clubs and societies were an important feature of social life; so that although London could not claim any special pre-eminence in musical talent or enterprise, it was natural for musicians to congregate there in search of patronage as well as appreciation.

As in painting, the fashion in music was to defer to Italian— and later, to German—taste. People who had been most critical of their own countrymen's performance were ready to accept foreign musicians at their own valuation. The musical Miss Crotchet, in *Dr. Syntax's Tour in Search of a Wife*,[3] when inviting the Doctor to join her 'garden Trio', told him:

> I have a foreign person here . . .
> As mistress of my harmonies;
> She plays the bass, blows the bassoon,
> And keeps the instruments in tune;
> Teaches the parish boys to sing
> Psalms, anthems, and God save the King.[4]

Had she been an Englishwomen she would probably have been Miss Crotchet's personal maid—at a far from 'handsome sal'ry'.

References to Italian opera singers can be found in the *Diaries* of both Samuel Pepys and John Evelyn, and the latter records

---

[1] Ed. C. K. Shorter. London (Navarre Society), 1924, vol. ii, p. 211.
[2] *Ibid.*, vol. iii, p. 262.
[3] By William Coombe. London, 1821, p. 302.
[4] This mention of 'God Save the King' is interesting. Its first-known performance was at Drury Lane on 28 September 1745, at a time when the Young Pretender was campaigning against George II. Yet this was the song that had been sung fifty years earlier in the interests of the fugitive Stuarts, James II and his son 'James III'. Its history as a National Anthem is fully discussed by Dr. Percy A. Scholes: *God Save the Queen!* London, 1954, *passim*.

what is thought to be the first performance of Italian opera in London on 3 January 1674. At first the singing was in a mixture of English and Italian, but by about 1710 the whole opera was rendered in Italian and the English songs were heard only between the acts. At the end of this year Handel came to England and produced *Rinaldo*, which was followed two years later by *Il Pastor Fido*. From this he went from strength to strength, and at last, in 1741, Drury Lane saw the production of the *Messiah*, with Handel himself as conductor.

There were grumblers, such as Addison, who thought that the new fashion was in some way connected with popery, but most of the fashionable world took to the opera most warmly, and in the nineteenth century, too, when Covent Garden Theatre was its home, to appear in a box at the opera was the visible sign of social success. It was, indeed, 'the *ton*', as young Mary Frampton wrote in her *Journal*.[1] It was, nevertheless, very expensive, and even the cheapest seats were far beyond the means of the great majority of music lovers. The Duke of Bedford was one of the subscribers at twenty guineas a year, but in 1742 he tried rather tentatively to reduce his contribution to half-subscription at ten guineas. The following year it was reported to him 'the Opera is a bankrupt', but he and others sustained their faith and their subscriptions and in 1746 delighted to see La Violetta in Gluck's *La Caduta de' Giganti* at the Haymarket,[2] which had commercial as well as artistic success.

Those who could not afford seats at the opera, or at fashionable concerts, and yet longed for good music, made a practice of attending Thomas Britton's weekly concerts held over his coal shop in Clerkenwell. Britton, also known as 'the musical small-coal man', was a remarkable character, who for many years, until his death in 1714, persuaded the greatest performers of the day to come and give their services in his Thursday concerts. He charged nothing for admission, and discerning Londoners and foreign visitors made their way to Clerkenwell to listen to Britton's concerts and to agree that the music, both vocal and instrumental, was 'the best in town'.[3]

[1] *The Journal of Mary Frampton . . . 1779–1846.* Ed. H. G. Mundy. London, 1885, p. 4.
[2] G. Scott Thomson: *The Russells in Bloomsbury 1669–1771.* London, 1940, pp. 289, 291. La Violetta afterwards became Mrs. David Garrick.
[3] John Ashton: *Social Life in the Reign of Queen Anne.* London, 1888, vol. ii, p. 36.

The great and the rich were able to indulge their musical tastes by adopting performers into their households, and such patronage was of course very profitable for those musicians who came to London to make a living, as painters and writers tried to do, by their art. The painter might earn his bread and butter, as the writer did, by hack-work—like Thornhill who was paid 40*s*. per square yard for painting the dome of St. Paul's[1]—and in the same way musicians could hire themselves out to play at a ball. Sometimes they formed their own orchestras, more often an agent collected the instrumentalists he needed and treated directly with the customer. On 26 April 1759 'for music for a ball at Bedford House' fourteen guineas were paid to one Barnard Rose who made a practice of supplying musicians, and he provided three violas, one hautboy, a pipe and tabor, and two basses. One single performer, however, who brought his French horn, was paid three guineas for his services.[2]

The German and Italian musicians and singers came *to* London but were not *of* London—that is to say, they came there to make their names and fill their pockets but never intended to identify themselves with the capital, as did those provincials who came thither to seek their fortunes and stayed to invest and spend them. Only Handel really became a Londoner[3] and found there his spiritual as well as his temporal home. The fact that he was able to do so demonstrates not only his personal qualities but also the genuine (as distinct from the fashionable) musical taste that permeated eighteenth-century London. From the 'small-coal man' in Clerkenwell to the Duke in Bedford House, in Court circles and suburban parlours, at Dr. Burney's and at Mrs. Thrale's, music was a part of life as it had not been since Elizabethan times. Country dwellers who were amateurs of music, people like Dr. Claver Morris of Wells and, in a lesser degree, the Oxfordshire John Hancock who bought himself the music of *The Duenna* when he came on a shopping visit in 1776,[4] drew their inspiration from London and looked to London to give them a lead in musical taste.

[1] John Ashton: *Social Life in the Reign of Queen Anne*, vol. ii, p. 43.
[2] *The Russells in Bloomsbury*, p. 284.
[3] This is the contention of Otto Erich Deutsch in *Handel: a Documentary Biography*. London, 1955.
[4] M. Dickins: *A History of Chastleton*, p. 54. For Dr. Claver Morris, see E. Hobhouse: *The Diary of a West Country Physician, 1684–1706*. Rochester, 1934, pp. 39–43.

By the middle of the next century London's welcome to foreign musicians had become proverbial, and in fashionable circles no one would have dared to say that he or she did not care for the opera, but the genuine, spontaneous response to music seems to have died down, and it became more of an accomplishment and perhaps less of a pleasure to play and sing.

IV. CLUBS AND GAMING

DEAR SIR, — It is inconvenient to me to come out, I should else have waited on you with an account of a little evening Club which we are establishing in Essex Street, in the Strand, and of which you are desired to be one . . . The company is numerous, and, as you will see by the list, miscellaneous. The terms are lax, and the expenses light . . . We meet thrice a week, and he who misses forfeits twopence . . .

Dr. Johnson to Sir Joshua Reynolds, 4 December 1784.[1]

It was Dr. Johnson who, Boswell tells us,[2] invented the word 'clubable'—a word much needed to describe those, of greatly varied interests and status, who felt strongly the need for companionship with their own kind. It has already been pointed out that the London clubs were the heirs of the old coffee-houses,[3] and at times it is difficult to draw any line between these two institutions. As early as 1693 the Italian Colsoni had 'two good Billiard Tables' in his Chocolate House, for the pleasure of his patrons, and it was early recognized that some such amenity would prove attractive.

Good talk, the exchange of views, and the association of congenial spirits in conditions of bodily comfort were the basic requirements of the early clubs, and to these attractions gaming was often added. There was nothing new about betting or gambling, but it was undoubtedly a very important feature of the early clubs and in many cases their avowed reason for existence.

Much has been written about the social life and manners of this time, and abundant material exists in the letters and diaries of Horace Walpole and others, in Boswell's *London Journal*, and above all in contemporary newspapers and novels like Fanny Burney's *Evelina*, to present the many-sided character of late Georgian and Regency London life in clubs and ballrooms.

---

[1] James Boswell: *The Life of Samuel Johnson*, ed. cit., vol. iii, p. 331.
[2] *Ibid.*, n.1.   [3] *Supra*, pp. 176, 179.

After 1659, when John Aubrey joined a political club named the Rota, with meetings at the Turk's Head in New Palace Yard,[1] a very large number of clubs were founded with enthusiasm, flourished for a while, and withered away when their originators died or lost interest in their doings. The very convivial 'mug-house clubs', where every man drank his ale from his own mug, became increasingly political in character and their members ceased to be clubable. Not until the second half of the eighteenth century were the famous Almack's Rooms opened, with a ten-guinea subscription for the twelve meetings, held once a week. The men's tickets were not transferable; they covered admission to the balls, and supper, and facilities for gaming. Stakes were high; often £10,000 in gold lay on the table. Some gamesters prepared for action by protecting their lace ruffles with pieces of leather, and turned their coats inside out for luck. Others found it necessary to put on masks in order to conceal their emotions when they played at quinze.[2] Every player had a neat little stand at his elbow, to hold his tea.

While their men-folk won and lost prodigious sums at the gaming tables, the ladies danced decorously with carefully chosen partners, for at Almack's they nominated the gentlemen members as the male committee did the ladies. It was all extra-ordinarily select and oligarchical, like the City Court of Aldermen. The rules of conduct and apparel were inflexible, and the Duke of Wellington himself was turned away from Almack's because he was wearing trousers instead of the prescribed knee-breeches.[3] When at last, at about the time of Queen Victoria's accession, the clique that had 'run' Almack's had disintegrated, the club changed its character, became known as 'Willis's Rooms', and was the scene of lectures, readings and concerts.

Other famous clubs, Brooks's and Crockford's, and many more, experienced varying fortunes. William Crockford, the son of a fishmonger at Temple Bar, retired from business in 1840 as a millionaire:[4] Brooks, the wine-merchant, died in poverty,[5] but both clubs continued because they were institutions the public

---

[1] J. Timbs: *Clubs and Club Life in London*. London, 1872, pp. 4, 13. There is a reference to 'Rota-men' in Samuel Butler's *Hudibras* (1664), part ii, canto 3.
[2] Timbs: *op. cit.*, p. 72.
[3] E. Beresford Chancellor: *Life in Regency and Early Victorian Times*. London, 1926, p. 50.
[4] *Ibid.*, p. 62.   [5] Timbs: *op. cit.*, p. 76.

15

wanted. There were also clubs for people of more specialized
interests, such as the Dilettanti, which was founded in 1734 by
rich men who had travelled in Italy, and the Roxburghe, another
rich men's club that consumed marvellous dinners and arranged
for the re-printing of rarities in literature.[1] The Travellers' Club
was started soon after the peace of 1814 and became so popular

William Hogarth and David Garrick

that it soon had a ten years' waiting list for admission;[2] more
exclusive was the Athenaeum (1824) and this with the Garrick
(1831) and the later Arts Club (1863) catered for amateurs and
patrons of all the arts as well as for professionals. In all cases the
number of members was strictly limited; the Arts Club, indeed,
fixed its original membership as low as 250,[3] although this was
afterwards increased.

[1] These probably inspired the foundation of the Camden and other publishing
societies.
[2] Timbs: *op. cit.*, p. 198.
[3] G. A. F. Rogers: *The Arts Club and its Members*. London, 1920, p. 1.

Women's clubs, except for society gatherings such as Almack's,
still lay in the future, and club life in London was a male prerogative
and institution. Thomas Hood in the *Comic Annual* for 1838 wrote a
long poem called 'Clubs, Turned up by a female hand', in which
the last verse summarized the supposed attitude of the wives:

> Of all the modern schemes of Man
>   That time has brought to bear,
> A plague upon the wicked plan
>   That parts the wedded pair!
> My wedded friends they all allow
>   They meet with slights and snubs,
> And say, 'They have no husbands now,
>   They're married to the Clubs!'

Perhaps the last of these 'clubmen' was an original member
of the Arts Club named Algernon Brent. At the age of ninety he
so resented the instrusion of ladies into the premises for a couple
of hours, twice a year, that he would barricade himself into one of
the principal rooms, alone but for the company of all the newspapers on which he could lay hands.[1]

It should not be supposed that clubs were altogether an upper-
class prerogative. Closely connected with the taverns and ale-houses
were the clubs formed among men of kindred interests that met
weekly in the inn parlour. The father of Francis Place the tailor
belonged to the 'House of Lords' which was held at the *Three
Herrings* in Bell Yard[2] and was the meeting place of the 'more
dissolute sort of barristers, attorneys, and tradesmen of what were
then called the better sort, but no one who wore a decent coat was
excluded'. There were also clubs less exclusive than this, where
thirty members might meet on Monday evenings at eight and stay
until the whole company was drunk—which meant a session of
some four to six hours—each member paying his shilling a night
even when he was absent. The qualification for this club seems to
have been mere conviviality, but others were based more firmly
on a common interest in sport or trade or science or card-playing.
'Cutter clubs' were founded by lads who shared a boat on the
river. Place himself belonged to one of these, composed of an unruly

---

[1] G. A. F. Rogers: *The Arts Club and its Members*, p. 59. He died in 1916.
[2] M. D. George: *London Life in the Eighteenth Century*. London, 1930, p. 272. Mrs.
George is quoting from the MS. autobiography of Francis Place in the Brit. Mus.
(Add. MSS. 35142–35147).

crowd of apprentices; it broke up some years later when the cox was transported for robbery and the stroke was hanged for murder.[1]

The 'cock and hen' clubs, where young men and young street-walkers met to drink and sing songs, also had a bad name. A silversmith named Brasbridge, repenting later of the wild youth he had spent, in 1824 wrote *The Fruits of Experience* in which he enumerated the clubs to which he had belonged, and described his interests as 'divided . . . between the tavern-club, the card-party, the hunt, the fight',[2] and recalled the political debates and arguments in the Cider Cellar of Maiden Lane. Actually, Brasbridge's clubs were moderately respectable, and Place contrasts them favourably with the *Spread Eagle* in the Strand, where the landlord said his customers changed completely every six months on account of the 'hangings, drownings, and sudden deaths'.

These raffish clubs represented a large section of London life, but there were many more whose conduct was unblemished by the violence and vice that won the others recognition in the records of the time. Francis Place referred at a later date to clubs 'attended almost wholly by labouring men', who discussed the matters of the day, drank their ale, sang their songs and smoked their pipes, and played dominoes or draughts in the warm atmosphere of friendship tempered with the aroma of tobacco and beer that still lingers in the best bar-parlours. These men indeed were 'clubable', and the great Dr. Johnson would have recognized them at once.

v. OUTDOOR PLEASURES

April, 1749. We have a New Entertainment to be introduced tomorrow Night at Ranelagh a Masque to be conducted as done at Venice, to begin at 3 in the afternoon and end at 10 or 11 o'clock, all the World will be there, as 'tis a new Thing . . .

Correspondence of John Collier.[3]

I missed you vastly last night at Vaux Hall because it was so vastly pleasant. I cannot say so of the masquerade, for it was very hot and disagreeable.

The Duchess to the Duke of Bedford,
May 1746.[4]

Like many other places designed for entertainment, Vauxhall, Ranelagh, and Cremorne were often so crowded with pleasure

[1] M. D. George: *London Life in the Eighteenth Century*, p. 279.
[2] Quoted *ibid.*, p. 274.
[3] Ed. Rev. W. V. Crane: *Sussex Archaeological Collections*, vol. xlv (1902), p. 104.
[4] G. Scott Thomson: *The Russells in Bloomsbury*, p. 290.

seekers that they created their own problems of congestion and embarrassment. Fanny Burney's spirited description[1] of her heroine's expedition, one June evening, to the gardens at Vauxhall, is worth repetition.

> The trees, [she wrote] the numerous lights, and the company in the circle round the orchestra make a most brilliant and gay appearance; and, had I been with a party less disagreeable to me, I should have thought it was a place formed for animation and pleasure. There was a concert, in the course of which, a hautbois concerto was so charmingly played, that I could have thought myself upon enchanted ground, had I had spirits more gentle to associate with. The hautbois in the open air is heavenly.

The most famous (and the most expensive) pleasure gardens in London were Cuper's (or 'Cupid's'), Marylebone, Ranelagh, and Vauxhall. All of them were well established by the mid-eighteenth century, and only Ranelagh was inclined to be exclusive. On ordinary evenings people could wander about the gardens or sit drinking tea and eating bread and butter; on gala nights there would be illuminations and concerts, and sometimes fireworks to enjoy. Other gardens with less renown but with their own individual charm were opened in different parts of London, with concerts by local celebrities: one of the most frequented was Finch's Grotto Garden in Southwark.[2] At the end of the century there were various imitations of Vauxhall—the Temple of Flora in Westminster Bridge Road, for instance—but these only attracted the raffish and the rowdy and were soon given up.

A number of these gardens adjoined mineral springs where people could drink the waters in pleasant surroundings. Sadler's Wells, Hampstead, Islington Spa and Bagnigge Wells were four of the most fashionable; of these the last three were little more than tea gardens, but Sadler's Wells provided amusement for its patrons in rope-dancing and pantomime. When Sophie von la Roche visited London in 1786 she made an expedition to Sadler's Wells and was delighted with what she found there. She wrote in her *Diary*[3] a description of 'the playhouse dedicated to the small

[1] In *Evelina*, published 1778, letter xlvi.
[2] W. Wroth: *The London Pleasure Gardens of the Eighteenth Century*. London, 1896, p. 5.
[3] Ed. and trans. C. Williams. London, 1933, p. 132.

middle-class . . . lakes with trees in front of the house itself, numerous avenues with delightful tables and benches for visitors, under trees hung with tiny lamps. In the open temple lower-class lasses, sailors, and other young people were dancing.' Sophie was surprised to find that the show lasted three hours. It included a comedy, a ballet, a rope-walker, pantomime, 'balancing tricks', an 'operette', feats by a strong man, and finally another comedy and another operette. One might have expected it to last three days! To sustain the audience, bottles of wine with cold chops, ham, and pasties could be bought and placed on a special shelf that ran along the back of the seats for the convenience of those in the row behind.

There were, too, simple tea gardens in such rural places as Highbury Barn and Hornsey, where on Sunday afternoons bowls and skittles could be played and tea drunk in vine-covered arbours. The patrons of the tea gardens were mostly city men—young lawyers, apprentices, and small shopkeepers—and they paid perhaps sixpence for admission and light refreshment, whereas at Vauxhall, Marylebone and Cuper's they would be charged a shilling, and at Ranelagh half-a-crown.[1] The more sophisticated Cremorne Gardens were not opened until 1843, when the other resorts were beginning to fall out of fashion and into disrepute. Humbler people resorted to Greenwich Park, which afterwards became a favourite place for school treats.

Sometimes residents in a highly respectable district would object to the organized dog-fights and the rough games played in near-by fields, and complain to their landlords of noise and damage. Some went further still, like the eccentric Miss Hester Capper who emerged from her house in the Tottenham Court Road armed with a great pair of shears to cut the little boys' kite-strings.[2] For the most part, however, there were green fields and open spaces where London youths were allowed to play undisturbed the games familiar in FitzStephen's day. The Duke of Bedford could still hunt hares on Mitcham Common[3] when George II was on the throne, and sheep still grazed in Bloomsbury and horses in the parks. The spa of Kilburn was, we read, 'but a morning's walk

[1] Wroth: *op. cit.*, p. 8.
[2] Scott Thomson: *The Russells of Bloomsbury*, p. 362.
[3] *Ibid.*, p. 289.

from the metropolis . . . the footway from the Mary-bone across the fields still nearer'.[1]

Then, as now, London's parks were one of her chief glories, and St. James's in particular made a deep impression on all visitors. Here (in 1780) there were benches for the weary to sit upon,[2] or the 'curious observers' who liked to watch the fashionable world go by. The Abbé Prevost remarked that St. James's Park was 'the public walk of London, and open to all ranks'. He appreciated too the gardens of Gray's Inn and Lincoln's Inn Fields, where fine company and courtesans took their evening walks.[3] Walking was not only a necessity but a pleasure to eighteenth-century Londoners, and family excursions were often made along the river bank to such places as the Chelsea Bun House. Swift speaks of this in the *Journal to Stella* as early as 1711,[4] and it was still popular when Victoria came to the throne. Indeed, in 1839 it was said that on Good Friday no fewer than 240,000 hot cross buns were sold there.

At the peace rejoicings in 1749 there was a great firework display in St. James's Park, and at least one employer found it impossible to keep his servants within doors, for they had 'declared one & all for the fireworks' and neither argument nor bribery could persuade them to stay away.[5] Many people viewed the displays from a distance; one Captain Murray wrote 'we go to Nightsbridge on Tuesday for air and a view of the fireworks',[6] and those who could not afford tickets for gala nights at Vauxhall and Ranelagh could still enjoy the brilliance reflected in the night sky. The peace celebrations of 1814 were illumined by two hours' display of fireworks provided by Woolwich Arsenal, which made London as light at midnight as at noon.

It was in Rowlandson's day that cricket came to London as a sport and as a spectacle; one of his best-known pictures shows a match in progress on the White Conduit Fields (in Islington) about the year 1790. Three years before this date Thomas Lord

[1] *The Public Advertiser*, 17 July 1773.
[2] *Benenden Letters, 1753–1821*. Ed. C. F. Hardy. London, 1901, p. 176.
[3] *Adventures of a Man of Quality*. Trans M. Robertson. London, 1930.
[4] On 2 May he wrote that he had bought 'one [bun] today in my walk; it cost me a penny; it was stale and I did not like it'. The Chelsea Bun House was revived for the Festival of Britain in 1951.
[5] 'Correspondence of John Collier', *Sussex Arch. Coll.*, vol. xlv (1902), p. 104.
[6] *Ibid.*, p. 105.

had opened the first of his three cricket grounds in time for the
two-day Middlesex *v.* Essex match which was played there for
two hundred guineas. The ground was sometimes used for other
purposes, for athletic meetings, pigeon shoots, and even hopping
matches. The pavilion was a wooden shed, and spectators stood
or sat within a wooden paling that fenced the field; they were
willing to pay 6*d.* for admission, and by the turn of the century
crowds of 4,000 to 5,000 might be expected—many of them came,
however, less to watch the cricket than to lay wagers. The second
Lord's ground was in use only from 1811 to 1814, when Lord
secured the lease of the land in St. John's Wood and established
'Lords' as we know it today, and here the Marylebone Cricket
Club set up its headquarters.

There was nothing formal about the costume required for this
early cricket; no one needed to wear the customary white top-hats
with deep black bands; those who wished could sport 'billycocks',
with striped or checked or spotted shirts, and in a picture of Regency
date one umpire is shown in a red frock-coat and the other in a
blue swallow-tail.[1] For the game itself, reference must be made to
the cricket histories; much curious information may be found in
the *Times M.C.C. Number*,[2] that celebrated the Club's second
centenary, concerning not only the famous players but also the
lesser clubs that formed the game's great anatomy. Wagers might be
small here and performance poor, but these club players trundled
the ball over the uneven ground and hit it lustily, accepting all
hazards in these gloveless, padless days. Spectators cheered, made
bets, and booed without inhibition, dogs barked and helped chase
the ball; but the game went on. Matches were between all sorts
of teams; in one of the more notable games, played at Ball's Pond,
Newington, all the players were women, and a print called *Rural
Sports or a Cricket Match Extraordinary* shows deep square leg
shaping to catch a skier hit by a buxom damsel playing bare-legged.[3]

The first test-match between England and Australia in this
country was held at the Oval in 1880, although it had been preceded by a game between the Gentleman of England and the

---

[1] See an unsigned article on 'Cricket Fashions' in *The Times*, 1936.
[2] 25 May 1937.
[3] This match was reported in *The News* 6 October 1811. The sides represented
Surrey and Hampshire, and it was played for 500 guineas a side. One of the Hampshire
players made 41.

Australians at Prince's[1] in June 1878. This was the beginning of a new era, Grace and Spofforth and other giants of the game became national heroes, and the excitement of test-match struggles, with their controversies and all-night queues of spectators, was already coming into view.

[1] Now Cadogan Square. See Sir Home Gordon's article in *The Times*, 19 May 1956.

Chapter Thirteen

EDWIN CHADWICK'S LONDON

1. 'LONDON'S SWEETE WATERS'

*I was yesterday . . . over the cholera districts of Bermondsey;
and, oh God! what I saw! people having no water to drink—
hundreds of them—but the water of the common sewer which
stagnates full of . . . dead fish, cats and dogs, under their
windows.*

Charles Kingsley to his wife, 24 October 1849.[1]

THE problem of London's water supply was not new in the
nineteenth century, nor in the sixteenth, nor in the thirteenth, but as London spread out beyond the city walls, so
did the need for a satisfactory system increase and intensify. Wells
and springs and even ponds where horses could be watered, like
the 'great water' in West Smithfield, were lost or hidden or built
over as the population of London grew, and Londoners were
forced, as Stow said, 'to seeke sweete waters abroad'.[2]

As early as the time of Henry I the citizens had asked permission
to pipe water from Tyburn to the City, and the Great Conduit in
Cheapside—a lead cistern reinforced with stone—had been begun
before the year 1285.[3] John Stow made a list of all the further
conduits made during the next three hundred years, and in his
Survey alluded proudly to 'Thames water conveyed into men's
houses by pipes of leade from a most artificial forcier standing
neare unto London Bridge',[4] but the river was full of impurities
and an Italian of Stow's generation described it as 'hard, turbid
and stinking'.

Half a century before the Great Fire a really serious attempt was
made to provide Londoners with fresh, clean water. In 1609, after
much pressure on the Corporation, Sir Hugh Myddelton[5] secured

[1] *Life and Letters*. Ed. F. E. Kingsley. London, 1879, vol. i, p. 177.
[2] *Survey of London*. Ed. C. L. Kingsford. London, 1908, vol. i, p. 16.
[3] *Ibid.*, p. 17.   [4] See *supra*, Chapter Seven, § ii.
[5] His work was rewarded with a baronetcy in 1622.

a contract to bring sweet and sparkling water to the City from Hertfordshire springs and streams. There were many problems of tunnel-making and of drainage to be solved before the water could be brought the whole thirty-eight miles of the course, by way of Islington, to the reservoir at the New River Head, and it took Myddelton five years to accomplish this, but on 29 September 1613 the great day came and the waters passed along their new channel. Sir Hugh's brother was Lord Mayor at the time, and he too was interested in the new project, which was financed partly by the Myddeltons and their Company and partly by the King: landlords had been greedy and intransigent, as they were again when the railway companies wanted to lay their tracks, so the royal protection proved very useful.

When London was rebuilt after the fire, owners of new houses were given the opportunity of laying on water either from the New River Water Company or from the London Bridge Water-works. That is, they could choose between water from a purer source or a more convenient one. Twenty years earlier the Corpora-tion had laid pipes of hollowed elm along the Strand, and in 1641 the Earl of Bedford paid ten shillings to have the connection made to his house. As the Bedford property in Bloomsbury was devel-oped and many new houses were built, these too were supplied with water by the New River Company and the price paid was fixed at £7 16s. 0d. per annum.[1] The use of wooden pipes persisted into the nineteenth century, and even after cast-iron mains came into use the water companies—by Victoria's reign London was partitioned between nine rival concerns—clung to their practice of allowing only an intermittent supply on the excuse that the mains might not be strong enough to withstand constant pressure. In the mid-nineteenth century the companies still allowed their customers water for only two or three hours, three times a week, and those who relied on the public fountains had to collect their supply in 'pails, fish-kettles, casks, cans, and even soup plates'.[2]

The quality of the water supplied grew steadily worse as the years passed, and filth accumulated in the river bed. The story of the Fleet shows very well the obdurate nature of Londoners when

[1] G. Scott Thomson: *The Russells in Bloomsbury*, London, 1940, p. 350.
[2] R. A. Lewis: *Edwin Chadwick and the Public Health Movement*. London, 1952, p. 50.

invited to forego their medieval habit of tipping dirt and rubbish
out of doors and into the river, with a disregard for health and
hygiene that was due to recklessness as well as to ignorance.
Originally the Fleet had been one of the most useful of London's
rivers, but it had deteriorated into an open drain, a mass of filth
and debris, and a constant danger to public health. It had been
part of Wren's plan to make a Thames Quay, that would give London her much-needed river frontage, and to clear and canalize the
Fleet as far as Holborn Bridge, but he was defeated by the Londoners' habits. As fast as the stream was cleared it filled again, and
the wharves could not be kept free from the rubbish that was
dumped there, or from coaches parked on the roadway for repair,
or piles of timber. In 1733, ten years after Wren died, the struggle
was given up, and the canal was arched over for part of its course.
The wharves were converted into roads, and, finally, the lower
reach also was covered in and the much-abused river disappeared
from sight.[1]

Although it had become invisible, the Fleet still carried its
sludgy burden, and other sewers also deposited their slime into the
Thames. The knackers' yards of Lambeth and the slaughter-houses
of Whitechapel contributed their refuse too, and for variety there
was the rubbish from tanneries and tar-works on both sides of the
river. From its general hue of greenish coffee-colour, the river
water deepened to the colour and density of black treacle near the
outfalls, and a viscous scum covered the mud banks exposed at low
tide. When there was a rainy season the sewage might be diluted
and its stench diminished; a southerly wind might bring relief to
Vauxhall or a westerly one to Chelsea, but the inescapable fact
remained: this was the water that Londoners had to drink, and
eighty-two million gallons were taken daily from the Thames for
London's needs. Sydney Smith might well claim that there were 'a
million insects in every drop', the wonder is that in the same letter
he could say: 'I am better in health . . . and drinking nothing but
London water.'[2]

The climax came in June 1858, when an exceptionally hot summer and unusually low rainfall combined to produce what all
London knew as 'The Great Stink'. Parliament was in a good

[1] Reddaway: *op. cit.*, p. 201 ff.
[2] To Lady Grey: 19 November 1834.

position to appreciate the nuisance, for the windows at Westminster had to be draped with curtains soaked in chloride of lime so that members could breathe.[1] To cross Westminster Bridge it was necessary to hold a handkerchief firmly over one's nose and mouth and those who travelled on the river steamers suffered greatly when the paddles churned the water into stinking eddies. No one

A Drop of London Water (From *Punch* 1850)

could face the refreshments offered on board, and few dared to travel at all in this way, so that the owners of these pleasure-craft found they were running at a loss, and laid most of them up. There was talk of moving the Law Courts to Oxford or St. Alban's, and a Select Committee was set up to report on the Stink and to find means for its abatement. One ingenious witness, a Mr. Gurney, wanted to seal the ends of the sewers—there were 369 of them

[1] Stanley Hyland: *Curiosities of Parliament*. London, 1955, pp. 65–75.

between Putney and Blackwall—and to lead the gas by means of pipes to chosen high points and then fire it so that it would burn away—he said—harmlessly. Gurney was particularly anxious to carry a pipe from the huge new Victoria sewer through New Palace Yard to the Clock Tower; this he was allowed to do, although a more practical engineer was able to prevent the subsequent explosion from utterly destroying the Clock Tower (and perhaps completing Guy Fawkes's plan). A more conventional remedy, the use of slaked lime in large quantities, and the coming of the rain cured the Great Stink, but it had served its purpose in awakening Londoners to the realities of their position and had even ousted the Indian Mutiny as the chief topic of conversation.

When a powerful smell was combined with the stifling, smoke-laden fogs that persisted (and still persist) in London's neighbourhood, it might be thought that the atmosphere would be totally insupportable, but, according to Dr. Alfred Carpenter who read a paper to the Society of Arts on this subject,[1] the fog mitigated the stench from the sewers by pressing it downwards! On a cloudless September day, with brilliant sunshine elsewhere, he had seen Byron's 'sea-coal canopy'[2] lying like a blanket on London, barely reaching the tops of the houses, and he advocated a tax on all fireplaces that did not effectively consume their own smoke. In this Dr. Carpenter was supported by the chairman at his meeting, who was Edwin Chadwick himself. When, thirty years earlier, Chadwick was preparing his weighty *Report on the Supply of Water to the Metropolis*,[3] turning from his general preoccupation with smoke-laden atmosphere to contaminated water, he was shocked by the levity of his witnesses, those who spoke jokingly of the diluted sewage that was being pumped into the cisterns of London houses to supply the needs of men, women, and children. Chadwick wanted to sweep away the nine water companies, replacing them by one, and to provide soft water, 'pure, filtered, and aerated',[4] gathered from Richmond, Farnham, and Bagshot Heath, that could be constantly supplied, he said, to all households at the inclusive charge of 2*d*. a week. He could not believe that the supply of so essential a commodity as pure water ought to be

[1] On 10 December 1880. See the *Journal of the Society of Arts*, 1881, pp. 49, 54.
[2] See *infra*, p. 246.
[3] Published in May 1850. Lewis: *Edwin Chadwick, etc.*, p. 258 ff.
[4] *Ibid.*, p. 259.

governed by considerations of profit, and he said so in no uncertain terms. The companies were alarmed and angered by his suggestions, vested interests proved far stronger than Chadwick had imagined, politicians were inimical, and Londoners apathetic, so the great reformer had to see his project impeded and shelved. And, since Chadwick was the least conciliatory of men, his recommendations were greeted with suspicion even by intelligent and idealistic colleagues. London still had to wait for her 'sweete waters' until the Metropolitan Water Board was born in 1903.

II. DRAINS AND DISEASE

I have gone to see the places myself . . . and I have cross-examined the witnesses there on the spot.

Edwin Chadwick to Lord Bramwell, 3 March 1885.[1]

Long before the summer of the Great Stink Edwin Chadwick had devoted himself to the cause of sanitary reform. He was a barrister, and he was interested also in the prevention of crime; he served on the royal commissions appointed to investigate the condition of factory children, and he was an assistant poor-law commissioner, but it was his work for a sane and hygienic drainage system that made him one of London's greatest benefactors. For most of his life Chadwick was exceedingly unpopular, even among those who most needed his help, for he forced people to face disagreeable and often horrifying facts, and made not the slightest attempt to render them palatable, or to appease the vested interests that obstructed the path to reform. Recognition came to him at last, but very late in life, for he was not knighted until just before his ninetieth birthday.

There was nothing tactful or conciliatory about Chadwick's methods, and he was uncompromising in his denouncement of anyone willing to turn a deaf ear or a blind eye to the abuses he revealed. Chadwick would accept nothing at second-hand; he himself poked about on Farnham Heath looking for springs of pure water, and he made his way personally into the sewers and explored their hideous and noisome recesses. Uncovered ditches connecting sink to drain, cess-pools in the cellars of houses both large and small, defective privies, drains paved with badly-laid

---

[1] Quoted by Lewis: *Edwin Chadwick, etc.*, p. 13.

bricks—sometimes running uphill and frequently round sharp corners—the 'rookeries' in congested areas[1] where between two and three thousand people might be crammed into fewer than a hundred houses—all these were explored by Chadwick and his surveyors and duly entered in their reports. He was able to show that it would be not only far better from a hygienic point of view, but also financially, to have a proper system whereby the large brick sewers could be replaced by smooth earthenware pipes at proper levels, the streets paved, water-closets substituted for privies and cess-pools, and a dust-bin put in every yard and a common urinal in every court. All this could be done, it was estimated, for an 'improvement rate' of thirty-five shillings a year, whereas the charge for water, for emptying the cesspools and paying the scavengers, amounted to more than twice that sum.[2]

This information, and much more, was either collected by Chadwick himself, or brought to his office[3] in Greek Street, Soho, at the time (1848) that his Public Health Act was making its arduous way through Parliament. The *Sanitary Report*, which sold more copies than any Government publication that had yet been issued, had been published six years earlier, and Chadwick followed it up with the grim and sombre *Report on Interment in Towns* that appeared in 1843. This was the strongest of all Chadwick's expositions of evil social conditions, and the one that roused the most violent opposition. The overcrowded cemeteries within the City walls had become raised far above street level, and 'in the 218 acres of London's burial grounds, 20,000 adults and nearly 30,000 youths and children were interred each year,'[4] so that the grave-diggers had to exercise great ingenuity in inserting new corpses into old graves, and resorted to dreadful expedients[5] in making room for future burials.

Many City churchyards had been destroyed, and the ground was used for building until the Disused Burial Grounds Act of 1888 made them into open spaces.[6] There were the pest fields and plague pits, too, where many people had been buried hastily in

[1] Lewis: *Edwin Chadwick, etc.*, p. 221. [2] *Ibid.*, p. 222.
[3] I.e. of the Metropolitan Commision of Sewers.
[4] Lewis: *Edwin Chadwick, etc.*, p. 66.
[5] Detailed *ibid.*, pp. 66–7.
[6] Mrs. Basil Holmes: *The London Burial Grounds*. London, 1896, p. 76.

shallow graves, all contributing to the unwholesome state of over-crowded London. Special provision was made for the burials of cholera victims, for instance the 196 bodies that were laid in one plot near the burial ground in Whitechapel.[1] In 1832 the large cemetery at Kensal Green was opened; land for this, and for twenty-four more founded later, was secured in the face of much local opposition. Dissenters tended to keep jealously the tiny graveyards attached to their own chapels. Much strong feeling was generated both for and against the new cemeteries, but the case—in 1838—of two men who died when digging a grave in Aldgate churchyard, 'poisoned by the foul air', strengthened the hand of the reformers against the traditionalists.

Such exhalations, together with sewer gas and smoke-laden fog, might well be expected to spread disease, although it is notable that the year of the Great Stink had a death-rate below the average and cases of fever and dysentery were distinctly fewer than was normal. The 'pythogenic theory'—that disease was caused by some quality in the atmosphere—was favoured by Chadwick and others, and although it was later proved to be false, those who believed in it were moved to fight against the conditions that undoubtedly did help disease to flourish, and by the reformers' efforts deaths from typhus, cholera, and typhoid were greatly diminished. Cess-pools under basement floors—out of sight but most certainly not out of mind—were agreed to be one of the main causes of the cholera outbreak of 1849, according to the report on *The Dwellings of the Labouring Classes, etc.*, drawn up by Henry Roberts eighteen years later; Roberts fought for their abolition no less strenuously than did Chadwick.

The most terrifying quality of cholera, apart from its dangerous and distressing nature, was this ignorance concerning its cause. London had plenty of warning of its coming, for the disease was already rife in the provinces, and it was clear that it must arrive in the City sooner or later. In 1848 the West London Medical Society met in a doctor's house 'to draw up a tabular form of interrogation as to the nature and treatment of every case of cholera that may appear in this part of London'.[2] They would

[1] Holmes: *The London Burial Grounds*, p. 131.
[2] *The Journal of Gideon Mantell, 1818–52.* Ed. E. Cecil Curwen. Oxford, 1940, p. 229.

16

have done better to pay attention to a sensible little pamphlet of 'plain rules' that Dr. Gideon Mantell had scribbled at the break-fast table some seventeen years earlier. This recognized both cause and effects, and when the epidemic broke out in 1849 Mantell was able to describe its course in his *Journal* with insight and intelli-gence.[1]

The cholera raged during the summer months, and Mantell wrote in his *Journal* that throughout September there were between 200 and 400 deaths daily from this cause.[2] Many earnest people were fired to enthusiasm for the cause of sanitary reform, and those who understood slum conditions, or who had worked among the poor in districts like Bermondsey, or doctors who saw the ravages of the disease, were ready to support Chadwick, but he took little notice of them and plodded independently upon his way. Outside the ranks of the reformers few voices were heard to attack the 'pride and ignorance, stupidity and stinginess' deplored by Charles Kingsley,[3] but occasionally a strident cry broke through the polite mumur of the upper middle classes, as in this letter to *The Times* that appeared above fifty-four signatures on 5 July 1849.

Sur,
   May we beg and beseech your proteckshion and power. We are Sur, as it may be, livin in a Wilderniss, so far as the rest of London knows anything of us, or as the rich and great people care about. We live in muck and filthe. We aint got no privez, no dust bins, no drains, no water splies, and no drain or suer in the whole place. The Suer Company, in Greek Street, Soho Square, all great, rich and powerfool men, take no notice watsomedever of our complaints.[4] The Stenche of a Gully-hole is disgustin. We al of us suffur, and numbers are ill, and if the Colera comes Lord help us. . . .

---

[1] *The Journal of Gideon Mantell, 1818–52*, pp. 99, 242.
[2] *Ibid.*, p. 240.
[3] Lewis: *op. cit.*, p. 114. The authors are indebted to Mr. R. A. Lewis for this reference, and also for the next quotation, and, indeed, have drawn most of the material in this section from his excellent book.
[4] The writers do Chadwick less than justice. Lewis: *op. cit.*, p. 221.

III. LONDON TRAFFIC

*We are very glad to watch an opportunity to whisk across a
passage, very thankful that we are not run over for interrupt-
ing the machine, that carrries in it a person neither more
handsome, wise, nor valiant than the meanest of us.*

SWIFT; *The Tatler*, 1710.

London pedestrians have always taken a stiff attitude towards the
traffic that threatened to deprive them of their rights, from the
time when Hugh Picard, riding a headstrong white horse, acci-
dentally rode over and killed a three-year-old child[1] and found it
necessary to 'flee' from the wrath of the neighbours, and when the
hackney-coaches were first seen there were many accidents because
people refused to give them passage. As the throng of vehicles
became heavier and more and more dangerous, foot passengers
had to give way, but their resentment grew and they sometimes
overturned a coach and broke its wheels. They certainly had good
reason for their anger: not only were people greatly impeded in
using the streets, they were often injured or even killed by being
crushed against the houses.

The problems of John Taylor's day[2] were current also in the
nineteenth century as, indeed, they still are, and there is not a
great deal to be added to his complaints in *The World Runs on
Wheels*, beyond pointing out some new types of vehicles that
brought with them fresh difficulties. The coaches still ran, at
improved speeds, and in 1785 the first mail-coach between London
and Exeter took the road. Twenty-one years later the Holyhead
mail was running 162 miles in twenty-seven hours, and by 1836
the journey was done in sixteen and a quarter hours; the time at
which the coach passed through Shrewsbury had not varied five
minutes in eighteen months,[3] such was its regularity. This improvement was mainly due to the excellent road surfaces, but partly
also to good organization, well kept and well trained horses, and
sober, in place of befuddled, drivers. Some of these were very
distinguished, for example, the 'Cambridge graduate' who drove

[1] In 1301. She was Petronilla, daughter of William de Wyntonia. See *Calendar of
Coroners' Rolls, etc.*, 1300–78. Ed. R. R. Sharpe. London, 1913, p. 28.
[2] *Supra*, Chapter Five, § i.
[3] 'Nimrod', *The Road, The Turf, The Chase* (new edn.). London, 1851, p. 27.

the Brighton coach[1] and handed his passengers glasses of sherry and sandwiches from a silver box while the horses were changed. Some of the horses became famous, too, like the pair of leaders that worked together over the same stage on the Dover Road for upwards of twelve years.

By the opening years of the nineteenth century the streets of London had been very greatly improved; there were no longer complaints of deep ruts and broken axles and broken bones, although there was still much to be done. Even as late as the time of the Great Exhibition the highways were mostly paved with stone, which was noisy, or with Macadam's new surface, which was muddy. Only in a few places, notably in Poultry and Lombard Street, were there the wood blocks that within a generation covered London's thoroughfares, giving a surface suited to high speeds in fine weather but occasioning many accidents when it became greasy.

The authors have described elsewhere[2] the advent of the early omnibuses and hansom-cabs that became so marked a feature of London life, well known also in provincial towns. The owners of the early omnibuses were not content with providing efficient transport, they thought it was also their business to provide amusement or distraction for their passengers—Mr. Shillibeer stocked his vehicles with books and newspapers. They insisted, too, upon great gentility on the part of the conductor. This phase soon passed, however, and conductors began to be selected from a wider field. Within twenty years *Punch* prophesied that there would soon be 'female buses' with a she-conductor and a row of infants on the knife-board. As for their social status, by the time Dickens was writing *Sketches by Boz* conductors were significantly called 'cads' and their rude behaviour was often a matter for complaint. Many of the drivers concentrated upon racing one another and overturning their rivals if possible, especially on the route from Putney to St. Paul's.

The cabs increased steadily in numbers, both hansoms and four-wheelers, right up to 1886, when licences were granted to 7,000 hansom-cabs, and to nearly 4,000 four-wheelers or 'growlers'.

[1] 'The Age'. There were 25 coaches to Brighton in the summer. 'Nimrod', *op. cit.*, p. 29.
[2] *A History of the English People*. London, 1950, pp. 451-2. See also G. A. Sekon: *Locomotion in Victorian London*. London, 1938, *passim*.

Omnibuses multiplied also, the numbers jumping to 400 in their first seven years. When it is considered that the population of London had increased during the first thirty years of the nineteenth century from 865,000 to one and a half million people, it can be realized how crowded were the streets and pavements. It is true that this growth was partly due to the extension of the boundaries, and that during the same period the population of the City proper fell by 30 per cent,[1] but this meant that all these extra people were making their way to and from their work through streets only wide enough to accommodate half their number in relative comfort. An articled clerk, working in a London attorney's office in the year 1820, noted in his diary that of his two employers one walked in daily from Islington and the other from Walworth, yet neither of them arrived a moment later than half-past nine. He himself had to be at work in the office by 9 a.m., and there he stayed until nine (or sometimes ten) o' clock at night.[2]

On special occasions—the visits of great celebrities, or coronations—the congestion was tremendous. At the time of Queen Victoria's coronation people came flocking in from the country; we read of 'hundreds of people waiting on the line of road from Birmingham to get lifts on the railway', and 'people . . . waiting at Exeter for places' on the coaches. The occasion provided a great harvest for the cabmen, who charged '£8 or £12 each, double to foreigners'.[3] This was against the terms of their licence, and in normal times cabmen had to conform to strict rules concerning both their charges and their behaviour. They were not allowed to smoke while they were on their stands, and the Lord Mayor once fined a cabman 20s. (or fourteen days) for refusing a fare because he wanted his tea.[4] They still retained, however, the habit of repartee inherited from the watermen and hackney-coachmen, and passed on in due course to the London taxi-drivers and bus-conductors of today.

[1] R. H. Mottram: in *Early Victorian England* (ed. G. M. Young), vol. i, p. 170.
[2] *The Times*, 30 September 1938.
[3] *The Journal of Mary Frampton . . . 1779–1846*. Ed. H. G. Mundy. London, 1885.
[4] C. L. Graves: *Mr. Punch's History of Modern England*. London, 1921, vol. i, p. 142.

IV. THE FACE OF LONDON

*It is the disaster of London, as to the beauty of its figure, that it
is thus stretched out in buildings, just as the pleasure of every
builder, or undertaker of buildings, and as the convenience of the
people directs, whether for trade or otherwise; and this has
spread the face of it in a most straggling, confus'd manner, out
of all shape, uncompact and unequal.*

DANIEL DEFOE: *A Tour through England and Wales,* 1724.

*A mighty mass of brick, and smoke, and shipping
   Dirty and dusky, but as wide as eye
Could reach, with here and there a sail just skipping
   In sight, then lost amidst the forestry
Of masts; a wilderness of steeples peeping
   On tiptoe through their sea-coal canopy;
A huge, dun cupola, like a foolscap crown
On a fool's head—and there is London Town!*

LORD BYRON: *Don Juan,* 1822.

From the eighteenth-century planners, London has inherited
two physical traits that have a social as well as a topographical
significance. First, the laying out of the squares, and secondly the
characteristic London villages that have triumphantly survived
not only two world wars but the far more dangerous activities of
reformers obsessed with ideas of tidiness and uniformity.

In the suburbs to the west and north-west of London estates
were being laid out by the great land-owners, and they chose to
conform to a general pattern that has left to posterity terraces of
comely buildings and open spaces for greenery to delight the
mind and rest the eye. Even when the grass and trees and shrubs
were rigorously enclosed within iron railings, and access to them
confined to the privileged dwellers in the Squares, no vested
interest could control the pattern of the trees against the sky, or
the dappled shadows cast on the surrounding houses. The Caven-
dishes and the Portmans, the Russells and the Grosvenors are
commemorated, among many others, in the Squares that bear
their names.

Behind these gracious houses, however, with no gardens to
insulate them, were closely-ranged houses and tenements of a baser
sort, so that the back windows of 'the Squares' looked out on a
sordid prospect and were looked in upon by many pairs of eyes,
some envious, some hostile. Immediately behind Orchard Street,

where a French visitor lodged in 1810–11,[1] there was a warren of courts and alleys, squalid and filthy, inhabited by the migrant Irish labourers who were a continual social problem and such a menace to the watchmen that none dared venture among them. The noise was indescribable, especially on Saturday nights when pay packets were dissolved into liquor and fights were frequent.

The movement of richer merchants and tradesmen from the City to the suburbs, that had begun much earlier,[2] was very marked during the eighteenth century, and many delightful houses were built in Hackney and Streatham, Stoke Newington and Canonbury, as well as further afield at Chiswick, Hampstead, and Blackheath. These were sometimes clustered round a village green or tiny common, and retained their rural character long after they had become linked with the city by roads lined on both sides with new buildings. The days persisted for a very long time

> When Bethnal Green was verdant
> And rye at Peckham grew.

As early as 1724 Defoe had noted that Westminster was 'in a fair way to shake hands with Chelsea, as St. Gyles's is with Marybone; and Great Russell Street by Montague House, with Tottenham-Court: all this is very evident, and yet all these put together, are still to be called London: Whither will this monstrous city then extend?'[3]

Daniel Defoe came from the village community of Stoke Newington, where most of the people were poor dissenters of his own type, unlike the wealthy residents of Hackney who kept, between them, 'near a hundred coaches'. The tendency was for each 'village' to keep its own character and individuality, and to attract like-minded newcomers. At a later date we find the 'Clapham Sect' originating in Wilberforces, Thorntons, and Macaulays, and their activities directed from the great houses standing round the Common left a deep impression not only upon London life but upon the country at large. Mr. E. M. Forster's recent biography[4] of his great-aunt Marianne Thornton, who lived in the house called Battersea Rise fronting on to Clapham Common,

---

[1] L. Simond, quoted by M. Letts: *As the Foreigner Saw Us*. London, 1935, p. 197.
[2] See *supra*, pp. 51–2; 175.
[3] *A Tour through England and Wales*, Letter v.
[4] E. M. Forster: *Marianne Thornton, 1797–1887*. London, 1956.

gives an extraordinarily vivid, if selective, picture of this group of earnest and intelligent people.

According to Sophie von la Roche, many Londoners in her day (she was there in 1786) 'who have no country-seat of their own, in summer move into Kensington houses for the sake of the good air, the gardens and the fine prospect'.[1] She herself found it 'a lovely village full of wealthy people'. Mme Sophie was inclined to like much that she saw of London, and carried away an impression, which would have astonished her inferiors, of the comparatively equal distribution of 'the good things of life . . . and . . . lack of class distinction among London's inhabitants'. She had roamed widely through the city and to its further suburbs, some of which moved her to great enthusiasm. At Romford, for instance the individual character of the cottage gardens delighted her, and she praised too the wide, clean pavements, exclaiming 'How happy the pedestrian on these roads!'[2]

Seven years after Mme Sophie went home, John Fordyce was appointed Surveyor-General of Crown Lands in London and immediately began to plan the development of Marylebone Park. He wanted a general scheme, with carefully distributed markets, that paid special attention to sewers. He also saw the necessity for providing space at the back of the houses for storage of coal, drying the washing, and keeping poultry.[3] This enlightened man died in 1809; it was his successor who employed John Nash to such excellent effect in laying out this region. Both from architectural and from the topographical points of view Nash changed the face of London more than any man since Wren, not even excepting the Adam brothers whose elegant work reached its peak, perhaps, in the Adelphi.

The shopping centres were still drifting westwards when the nineteenth century opened, but the shops themselves had altered little since the time of Chippendale. Plate glass for windows was just beginning to come into use. It was a Ludgate Hill shop that first carried its window up to the first floor and showed the possibilities of window-dressing, especially when gas-lighting gave the necessary illumination.[4] Exciting window-displays and the early —and often ingenious—examples of advertising altered the whole

[1] *Sophie in London in 1786*. Ed. C. Williams. London, 1933, p. 136.
[2] *Ibid.*, p. 86.
[3] John Summerson: *John Nash*. London, 1935, pp. 104-5.
[4] R. S. Lambert: *The Universal Provider*. London, 1938, p. 27.

technique of salemanship, and encouraged, too, inquisitive crowds of what are now called 'window-shoppers'. It was for this class that the new bazaars of fancy-goods particularly catered. The Soho Bazaar in Soho Square required 'a plain and modest style of dress on the part of the young females'[1] who sold millinery and gloves, but the Pantheon in Oxford Street was less particular, more garish, and much more versatile. Here you could buy almost anything from feathers to pictures, although far more people visited the Pantheon with the intention of looking than of buying.

There were still shops and showrooms in the City; and here too were warehouses and offices that might sometimes occupy the sites that had carried noblemen's houses in the days before the fire. In Ironmonger Lane[2] where once there stood the Black Prince's chief City residence, with its hall and chapel surrounded by a garden and orchards, a large house was built that for more than a hundred years[3] was occupied by a firm of linen factors. They imported their goods from Northern Ireland and stored them in the four ground-floor warehouses, or over the stables across the yard. On the next floor were the offices, and at the top of the house there lived the owner and his family. Here they stayed until the 1830s, when the head of the firm sold his business and retired to Londonderry and the premises became a boarding-house for City clerks. Before the Black Prince lived here, and before the expulsion of the Jews in 1290, this had been the Jewish quarter: the name is recorded of a thirteenth-century Jew[4] who held the property from St. Paul's Cathedral. This gives No. 11 Ironmonger Lane a venerable history, but that there was a house on this site in even earlier days has lately been established, for a mosaic pavement was revealed there by bomb damage, and the remains of a large Roman house came to light by excavation.

The coming of the railways to London did even more to alter the City's appearance than did the canals. When the great Doric colonnade at Euston was erected in 1837 it was claimed as the eighth wonder of the world,[5] and St. Pancras with its Gothic-panelled booking-office was also praised extravagantly: these

---

[1] R. S. Lambert: *The Universal Provider*, p. 54.
[2] Donovan Dawe: *11 Ironmonger Lane*. London, 1952. See also review by M. D. George in the *Eng. Hist. Review*, July 1953.
[3] From 1716.   [4] He was called Lusbert; Dawe: *op. cit.*
[5] W. Sansom: 'Palaces of Steam', *Geographical Magazine*, December 1944, p. 342.

railheads made a profound impression on the general public, and
a great many of those who travelled from London bought their
tickets (which at first were copper discs) with the idea that they
were making history. The physician, Dr. Carus, who accompanied
the King of Saxony on his visit to England in 1844, observed that
Paddington Station 'has called into life a completely new and
continually increasing district of the town in its immediate neighbourhood',[1] but there were few who realized that new slums were
being born in the mean terraces of houses adjoining the tracks,
where the rumble of the brightly-coloured engines heralded the
belching of smoke and fumes into rooms already ill-ventilated
and overcrowded.

Not only did the new railways drastically change the physical
face of London; as Dr. Carus pointed out, their construction profoundly affected the social life of large numbers of people. If
their dwellings happened to lie in the path of the railroads, the
tenants were evicted and the houses demolished with very little
thought of where new homes could be found. It would be a mistake to suppose that the destruction of houses began with the
railways; many had been knocked down to make way for street
widening, or rebuilding projects, or the making of docks in
riverside areas; but these demolitions had been piecemeal and
were different in kind from the swathes cut through closely populated districts, deep into the heart of London.[2] Charles Manby
Smith in 1853 wrote in his *Curiosities of London Life* of 'the deep
gorge of a railway cutting, which has ploughed its way through
the centre of the market-gardens, and burrowing beneath the
carriage-road, and knocking a thousand houses out of its path,
pursues its circuitous course to the city'.[3] This was no exaggeration; it was estimated that the North London Railway Company
had destroyed some nine hundred working-class houses in the
construction of only two miles of track. Indeed, one report
claimed that the Midland Railway's terminus in the Euston
Road displaced no fewer than 20,000 people.[4]

[1] *The King of Saxony's Journey, etc.* Trans. S. C. Davidson. London, 1846, p. 68.
The terminus at this time was at Bishop's Road; the modern Paddington Station was
not built till eight years later.
[2] H. J. Dyos: 'Railways and Housing in Victorian London', I, and II: two articles in *The Journal of Transport History*, vol. ii, May and November 1956, p. 11.
[3] Quoted *ibid.*, p. 12.
[4] *The Working Man*, 8 September 1856. Quoted *ibid.*

The railway companies were supposed to provide accommodation for those that they turned out of their houses, but there was
nearly always a time-lag and the companies tended to evade their
responsibilities. As late as 1898 seventeen hundred and fifty families
lost their homes to give space for the new Marylebone Station and
had to crowd into the Lisson Grove district—already far too congested—because their housing scheme was not yet ready. Even
when the new accommodation was offered, the rents were much too
high for the dispossessed, and a different class of worker from a
higher stratum of society replaced the old. In this way whole districts were, from a social point of view, transformed: higher-paid
and higher-living people came to the new dwellings while those
who had been evicted went to swell the ranks in the already overcrowded slums and cheapest suburbs.[1] H. J. Dyos speaks of the
'ripples of migration'[2] set up by the displacements, and these
ripples spread to a very wide perimeter.

Weekly tenants had no legal claim to compensation, but in
practice small sums were in many cases given and these helped to
tide people over the expensive and anxious time when they had to
move house; the hardship was recognized, and with a good deal
of sympathy, but there was no compulsion to relieve it in any way.
Opinion was divided as to the amount of compensation it was
right to pay, amounts suggested varying from 1s. 6d. to £2 or £3[3]
payable to each tenant.

Meanwhile, great efforts were being made to solve the question
of housing the London poor; men like Chadwick and Dickens and
Charles Booth were very far from callous in their outlook and
refused to be daunted by the magnitude of the problem. Cheap
workmen's fares were an obvious means of enabling workers to
live in the suburbs and work in London—'facile transit' as the
great engineer William Bridges Adams called it, in his vision of
the transference of the slum-dwellers of South London to the
Surrey hills.

The first underground railway—'the Sewer Railway' as *Punch*
called it—was opened in 1863 and ran between Paddington
(Bishop's Road) and Farringdon Street, with carriages of open

[1] C. Booth: *Life and Labour of the People of London.* London, 1903, 3rd series,
vol. iv, p. 166.
[2] *Op. cit.*, p. 90.
[3] *Ibid.*, p. 96.

trucks; by this time Londoners were so used to rail travel that 30,000 of them ventured upon it on the day of its opening. Other lines were being excavated too, some with very great difficulty, as in Clerkenwell in 1861 where there was a dangerous sequence of wells and springs and buried rivers, but at last in 1884 the Inner circle was completed and the future intricacies of the modern web of electric rail could be discerned.

A hundred years had passed since a visitor to London had observed the prodigious number of shops where 'scourers [are] busied in scouring, repairing and new furnishing the cloaths that are smoked'; at that time Londoners had to contend only with the 'horrid smoake' noted by Evelyn; now, the face of London was to be streaked and obscured also by the grime from a hundred locomotives.

Chapter Fourteen

CHARLES DICKENS'S LONDON

1. MISERY AND REFORM

*. . . out of the Borough has come the still, sad music of Dicken-
sian prison-thoughts, and the Cockney lyric that is the heart of
Mr. Weller.*

IVOR BROWN: *Winter in London*, 1952.

*And what equalytye is in bargaynynge, I praye you, when the one
partie is famished, and the other is hoggesty fed?*

THOMAS WILSON: *A Discourse upon Usury*, 1572.[1]

WHEN misery becomes articulate it is generally a sign that
the worst is over, and when Dickens wrote as the champion of the oppressed the conditions he described were
already passing. People were increasingly conscious of the brutality
of the poor-laws, of the horrors of prison life, of the insanitary
nature of the surroundings in which many Londoners still lived:
that is why his novels had so powerful an effect. It has been said
of Dickens that he generated more emotion than he could consume, but there can be no question about its intensity, nor can
there be any doubt that he awoke in his hearers and readers a
genuine response.

Many of the ills of the time were a legacy from much earlier
days, from Stuart or even Tudor times, although they were
brought into sharp relief by the industrial revolution to which
they have so often been attributed. The fearful brutalities of life
in these earlier centuries have not always been given sufficient
weight, because the evidence for them is less abundant and not
very readily accessible. So profound a student of the eighteenth
century as Dr. Dorothy George is of the opinion that—although
there was a notable set-back after the peace of 1815—once the
influence of gin-drinking began to diminish there was progressive
improvement.

[1] Ed. R. H. Tawney. London, 1925, p. 287.

Perhaps the greatest evil of all, and the one that was most easily recognizable in London life, was sweated labour in all its many forms, and in one of his most striking pamphlets, entitled *Cheap Clothes and Nasty*, Charles Kingsley compared 'sweated' clothes to garments made of human skin. Irregular supplies of work contributed to this evil, so did the powerful effect of custom and tradition in many different trades, and the willingness of women (in particular) to accept on behalf of themselves and their children 'home-work' in return for a wretched pittance. They were unorganized, ignorant, and often inept—where, indeed was their 'equalytye in bargaynyng'? The 'sweating' applied most of all to women's work, particularly needlework of all kinds from skilled millinery to unskilled shirt-making,[1] from the stitching of stays to the sewing of quilts.

As early as 1686 a contemporary pamphlet tells us *Sad and Dreadful News from Duke's Place near Aldgate*, recording the suicide of one Dorcas Pinkney, a single woman aged about forty, who was evidently a highly skilled needlewoman for she made children's coats for 'divers eminent shops in and about London'. Dorcas had expressed a 'fear of wanting e'er she died' and rather than face the future she hanged herself from her bed-post.[2] This pamphlet is interesting also in showing that the ready-made clothes trade flourished at an earlier date than is sometimes supposed.

One of the worst-paid trades in the eighteenth century was silk-weaving, and employment here was precarious not only from unpredictable changes of fashion but because the raw material came from abroad and supplies might be interrupted. The weavers of Spitalfields were accustomed to take on far too many apprentices, who provided cheap labour for their employers but when their term of service was finished could not possibly all find work. The position was made worse, as we have seen,[3] by the intrusion into this market of Irish labourers ready to work at even lower wages. Foreign visitors might (and mostly did) comment upon the rosy cheeks and general well-being of what they imagined to be 'the lower classes', but the lowest and most miserable they never saw for the simple reason that the really poverty-stricken

---

[1] As late as 1859 'sweated' shirt-makers were paid only 4*s*. 6*d*. a dozen.
[2] Ashmole Collection, Bodleian Library, Oxford, no. ccxxvii.
[3] *Supra*, pp. 212, 247.

were far too busy in their garrets or cellars, trying to earn a few pence to buy bread, to waste time wandering abroad in the fresh air and sunlight: only the privileged tradesmen could afford to do that.

It has been shown that Sir John Fielding was able to stimulate well-to-do ladies to take an interest in his schemes for the help and reform of the poor and the wicked, and there were also many who were prepared to make individual gestures of charity. Of these was the famous Mrs. Montagu, who on May Day used to give roast beef, plum puddings, and beer to all the chimney-sweepers' boys in London. 'The scene', wrote an observer in her *Journal*, 'was very pretty and gratifying.'[1] Such charitable acts may have been pretty, but it was more gratifying to the climbing boys when public opinion (educated by Lord Shaftesbury) and the watchfulness of the stipendiary magistrates at last put an end to their employment in London,[2] although it persisted for a long time in the provinces. In 1853 it was reported that there were no climbing boys in London, but a few years later the practice of employing them was creeping back again,[3] and it was not until Shaftesbury's Bill was passed in 1875 that the reform advocated by Jonas Hanway, eighty-seven years earlier, became effective.[4]

When misfortune overtook the Dickens family and young Charles's father had to go to the debtors' prison of Marshalsea, the boy himself worked miserably in a blacking factory, endlessly sticking labels on to bottles, and visiting his father in prison every week.[5] These experiences profoundly influenced Charles Dickens throughout his life, and he felt the mortification of them so strongly that he could scarcely bring himself to mention the factory, although his personal unhappiness during childhood had an important place in his passionate regard for the woes of humanity.

The reforms of the prisons that had followed the efforts of Howard and others had less result in London than in almost any other place:[6] nearly all the old abuses persisted, and Peel's Bill of 1823 did not touch the London debtors' prisons at all.[7] Public

[1] *The Journal of Mary Frampton . . . 1779–1846.* Ed. H. G. Mundy. London, 1885, p. 2.
[2] J. L. and B. Hammond: *Lord Shaftesbury.* London, 1923 (repr. 1939), p. 204.
[3] *Ibid.,* p. 213.   [4] *Ibid.,* p. 217.
[5] G. K. Chesterton: *Charles Dickens.* London, 1913, pp. 30–3.
[6] S. and B. Webb: *English Prisons under Local Governement.* London, 1922, p. 62.
[7] *Ibid.,* p. 71.

opinion was indeed veering round to the need for humanity in the treatment of prisoners, but progress was extremely slow, and throughout most of the nineteenth century the London gaols were as bad as any in the country. The prisoners do, however, seem to have been in better heart than formerly; a French visitor to Newgate in 1810 found them playing fives 'with great briskness and glee'[1] still with irons clamped on one leg.

John Wesley in his *Journal* gave an unforgettable description of Newgate when he went there in 1784 to preach the condemned criminals' sermon; 'Forty-seven were under sentence of death', he wrote. 'While they were coming in there was something very awful in the chink of their chains.' Twenty years later the grim ceremony was illustrated in *The Microcosm of London*.[2] Here, Newgate chapel is shown on the Sunday before execution day with the condemned sitting and kneeling round a symbolic coffin, the preacher about to climb into the pulpit to make his oration, and the governor and his wife insulated from the ordinary prisoners in a large box pew. Visitors sometimes attended these ceremonies, and Dickens himself went to the gaol in Horsemonger Lane to witness the execution in 1849 of Mr. and Mrs. Manning for murdering their lodger. He was so moved by the experience that he wrote to *The Times*: 'I do not believe that any community can prosper where such a scene of horror as was enacted this morning . . . is permitted.'

Six years earlier than this, however, a new model prison had been built at Pentonville, and when the Duke of Saxony went with his party to see it his medical attendant Dr. Carus was greatly impressed by its cleanliness and order. He noted the hammocks and wash-basins in the cells and compared the building very favourably with German prisons that he knew.[3] Dr. Carus also visited the lunatic asylum at Hanwell and approved 'the care and attention paid to the food and protection of the inmates', of whom there were at this time a thousand. In the seventeenth century Bedlam had been one of the regular 'sights', and mocking the lunatics there an ordinary occupation for Londoners, but by

[1] L. Simond; quoted by M. Letts: *As the Foreigner Saw Us*. London, 1935, pp. 203–4.
[2] Plates by T. Rowlandson and A. C. Pugin, repr. London, 1947, with introd. by John Summerson.
[3] *The King of Saxony's Journey, etc.* Trans. S. C. Davidson, London, 1846, p. 138.

GINGERBREAD SELLERS

Chelsea Pensioners

The Wallflower Girl

The Birds' Nest Seller

The Lieutenant of the Yeomen
of the Guard

LONDON CHARACTERS

the end of the eighteenth century the new humane attitude had prevailed to a striking degree. Mme Sophie of course went there and was as pleased at what she saw as Dr. Carus was at Hanwell. She found that the patients in Bedlam had bright and spacious quarters, and were treated with great gentleness and kindness, so that 'the worst attacks improve within a fortnight or three weeks and a number are cured'.[1]

II. HOUSES AND HOUSING

. . . public buildings, houses, and shops, all appeared to me little, monotonous, and meanly ornamented; everywhere columns, large and small, pilasters, statuettes, and embellishments of all kinds; but the whole strikes by its extent. London conveys the idea of unlimited space, filled with men incessantly and silently displaying their activity and their power. And in the midst of this general greatness, the extreme neatness of the houses, the wide footpaths, the effect of the large panes of glass, of the iron balustrades, and of the knockers on the door, impart to the city an air of careful attention and an attractive appearance, which almost counterbalance the absence of good taste.

François P. G. Guizot, in 1840.[2]

Guizot was a shrewd and detached observer, he could take a much more objective view of the spread of London than could Londoners themselves. To those of his generation, London was the centre where fortunes were to be made and spent, and they rightly regarded their city as the centre of trade for the whole country and the port of London as the greatest in the world. To Cobbett, on the other hand, it was 'the Wen' and he gives disagreeable pictures of the London approaches in his *Rural Rides* of the eighteentwenties and 'thirties. Coming towards London from Sutton he claims that 'there is, in fact, little beside houses, gardens, grass plots and other matters to accommodate the Jews and jobbers, and the mistresses and bastards that are put out a-keeping'[3] but he cannot refrain from giving glimpses of the gardens and orchards that still survived. When making for his Kensington farm, 'I came up by Earl's Court', he wrote in 1823, 'where there is amongst the market gardens, a field of wheat'.

It was this composite character of London that struck so

---

[1] *Sophie in London in 1786.* Trans. C. Williams. London, 1933, p. 167.
[2] *Embassy at the Court of St. James, 1840.* London, 1862, p. 3.
[3] 10 August 1823.

17

forcibly an intelligent visitor like Guizot, the majesty and squalor, the filthy slums and the oases of beauty, but above all he was impressed by its size and growing extent. Another point that foreigners noticed was the Londoners' fierce individuality, where monotonous rows of identical featureless houses would have suggested complete uniformity. 'In our country a man thrusts his head out of the window, and he is right in the street. But the English home is separated from the street not merely by a curtain in the window, but also by a garden and a railing, ivy, a patch of grass, a door-knocker and age-old tradition.' These words were written in 1923, but they apply just as well to the age of Dickens, or earlier.[1]

No two homes were identical within, however similar their exteriors, and in their furnishings and household treasures they differed very widely indeed. It was not merely a question of one family keeping a linnet in a cage where another had a bullfinch, or the difference between towsled blankets and a neat patchwork quilt, the whole standard of living varied greatly. At a time when many of his fellows were just existing above starvation level, in 1768, a man's goods were seized by the parish of Brentford to defray the cost of keeping children he would not maintain. The value of his belongings amounted to £11 5s. 4d., and they included a four-poster bed, with feather beds, bolsters, and quilts, a 'wains-cott' dining table, leather-covered elbow chair, and a mahogany tea-chest. He had pewter dishes and plates as well as stoneware ones, a silver spoon, a copper tea-kettle and a coffee-pot. He also owned books and prints, and the clothes included a woman's striped silk gown.[2]

Some people were very particular about their quarters and wanted, then as now, a great deal for their money. Thomas Rumney, the younger son of a Cumberland farmer, was an ordinary clerk to a West India merchant in London and, as he told his family when excusing himself from sending them better presents, 'not full of money'.[3] Yet he wrote a letter to the owner of a house in Highgate in December 1797, that shows that his standard was high indeed.

[1] Karel Capek: *Letters from England.* Trans. Paul Selver. London, 1925.
[2] E. W. Gilboy: *Wages in Eighteenth Century England.* Harvard Economic Studies, 1934, vol. xiv, p. 58.
[3] *From the Old South Sea House.* Ed. A. W. Rumney. London, 1914, p. 111.

Sir, [he began] The house you have to let at the end of a row only suits me in some respects. The water not being supplied within doors [few houses in Highgate had this amenity at the time] the smallness of the principal garden, and there being no stable etc. are great objections, but if they could be removed in a certain degree, I might be induced to think more about it. I shall not, however, have occasion for a country residence before Lady Day next . . .[1]

Patrick Colquhoun, the enlightened police magistrate of a later generation than the Fieldings[2] was a man of very wide experience and his opinions were based firmly upon it. He claimed that in his day there were more than 20,000 people who rose every morning without any knowledge of how they would be supported during daylight or where they would pass the next night.[3] No doubt many of these could earn the price of a bed in a common lodging house, but there were always some who could not find work or do it if it were offered. Those who could not afford any lodging at all had to 'sleep rough' in warehouses and dark alleys, under archways or in sheds and huts and boathouses. A number of homeless children, too, were found to be living a wretched nomad life in 1843, when Lord Shaftesbury threw himself whole-heartedly into the Ragged School movement designed to help these outcasts. In a masterly understatement to the House of Commons five years later, Shaftesbury said: 'Curious indeed is their mode of life', and went on to describe how one boy spent 'the inclement season of last winter' lying 'in comparative comfort' inside an iron roller in Regent's Park.[4] Most people who slept outside did so from necessity, but a few from choice. Such was the waterman named Holmes who bought a barge and lived in it with his family, mooring it at various places and thus 'eluding all taxes'.[5]

There was no opportunity for the poor, or even for middle-class Londoners, to live outside the City or to migrate to the country at weekends as did increasing numbers of merchants and tradesmen. The open spaces that they did frequent were often fever-ridden and as dangerous to health as the airless streets whence they had come—the undrained marshes of Bethnal Green were cited as

[1] *From the Old South Sea House*, pp. 278–9.
[2] He died in 1820, after living in London from 1789: he was a magistrate for 26 years.
[3] M. D. George: *London Life, etc.*, p. 94.
[4] J. L. and B. Hammond: *Lord Shaftesbury*, p. 232.
[5] *New Town and Country Magazine*, 20 June 1787.

highly insanitary by the Commissioners under the new Poor Law of 1834. Dickens thought that London could be made 'an immeasurably healthier place' if large well-planned buildings were put up to house the poorest inhabitants and the open spaces properly laid out and drained, as he wrote to the Baroness Burdett-Coutts in 1854.[1] Dickens acted as her almoner in many cases of private charity and as her adviser in more ambitious schemes; they both recognized the paramount importance of the housing problem and were anxious to solve it in their own way. They were particularly severe upon the small builder or carpenter with a few pounds to spare who employed his capital to run up small dwelling-houses. In the early eighteenth century it was common practice to build a brick shell, with floors and a roof, and then offer this 'carcase' for sale; the Westminster Fire Office used to insure these carcase-houses for builders and then issue policies for higher values when they had been finished to the purchaser's taste.[2] Naturally it was to the builders' interest to do their work as cheaply as possible, and there are many instances of houses that collapsed over the heads of their inhabitants, often with loss of life.[3]

Among the many projects started at this time—the Ladies' Sanitary Association, the Female Domestic Mission, Meetings for the Instruction of Mothers, and many more—was the Society for Improving the Condition of the Labouring Classes, which was founded in 1844 with Prince Albert as its President. Their first set of model dwellings was built near Bagnigge Wells, a double row of two storey houses meant to accommodate twenty-three families and thirty single women. Within a few years of this, Pickfords (the carriers) made a lodging-house in Camden Town for their unmarried employees; by 1867 there were sixty men and boys there, paying half-a-crown and eighteen pence per week respectively, and the Society visitors were greatly impressed by the improvements in appearance and manners of the inmates and duly recorded that they had noticed 'a common carter carrying a piece of music'.

[1] *Letters of Charles Dickens to the Baroness Burdett-Coutts*. Ed. C. C. Osborne. London, 1931, pp. 110, 142.
[2] E. A Davies: *The Westminster Fire Office*. London, 1952, p. 41.
[3] See the excellent account of housing conditions and difficulties in J. L. and B. Hammond's *The Bleak Age*. London, 1934, chapters v, vi, and xii.

The author of the Society's report, Henry Roberts, gives re-markable figures concerning overcrowding in the parish of St. George's, Hanover Square, where he made a house-to-house visitation in 1842 at the instance of Lord Harrowby.[1] Here, 1,465 families had only 2,174 rooms, and between them all there were only 2,510 beds. Roberts saw in one house a low room about 22 feet by 16 feet, unventilated except for 'some half-patched broken squares of glass', where forty to sixty men and women and children were constantly lodging, 'besides dogs and cats'. These two examples have been selected as a fair sample from the great mass of material available: there are others so sordid as to be scarcely credible. Roberts was concerned also with fittings and made some interesting specifications that throw light on the domestic arrangements. Iron pumps were to be installed at 35*s.* each for supplying the reservoir of each water closet, also iron pipes and sinks. Fire-clay ovens that could bake a batch of five quarterns of bread at one heating were recommended, and for an obvious reason iron bedsteads were preferred to wooden for all lodging houses. Roberts was a humane and practical man; in many ways his report is a model and it was, in fact, the basis of nearly all the later efforts at improvement.

The great pioneer of housing reform in London was Octavia Hill; she lived on until 1912 but much of her work was done before the formation of the London County Council began a new era in this as in other respects. Octavia Hill interested Ruskin in her projects and it was through him that the first houses for improvement were bought in 1865. Being an admirable business woman, she soon had her undertaking on a sound financial footing and persuaded her friends to give her plan their support. Her best work was done after 1884, when the Ecclesiastical Commissioners had appointed her manageress of their Southwark property, the territory of the 'Winchester Geese'[2] of an earlier day.

---

[1] Henry Roberts: *The Dwellings of the Labouring Classes, etc.* 4th edn. 1867.
[2] The stews in Southwark belonged to the Bishop of Winchester, and the bawds there went by this name. See Shakespeare's *Troilus and Cressida*, act v, sc. xi.

III. STREET TRADERS

Some hundreds of people went on Wednesday to visit him, and knew him to be the same person that used to crie Apples about the Street, and say a Lump, a Lump, a Lumping Penniworth.

A pamphlet of 1685.[1]

I get the eggs mostly from Witham and Chelmsford, I know more about them parts than anywhere else, being used to go after moss for Mr. Butler, of the herb shop in Covent Garden.

The Birds' Nest Seller, 1851.[2]

Street traders were a commonplace in London as far back as the days of the *London Lickpenny*;[3] even the name 'coster-monger' (from costard = a large ribbed apple) was well-known to Shakespeare and his contemporaries. When Henry Mayhew was collecting material for his great book on *London Labour and the London Poor*, which he completed and published in 1861, he took particular care to find out everything he could about the London hawkers and street traders, who formed a distinct community among themselves although they were of widely varying types. It was difficult for Mayhew to estimate their number; he knew that the official census of 1841 gave far too low a figure when it quoted the number of 'hawkers, hucksters, and peddlers' as 2,045, for many were too distrustful to fill in the forms and many more were uncaring or illiterate.[4] His own estimate was that there were not fewer than 13,000, of whom nearly a quarter were Irish. This total includes also the seasonal workers.

Some of the lowest and roughest types of nomad scavengers were found at the water's edge, beachcombers on the muddy verges of the Thames who penetrated far into the sewers in search of saleable lead, iron, or bottles. If they were lucky they might even find money or lost trinkets. These sewer hunters, hardened to the stench and living in mortal fear of the fierce rats, were quite distinct from the dredgermen who searched for lost articles in the river mud and were more allied to the fisherfolk. 'Dredgers' might smuggle goods on occasion from the East Indiamen lying at

[1] *A True Account of a Bloody Murther committed by three Foot-Padders in Fig Lane near S. Pancras Church*. From the Ashmole Collection in the Bodleian Library, Oxford, no. ccxxv.
[2] Henry Mayhew: *London Labour and the London Poor*, 4 vols. London, 1861, vol. ii p. 73.
[3] *Supra*, Chapter Two.　　　　[4] Mayhew: *op. cit.*, vol. i, p. 4.

anchor in the river, but on the whole they were steady hard-working men, and to them fell the grim task of recovering dead bodies from the river: for this they received 'inquest money' and sometimes rewards.[1] Most miserable, despite their cheerful-sounding name, were the Mud-larks. Some of these were gangs of boys who had never known any other life but picking up pieces of coal and so on and bartering them for a meal, but most of them were filthy old women long past any other activity. Of the younger mud-larks a few succeeded in rising above their conditions if anyone gave them a chance; Mayhew mentions a boy who was taken by a printer into his business and did very well.[2] Dust-collectors held their heads high; they owned the horses and carts that carried rubbish to the dustyards where it was sieved by women, the pure dust being used for manure or brick-making and the residue sold as rags, bones, cinders, and so forth.

The street sellers kept rigidly to their own line. Costermongers would only sell fish, fruit and vegetables at their stalls or from a barrow on their regular rounds. They had some contempt for the artisans who asked to be taken on as assistants when they could not find work, for the technique of salesmanship was very important. They were noted for their freedom of language at an early date; in Beaumont and Fletcher's *The Scornful Lady* (1616) a character says:

> And then he'll rail like a rude costermonger.

With glowing fruit piled on the stall, illuminated perhaps by one of the new 'self-generating gas lamps' or more humbly by a candle stuck into a bundle of firewood, the costermonger's wares must have looked attractive, and his cries of 'Twopence a pound grapes! Three a penny Yarmouth bloaters!'[3] readily drew the attention of passers-by.

When they were not working the costers would gamble at card-games or pitch-and-toss; the men would play shove-halfpenny while the girls disported themselves at the dances or 'twopenny hops'. They visited the galleries of theatres sometimes, and a properous coster might go to three hops or theatres in one week. Most of them kept dogs, and fights and rat-killings were organized

---

[1] Mayhew: *op. cit.*, vol. ii, p. 150.
[2] *Ibid.*, vol. ii, pp. 170 –1. [3] *Ibid.*, p. 10.

as holiday amusements. Only about one-tenth of this community were married, although Mayhew found that the couples remained faithful as a rule; in Clerkenwell where the parish incumbent married people free of charge at Easter and in Advent, double the number of married couples were found. Few, except the Irish Papists, had any real interest in religion, and one coster told Mayhew 'If a missionary came among us with plenty of money, he might make us all Christians or Turks or anything he liked'.

The costers were fond of their donkeys, which were bought at Smithfield on Friday afternoons and cost anything from three to five pounds. They fed the animals well, and gave them bright harness. They were particular about their own appearance, too, and paid great attention to their silk neckerchiefs and the quality of their boots. Young dandies would have embroidery of 'a heart or thistle, surrounded by a wreath of roses' worked on their boots, just as the canal boatmen painted castles and roses on their barges: both these classes of people formed distinct communities with individual standards of character and conduct.

When English fruit was out of season, the costers stocked their stalls mostly with fish bought from Billingsgate—plaice, flounders, cockles, and sprats—or oysters straight from the holds of the boats moored along the wharves. They sold imported fruit, too, the nuts and oranges being sold by the poorest types, mostly women and children, and many of them Irish. The oranges were all imported by Jews and stored in warehouses under their own dwellings; they sold them to the costers on Sunday mornings and were reputed to make high profits; Mayhew affirms that nearly $15\frac{1}{2}$ million oranges were sold annually in the London streets. There was an astonishing increase in the number of pineapples sold in London since their first introduction from the Bahamas in 1842. Their wholesale price was fourpence and the costers did well to re-sell them for a shilling, or to poorer customers at a penny a slice.[1] Cherries remained the most popular of all fruit, but strawberries were out of favour except with suburban housewives.

There were, too, the sellers of street literature who derived from the ballad-mongers and were of different types. The 'standing patterers' sold ballads and 'penny histories' from a stall, while the 'running patterers' had no regular pitch; the 'screevers' were

[1] Mayhew: *op. cit.*, vol. ii, p. 84.

writers of begging letters; the 'straw sellers' hawked indecent literature in covers that sometimes, as their outwitted customers found, contained only blank paper. Flower-sellers and bird-catchers brought the country to the town and bridged the widening gap between growing industrial London and the receding country-side. On a fine Sunday in summer there would be about four hundred girls selling flowers in the streets. An Irish girl told May-hew that moss roses had the best sale, and 'Gentlemen are our best customers'. Lavender was popular, too, and wallflowers, mignonette, violets, stocks, and lilies of the valley—all of them sweetly and strongly scented. Then there was the Groundsel Man, who brought chickweed 'and grunsell and turfs for larks' from Chalk Farm and sold them to houses where they kept canaries, or goldfinches, or linnets, or larks. The seller of birds' nests was usually a gipsy; he also traded in live snakes, lizards and hedgehogs (for killing black beetles). He brought bulrushes from the water meadows of Essex and sold them to the bird-stuffers at a penny a dozen; the hedge-sparrows' nests and eggs were intended for glass cases, but the linnets' eggs were to be put under canaries for hatching. This boy went bird's-nesting three times a week and walked the twenty miles to London during the night, carrying with him his spoils—the moss for Mr. Butler in the herb shop at Covent Garden, the special order of six dozen frogs for the French hotel in Leicester Square, and the three dozen weekly for a certain Frenchman who kept a cigar shop. Occasionally he brought a squirrel's nest complete with young. This item yielded him six to eight shillings. The boy had no joy in the capture of the squirrel or in robbing the nests; he told Mayhew: 'oftentimes I wouldn't take them if it wasn't for the want of the victuals.'[1] Mayhew, busy with his calculations, reckoned that 41,750 English birds were sold annually in London at a tariff of half-a-crown for a bullfinch down to sparrows at a penny each.

All these traders were more or less genuinely earning their living, and their number was increased by dock-labourers and others who supplemented their wages by dealing in sporting dogs they had trained in their spare time, or by selling walking-sticks on Sundays to the crowds in Battersea Fields. There were also mendicants, blind or disabled, who hoped to earn a few pence as

[1] Mayhew: *op. cit.*, vol. iii, p. 73.

musicians or bootlace sellers but who really depended on the charity of passers-by. Some of the City Companies—notably the Cordwainers and the Painter Stainers—had funds for the blind, and in London there was one 'School for the Indigent Blind' that had been opened in 1799, but it had accommodation for only thirty-five men and seventeen women. The problem of these unfortunates' welfare, even of their bare existence, was to remain unsolved for several generations.

There was a world of difference between Mayhew's grim pictures of the London street-traders and Wheatley's charming series of the *Cries of London*, though they were separated by less than seventy years. The set of thirteen prints appeared between 1792 and 1795[1] and show a London calm and dignified. Wheatley's models are well fed and well clad; they are in strong contrast to the ragged, hungry people Mayhew grew to know so well. But Wheatley was giving people what they wanted to see—with an eye on the French market the titles were reproduced in French— whereas Mayhew tried to force people to listen to what he wanted them to hear. There can be little doubt which set of portraits is the more realistic.

IV. Holidays

> *John Gilpin's spouse said to her dear,*
> *Though wedded we have been*
> *These twice ten tedious years, yet we*
> *No holiday have seen.*
>
> *Tomorrow is our wedding-day,*
> *And we will then repair*
> *Unto the 'Bell' at Edmonton*
> *All in a chaise and pair.*
>
> *My sister, and my sister's child,*
> *Myself, and children three,*
> *Will fill the chaise; so you must ride*
> *On horseback after we.*
>
> WILLIAM COWPER: *The Diverting History of*
> *John Gilpin*, 1782.

Twenty years is a long time to wait for a holiday, and it seems a pity that Mr. and Mrs. Gilpin did not have a more successful

---

[1] Faked sets and reproductions are abundant, genuine sets are rare.

outing. In real life, however, citizens 'of credit and renown' did enjoy their leisure and were able to roam abroad with their families any evening and every Sunday[1] and, if they chose, to take holidays as and when they pleased. Within ten years of the invention of 'John Gilpin', a correspondent was writing to *The Lady's Magazine*[2] to complain of the superior tradesman's neglect of his business: in the old days he had been 'almost as stationary as his shop', only once or twice in the summer would he indulge his family with an expedition to Hornsey or Edmonton. Nowadays, however, he 'is as seldom found in his shop as in church' but goes to coffee-houses, concerts, and 'disputing clubs' every night of the week, and entertains his guests on claret and madeira. The writer prophesies that this shopkeeper will appear as a bankrupt in the *Gazette* before retiring to the Marshalsea or King's Bench, his wife will go to the parish workhouse, his daughter ('if handsome') to a brothel, his sons to Botany Bay. Such will undoubtedly be the result of taking excessive holidays. For labourers and shop assistants the 'fortnight's holiday with pay' was unheard of; even without pay it was not thinkable, and *Punch* was still fighting for a Saturday half-holiday at the time of the Great Exhibition.

The great crowds that attended coronations, the early ascents of air balloons and so on, could also be seen on the occasions of State funerals, which always drew spectators from every class of society. Lord Nelson's funeral was perhaps most popular of all; those who could not bear to mix with the common throng could answer the advertisement that appeared in *The Times* of 2 January 1806. 'A few respectable Families may be accommodated with Three Front Rooms on the N. side of Ludgate Street near St. Paul's. First Floor £20.0.0., 2nd and 3rd £15.0.0.' No doubt there were some who mourned the passing of a great man, but far more who simply wanted to see the procession, and the usual collection of pick-pockets and ballad-sellers looked upon it as upon any crowd intent upon a spectacle, whether a state occasion, a fashionable ball, a hanging, or a dog-fight.

About the year of Waterloo, steamers first appeared on the Thames, and they very quickly became popular. Londoners loved

[1] Although a fair proportion of London shops did open on Sundays, after 10 a.m. Conditions of work were improved by the Shop Hours Act of 1886, but only for the younger assistants: those under 18 were limited to a 74-hour week.

[2] April 1792.

their river as much as ever, for all its noisome smell and murky colour. They loved ships too, hence the crowd of 'full grown men of the mechanical walk of life' who sailed their model yachts on the Serpentine, 'a . . . fleet of mimic sloop-rigged yachts, some of them large enough to carry a hundredweight, and rigged with the most scrupulous attention to all the nautical proprieties'.[1] Gideon Mantell noticed (in 1842) that Battersea Fields were covered on Sundays with 'tens of thousands of mechanics, little tradesmen, apprentices, and their wives and sweethearts' and that all who could were crowding on to the steamers for trips up and down the river; those who could not, took refuge in the inns and beer-shops.[2] He regretted that they would go home to their weekly toil without 'their hearts and minds improved', but as a doctor it might have occurred to him that fresh air and relaxation could greatly improve their bodily health.

A young attorney's clerk who came to work in London in 1820 has left a diary that tells us something of how he spent his holidays. He, too, went by steamer to Greenwich Fair and to dine at Richmond; he watched the fireworks at Vauxhall and applauded a female rope-climber; he went to see Kean play at Drury Lane, and in the winter he used to shoot snipe and hares on Wimbledon Common.[3] His activities illustrate the variety and liveliness of his tastes; no doubt duller individuals had duller holidays.

By the middle of the nineteenth century it was becoming increasingly the custom for families to migrate to the country in the summer months, middle-class families who would never have thought of doing so a few years earlier. This had its effect on the shopkeepers, for trade became very slack, and they too began to take their ease. Dickens was in London during September 1853, and he wrote to a friend that he had never known the city so empty—he called one morning on two tailors with whom he usually dealt and found one playing the piano upstairs with his family and the other departed to Brighton because 'he couldn't bear the silence'. Dickens then called on his hosier in New Bond Street, found him out, and the shop in the charge of two young

---

[1] Quoted by R. S. Lambert: *The Cobbett of the West: A Study of Thomas Latimer.* London, 1939, p. 177.

[2] *The Journal of Gideon Mantell . . . 1818–52.* Ed. E. Cecil Curwen. Oxford, 1940, p. 160.

[3] See 'An Articled Clerk's Diary', *The Times*, 30 September 1938.

assistants who were playing draughts in the back parlour.[1] Few people had more sympathy with holiday-makers than Dickens, and no one has ever described their activities so well.

It is generally conceded that if Dickens did not exactly invent the merriment of the Merry Christmas he was its most distinguished exponent. This is true up to a point, but he must not be blamed for the commercialization of the Christian festival—he is not even responsible for the Christmas card. As early as the 1840s boys from Charity Schools used to carry Christmas 'pieces', or broadsides, with them and ask passers-by for a few pence in reward for writing on them a seasonable motto or greeting.[2] The *Christmas Carol*, like *The Chimes*, is an appeal for charity and joy; Chesterton says it is a Christmas war-song directed by Dickens against the kill-joys, a plea for the poor man's pleasure and a weapon against the 'benevolent bullies' who would deny it him.[3]

[1] *Letters of Charles Dickens to the Baroness Burdett-Coutts*, p. 126.
[2] G. Buday: *The History of the Christmas Card*. London, 1954.
[3] G. K. Chesterton: *Charles Dickens*. London, 1913, pp. 131-3.

Chapter Fifteen

PRINCE ALBERT'S LONDON

1. THE ROYAL FAMILY

*Her Majesty, upon this occasion [the King's birthday], was
dressed with more magnificence than we remember to have ever
seen her before.*

*The petticoat was of green silk, entirely covered with Brussels
point, . . . with a loose drapery of lilac silk, covered also with
lace, and drawn up in festoons with large bouquets of diamonds,
each bouquet consisting of one large rosette, from which rise
bending sprigs in imitation of snowdrops. From each rosette fall
two large diamond chains and tassels; and upon each festoon of
drapery is a chain of large diamonds.*

The Lady's Magazine, June 1792

LONDONERS liked their royal family to look the part; it was
the homeliness of George III that made him so frequently
the butt of the caricaturists. Gillray in one of his cartoons
showed the royal household in two compartments, King George
toasting his muffins for breakfast, and Queen Charlotte in a very
commonplace unfashionable dress—but with money overflowing
from her pocket—busily employed in cooking sprats for his
supper.[1] Society looked to royalty to give a lead in behaviour as
well as in dress, and the King's rather endearing simplicity in
wondering how the apple got inside the dumpling was not thought
amusing but exasperating, and was the subject of another of
Gillray's cruel caricatures.

Magnificence alone was not enough to please Londoners, and
their response to a fine spectacle was quite unpredictable. No one
could claim that George II had a glamorous personality, yet his
coronation procession—which was very gorgeous and took two
whole hours to pass—attracted a mob of spectators, and the stands
and platforms outside the Abbey were crammed to overflowing.
Indeed, a foreign visitor[2] making his way to his reserved seat in

[1] T. Wright: *A History of Caricature and Grotesque in Literature and Art.* London,
1865, p. 471.
[2] César de Saussure: *A Foreign View of England in the Reign of George I and George II.*
Trans. Mme Van Muyden. 1902.

New Palace Yard left his lodging at 4 a.m., not a moment too soon. On the other hand, the coronation of George IV, in July 1821, was agreed to be 'imposing and very splendid', but people took little or no interest. Shops remained open, trade went on as usual, people stayed indoors or went about their business. In spite of the brilliance of the scene, 'it passed off exceedingly dull'.[1]

This lack of interest in the Regent's coronation most probably had a political significance; the general public's lack of response on this occasion was in strong contrast to the enthusiastic scenes that greeted the news of Queen Caroline's acquittal, and the dejection that followed the news of her death.[2]

The presence of children of the royal household, on both formal and informal occasions, was generally welcomed by Londoners. They were not expected to wear bouquets of diamonds or to behave in any way that was not simple and natural. A provincial visitor to Covent Garden in 1744 to see Shakespeare's *Henry VIII*, was pleased to observe the Prince and Princess of Wales there with their children,[3] and when the children were taken to outdoor entertainments and fireworks this too excited favourable comment. At a later date Queen Victoria and other members of the royal family ordered toys from Whiteley's, and the Duke of Edinburgh used to visit the Christmas bazaar and buy presents for the royal children,[4] to the furtherance of trade and the increase of royal popularity.

During his lifetime Prince Albert encountered mistrust and lack of understanding, but public opinion was veering to his side before his death in 1861, and thereafter his name was perpetuated in many districts, where cottages, terraces, streets, mews, and gardens were called after him. New institutions such as the Embankment and the great Westminster sewer were named after Victoria, too, but of late years many of these names have been changed or swept away. In some cases Albert has been changed to 'Alberta', or 'Consort', or replaced—perhaps fortuitously—by 'Darling',[5]

[1] *The Journal of Gideon Mantell . . . 1818–52*. Ed. E. Cecil Curwen. Oxford, 1940, p. 36.
[2] *Ibid.*, pp. 28, 36.
[3] 'Correspondence of John Collier', *Sussex Arch. Collections*, vo. xlv (1902), p. 104.
[4] R. S. Lambert: *The Universal Provider: A Study of William Whiteley*. London, 1938, pp. 122–3.
[5] *Names of Streets and Places, etc.* L.C.C., 1954.

but although the official title has been altered, the old names sometimes linger on in the minds of ancient inhabitants.

In all these ways Londoners were made conscious of the presence of the royal family in their midst, and they counted upon it as a regular feature of London life. Although this was external to the life of the City, its effect if imponderable was nevertheless very considerable. Even when Queen Victoria became practically invisible after the death of her Consort, every Londoner knew that she was there, behind one of the blank windows of the Palace, and that if she happened to be away at Osborne, or Balmoral, London remained solidly her capital, and the seat of her Empire.

II. INVENTIONS AND EXHIBITIONS

23 May 1851. The Exhibition engrosses everybody, and disarranges everything; it has literally driven all the London world mad.

Journal of Gideon Mantell, 1851.

We publish in another column the extraordinary new uses of which this invention (the telephone) has been found capable. By its means the human voice can be conveyed in full force from any one point to any other five miles off, and with some loss of power to a very much more considerable distance still.

The Times, 8 September 1879.

Two days before this leading article appeared in *The Times* an event took place that is symbolic of the great age of invention and discovery that made possible even more profound extensions of knowledge in our own day. The first telephone exchange in London was opened in Lombard Street, and no fewer than ten subscribers were connected and proudly accepted their numbers. Chubb's Lock and Safe Company of St. Paul's Churchyard was among these pioneers, with the number: London 9.

At a time when ingenuity of invention was seen everywhere, and 'progress' was the rage in all grades of society, the new problem arose of making known unaccustomed processes, and of familiarizing the general public with their new opportunities, before the days when advertising had become the first of the illiberal arts. Six years before the date of the Great Exhibition a successful 'Bazaar of British Manufacturers' was held in Covent Garden, in aid of the Anti-Corn Law League, which was attended

PRINCE ALBERT'S MODEL HOUSES

GREENWICH PARK ON WHIT MONDAY

A SUMMER'S DAY IN HYDE PARK

by thousands less interested in buying the goods than in seeing what these were. Exhibitions, too, were organized by the Society of Arts, and the famous Paris Exposition in 1849 gave English manufacturers a lead, so that the project for a gigantic show in London in 1851 was by no means original, although it was to be on a far larger scale than anything that had been attempted before. From the first, Prince Albert was convinced of the value and rightness of the idea, and it was due far more to his sustained enthusiasm than to any other cause that the Exhibition at last came into being. The Prince was a most sincere believer in 'Progress', as he made clear at the Mansion House dinner when he told the company that this Exhibition would bring them 'a living picture of the . . . development at which mankind has arrived, and a new starting point from which all nations will be able to direct their future exertions'.[1]

As a result of the Prince's efforts a Royal Commission was appointed and subscriptions invited from local bodies. These were very slow to come in, and there was practically no response at all until £50,000 was guaranteed by the head of the firm of contractors who had constructed the earliest railway lines.[2] There was much obscurantist opposition to the scheme, some of it inspired by dislike of Prince Albert, but most of it arising from self-interest. There were many people who felt that Lord Brougham had expressed their view when he said in the House of Lords that 'he marvelled that English tradespeople were such fools as to subscribe their money to provide accommodation for the traders of all nations to come over and undersell them in their own market'.[3]

The stories of the great controversy about the site, and of Paxton's brilliant idea for the design of the building, and of the gigantic conservatory itself, have all been told many times, but there are two points that should be mentioned here. First, that there was never the slightest question that the Exhibition should be held anywhere but in London—yet another illustration of London's 'effortless superiority'. The other is that here again was an opportunity for the country to come to town, a chance of fugitive contacts before the country-people slipped away from

---

[1] Quoted by C. Hobhouse: *1851 and the Crystal Palace*. London, 1937, p. 14.
[2] *Ibid.*, p. 12.
[3] *Ibid.*, p. 18.

18

London.[1] Some account is given by the authors in an earlier book[2] of the country visitors, of the working men's clubs subscribing for an outing, of parties of schoolchildren, and the activities of the young pioneer travel agent, Mr. Thomas Cook. London lodging-house keepers gathered in a rich harvest, and never before had London been so crowded. There were as yet comparatively few hotels, though more than is commonly supposed. Some family letters of 1797[3] refer to 'Webb's Hotel' in King Street, Covent Garden, of which there is now no trace, and several foreign visitors to London mention hotels that catered for wealthy continentals, such as Brunet's in Leicester Square; but ordinary people had to be content with the small boarding-houses that were appearing in less fashionable quarters. People who could not find a roof to shelter them camped out in the open or rigged up some kind of tent; it was like a return to the days immediately following the Great Fire when London went to sleep in Moorfields, and something of the comradeship of those times burned up afresh as it always seems to do when Londoners and their visitors meet in strange conditions.

Here, however, there was no hideous background of calcined buildings and hot ashes: London must have looked vast and grand to the eyes of the countryman, stupendous perhaps but not forbidding. One visitor found that the Exhibition itself was 'quite overpowering',[4] and surpassed all his expectations; he said that he could not express the effect it had left upon his mind, but in fact he devoted some pages of his *Journal* to describing what he saw. On the last day his impression of the 50,000 visitors was of a sea of black hats, for men outnumbered women by ten to one, and at five o'clock came the closing time. This was something of an anti-climax, for, when the organs pealed out the National Anthem everyone wanted to sing and although the first stanza was rendered 'in tolerable accord', by the second verse and after 'by no chance did any two organs or choirs play or sing in unison, and amidst the most incongruous medley of sound, anything but sweet, the

[1] Within the last fifty years the country has come back to town in ever-increasing force. Trains and coaches bring crowds to attend cup-ties and international matches, people come to horse shows, dog shows, pantomimes and concerts, and Womens' Institutes in remote villages send their representatives to the Albert Hall.

[2] *A History of the English People.* London, 1950, pp. 446–7.

[3] See a letter in *The Sunday Times*, 26 January 1936.

[4] *The Journal of Gideon Mantell*, p. 267 ff.

anthem was concluded . . . It was great mismanagement, but no order was observed for the closing scene of the most marvellous display the world ever beheld !'

Victoria had indeed some justification for writing ecstatically to her uncle[1] of 'the triumph of my beloved Albert . . . It was the *happiest, proudest* day in my life, and I can think of nothing else'. By the time of Albert's death, ten years later, his vision and probity had been widely recognized, and *The Times* was moved to commend his 'inestimable value to this nation'.[2]

The model houses for labouring families, called after their promoter Albert Cottages,[3] were erected in Hyde Park outside the main structure, and attracted much attention. Three hundred and fifty thousand people, among them many foreigners, came to see these excellent houses—in this way the Prince's influence reached overseas and his pioneer efforts were probably appreciated quite as much abroad as they were (by this time) at home. Similar new model dwellings were being shown in Paris, Berlin, Bremen, and St. Petersburg within the next twenty years.

These model dwellings and the new residential flats of the 1850s (or sometimes perhaps a little earlier) were undoubtedly the fruit of the new ideas on the circumstances of life in a great town. The project, however, of planning and building blocks of flats, was thought daring in the extreme. In one sense the flats were not new at all, for their prototype could be seen in the chambers of the Inns of Court.[4] As early as 1855 a pamphlet was published[5] concerning the building of flats for the poorer artisans, with sound practical advice about making them fireproof, and only thirteen years later they were being built also for other classes of society and were becoming positively fashionable.[6] Some of the earliest and most successful were the flats in Victoria Street (Westminster) which were being furnished when the Great Exhibition opened.[7]

---

[1] The King of the Belgians. *The Letters of Queen Victoria.* Ed. A. C. Benson and Viscount Esher, London, 1908, vol. ii, pp. 317–18.

[2] 16 December 1861.

[3] Henry Roberts: *The Dwellings of the Labouring Classes, etc.* p. 63. See also H. Roberts: *The Model Houses for Families built in connexion with the Great Exhibition of 1851 by command of H.R.H. Prince Albert.* London, 1851.

[4] S. Perks: *Residential Flats of all Classes.* London, 1905, p. 16.

[5] By A. Ashpitel and J. Whichcord: *Town Dwellings: An Essay on the Erection of Fireproof houses in Flats, etc.*

[6] *Building News,* 1868. Quoted Perks: *op. cit.,* p. 25.

[7] They were opened 6 August 1851. Perks: *op. cit.,* p. 27.

Mechanical inventions shown for the first time in 1851, or made known then to the general public, were many and varied, and from an artistic as well as from a utilitarian point of view many homes were transformed by objects bought or ordered or imitated; but it would be wrong to claim that the London people were more strongly influenced by the Exhibition than anyone else. Londoners, it is true, had more opportunities to visit the display in Hyde Park, just as they could go as often as they pleased to the Egyptian Hall to see the midget Tom Thumb who so delighted Queen Victoria, or to concerts or to the theatre, or take a boat down the river, but they did not necessarily do all or any of these things.

Those who could not afford expensive pleasures might wander in the Parks[1] or, in wet weather, in the Lowther Arcade. There were, too, many cheap exhibitions and shows within the reach of all but the very poorest. There was the 'Colosseum' in Regent's Park with its pseudo-Swiss scenery, and the new attractions that were appearing in the Zoological Gardens near by; the reptile house was opened in 1850 and the monkey house fourteen years later, additions which immensely increased the 'Zoo's' popularity, for enthusiasm had been tepid in the years following its foundation in 1826, compared with its enormous popularity thereafter. Another show, imitated in the provinces but never rivalled, was Madame Tussaud's collection of wax models. *Punch* in the 'forties spoke sourly of the Chamber of Horrors, saying that it ministered to the cult of monstrosity and likening Madame herself to the witches who made wax images of those they wanted to destroy.[2] Certainly Londoners in Victoria's reign had great choice of shows and exhibitions, some edifying, others less so, and opportunities too for more serious self-improvement.

[1] See a brief but interesting survey of these in Richard Church: *The Royal Parks of London* (Stationery Office), 1956.

[2] C. L. Graves: *Mr. Punch's History of Modern England*. London, 1921, vol. i. pp. 157–8. In the early eighteenth century there had been two well-known wax-work shows, Mrs. Salmon's and Mrs. Goldsmith's, and of course the wax figures of the Kings at Westminster. See J. Ashton: *Social Life in the Reign of Queen Anne*. London, 1882, vol. i, pp. 282–3.

III. POPULAR EDUCATION

Schools are the seed plots of all learned arts
And doth enrich our lives, our tongues, our hearts.

Mary Derrow's Sampler, 1723.[1]

When Caroline Fox came up from Falmouth to London in 1851 she recorded in her *Journal* that she attended on successive days Thackeray's lecture on the 'English Humourists' and Faraday's on 'Ozone'.[2] The range and scope of lectures that were available at this time are remarkable, and so is the eagerness with which they were attended. Many supposedly educated people became aware of great gaps that needed to be filled, some felt a real thirst for knowledge, many more felt the stirrings of intermittent curiosity and attended lectures because it seemed to be the thing to do. It occupied their time and made them feel 'improved'. For good measure there were always the Dickens readings, when the author declaimed his own works with a passionate enthusiasm that was highly infectious.

The learned lectures on scientific subjects, the more generally popular ones on literature and the arts, and the serious instruction for those who had had no opportunity for proper education in their youth—each appealed to different classes of the public, so that lecturers were obliged to grade their material to the right level for their audience, and lecturing was rightly looked upon as a fine art. The scarcely literate adults who had been denied opportunity and who needed the utmost encouragement and sympathy in their efforts to expand their minds deserved the very best instruction although it was not always to be had.

Something has already been said of the Ragged Schools, which were not, of course, peculiar to London any more than were the Sunday Schools, or Chapel schools, or the Charity schools which had descended from medieval times. An essentially 'London' institution is found, however, in the new University that was given its charter the year before Victoria came to the throne and developed power and impetus throughout her reign. For many years past it had been a subject of regret to many young men that they could not enjoy a university education at Oxford or

---

[1] Of St. Clement Danes Charity School.
[2] H. Wilson Harris: *Caroline Fox*. London, 1944, p. 34.

Cambridge because it was too expensive, or because they would not be able to study their own chosen subject, or because they were dissenters.

To enter either of these universities—and there were then no others in England—it was necessary to be a member of the established Church. Moreover, there was no satisfactory provision for studying either medicine or law, so that very few doctors were graduates and virtually no attorneys. The question of expense was not so much a matter of fees, as that the general living standard was extremely high. Promoters of the idea of founding a new university in London enraged the older institutions by asserting that they were 'provincial' and remarking—quite truly—that London would be the most convenient centre not only for Londoners themselves but also for young men from abroad and from the Colonies. By 1827 the scheme was drawn up, and certain professors already appointed, but the mistake was made—which was afterwards to prove a serious weakness[1]—of failing to define properly their duties, the limits of their subjects, and their rights. The site had been acquired at a cost of £30,000 and on 30 April 1827 the Duke of Sussex laid the foundation stone of the new building. Some initial quarrels resulted in the resignation of a number of the professors, but their status improved as first three, and then six, were made members of the council.

The earliest women's college was Bedford, and the foundation of Westfield and Holloway followed soon afterwards. Women were, however, kept carefully segregated from the male students, and when, in the 'seventies, some women wanted to read physics and chemistry special classes were held for them which always began and ended at the half-hour so that neither they nor the men should be embarrassed by close association. In 1872, however, the authorities were faced by a lady who insisted upon reading jurisprudence, and she was admitted to the ordinary classes with, apparently, no ill effects. Thereafter, prejudice dwindled, and by 1878 women were admitted to examinations and classes on exactly the same terms as men.

It seemed that London University had avoided most of the difficulties and stresses inherent in a project of such magnitude,

[1] Sir Gregory Foster: 'Those Hundred Years', 25 March 1926. See the Bodleian Collection of London Pamphlets (Lond. 8vo 1215).

although steps were sometimes taken that had to be retraced. When King's College in the Strand was founded in 1829 on their own model, Oxford and Cambridge objected to the granting of degrees by the new university and succeeded in holding up the issue of its charter to the University : this was not obtained until 1836. At last good sense prevailed, and two charters were given simultaneously, the one setting up London University with power to give degrees, the other incorporating the existing institution as University College.[1]

Ribald people might call London 'the Godless University' because of the religious freedom it allowed, but even those who had most bitterly opposed the idea of its foundation had in the end to admit its success. From the first London insisted upon the importance of the study of English and included this as a compulsory subject for an arts degree instead of being satisfied—as were the older universities—with Greek and Latin. This university also founded the first faculty of science, admitting the first doctor in 1862, and six years later giving its first doctorate in literature. The success of London University was the triumph of a great idea, and a fitting reward for those who had the foresight to plan, and the tenacity to carry out their scheme, in the face of very considerable opposition.

It could not be said that the British Museum did much in its early days to further popular education, although it had from its beginnings the Cotton, Harleian, and Sloane collections that form the nucleus of today's library. It was first opened in 1759, in Montagu House, Bloomsbury, but in a very limited way. For nearly fifty years it was necessary to make formal application for admission, and only five parties of fifteen persons were admitted on Mondays, Wednesdays and Fridays, under the supervision of a guide. Pastor Moritz, in 1782, had to give a fortnight's notice, and he and other foreigners were discouraged by the bells that were rung to notify visitors that they had stayed long enough in one department. A certain Frenchman complained that the guides were unable or unwilling to answer sensible questions and merely repeated their facetious patter 'in a style of vulgarity and impudence which I should not have expected to meet with in this place

---

[1] Bodleian Collection of London Pamphlets. Address by Sir Philip Magnus on 'The Birth of University College, London, 100 Years Ago' (27 April 1920), p. 18.

and in this country'.[1] Fifteen years later, when the rules of admission had been somewhat relaxed (although children still could not, under any circumstances, be admitted) a German traveller found the whole collection muddled and tasteless; he called it a 'mischmash' and complained that the Elgin Marbles were housed in a shed.[2]

There was still a long way to go, but the first stirrings of the strong and widespread desire for popular education had been noted with real sympathy, not only by philanthropists bent on improving their fellow men, but by those who felt a compulsion to share with others the pleasures and privileges they had themselves enjoyed, and to spend their own time, money, and personal effort in so doing. Museums and picture galleries were not yet fulfilling their functions as well as they could, although increasing numbers of people were realizing what a splendid heritage these might become under enlightened management: Charles Kingsley said that galleries 'should be the workman's paradise',[3] and once the matter was pointed out there were many to agree with him.

By the late 'sixties and early 'seventies it was beginning to be apparent that education is the means by which ambitious men can climb to what height they will; class distinctions were still rigid, but in places they were beginning to crack. Perhaps the position is best summed up by the hero in Robertson's play *Caste*, first produced in 1867.

'Caste', says George, 'is a good thing if it's not carried too far. It shuts the door on the pretentious and the vulgar; but it should open the door very wide for exceptional merit. Let brains break through its barriers, and what brains can break through love may leap over.'[4]

---

[1] This was in 1810. M. Letts: *As the Foreigner Saw Us*. London, 1935, p. 202.
[2] *Ibid.*
[3] *Collected Works*. London, 1901, vol. i, p. 176.
[4] T. W. Robertson: *Caste*, repr. in *Nineteenth Century Plays*. Ed. G. Rowell. Oxford, 1953.

IV. LONDON AUDIENCES

When Crummles played he never knew
Those pretty arts which charm the few;
He painted with an ampler brush
The coal-black frown, the crimson blush.
No psycho-analytic sage
Had set the farmyard on the stage,
The simple Circles did not itch
To see the bedrooms of the rich;
He kept the awful 'gods' in view
So every devil got his due,
The bigamist was hissed at sight,
And black was black and white was white
When Crummles played.

A. P. HERBERT, 1927.[1]

Just as the audiences in Ben Jonson's London craved for thrills
and horrors, so did Londoners of mid-Victorian times passion-
ately desire a particular type of melodrama: the ingredients, so
to speak, were the same but the cooking and serving very different.

The quarrels of the eighteenth century had resulted in the
licensing of only two London theatres for 'straight' drama so
that the others could present only variety or 'burlettas'—that is,
plays with music, or 'turns' of any kind, between the acts. It was
quite possible to play anything from *The Rivals* to *Macbeth* if
enough 'musical pieces' were included, and such incongruities
occurred as 'The nigger melodists will shortly commence their
unrivalled entertainment, preliminary to the orchestral selection
from Beethoven's Pastoral Symphony.'[2] Among the publisher's
advertisements on the back cover of one of these plays, published
in 1860, is a list of others that were available; copies could be
bought for 6*d.* each, post free. There are 292 of them, and they
include *Antony and Cleopatra* (played as a farce), *King Richard ye
Third, Oliver Twist, The Beggar's Opera, Uncle Tom's Cabin,* and
The Rape of the Lock. Interspersed among these titles are to be
found also those of contemporary plays, which throw a strong
light upon public taste. Some are facetious and show the rage for
puns and supposedly phonetic spelling; of these *Virginius the*

---

[1] Epilogue to the printed version of Lillo's tragedy of *The London Merchant* in Sir
Nigel Playfair's production at the Lyric Theatre, Hammersmith, in 1927. *When
Crummles Played.* London, 1927, p. 126.

[2] From Tom Taylor's *The Ticket of Leave Man* (1863), repr. in *Nineteenth Century
Plays.* Ed. G. Rowell, Oxford, 1953, p. 278.

Rum-un and *Bould Soger Boy* are fair samples. Others have such fascinating titles as: *My Wife's Dentist, Unprotected Female, The Negro of Wapping, The Death Plank,* and *The Phantom Breakfast.*

The unwieldy size of the licensed theatres, where sometimes an audience of three thousand might be pushed in, had its influence upon the drama as well as upon the audience. There was no possibility of achieving anything but broad effects; poetry and philosophy were abandoned in favour of sensation and spectacle. Ingenious stage machinery, unrolling dioramas, ambitious scenery and realistic thunderstorms took the place of refined acting. Lines

Trio ... · "My Heart is full of sorrow" ...   Miss SENNETT, Miss HASLEWOOD, Miss SLADE.
The Tortured mind—Mark in another character—a rather strong pull—Winnifred makes a mistake.

*** AN UNPLEASANT RECOGNITION.
Potts in a Fog—a rather loose habit.

☞ SIR ERNEST POISONS THE WINE.
Mark takes the name of Smith for want of a better—the little packet.

MARK RAISES THE GLASS, WHEN ▉▉▉▉▉

CHARLES ACTON BEFORE SIR ERNEST.
Mark sees his Brother—the heart-sticken Mother—Mabel avows her love

A WITNESS FOR THE DEFENCE.
The Rage of Sir Ernest.—The Malediction.

SUDDEN APPEARANCE OF ▉▉▉▉▉
MARK REVEALS ALL, AND SUES FOR MERCY.
A Brother's Pardon—Meda seeks shelter in Holly Bush Hall—Jafed Caught.

*** THE FRATRICIDES DOOM!
A Repentant Individual—Dame Acton pleads for her Son—joy and hope beam on all in

HOLLY BUSH HALL.

Programme of a Melodrama, 1860

had to be bellowed if they were to reach the extremes of pit and gallery, and the dramatist was not only subordinated to his actors but to his effects man. The theatres themselves were cold, dirty, and uncomfortable. Even after the smaller theatres were licensed, in 1843, there was little improvement, and although the songs and dances were no longer obligatory, they were often retained within the framework of the plays because the public had grown so used to them. The mob had taken charge of the theatres; these gaunt buildings filled with uncouth and noisy people were so unattractive that polite society deserted them in favour of concert halls, or read the new novels comfortably in their own homes instead of watching distorted versions of familiar stories upon the stage.

The new audiences who flocked to the plays were as generous in applause as they were vociferous in disapproval. They were, however, something more than undisciplined 'rowdies', for they were able to organize theatre riots—as they did on several famous occasions—so as to impose their will on the managers, either to make them lower their prices or to engage or dismiss artists according to the audience's taste. For the most part the spectators only wanted 'the mixture as before': they were quite uncritical of absurdities and crude contradictions in the plot, which tended to run on well-established lines. The basic characters were the aristocratic villain, recognizable immediately he appeared, the golden-haired hero who was probably the missing heir, a heroine of incomparable idiocy, and a faithful old servant. Blood-stained knives, missing wills, mysterious 'papers', all these were favourite properties, and a play with a nautical background was almost certain of success. Douglas Jerrold's *Black-Eyed Susan*, produced at the Coburg Theatre in 1829, was one of the first English plays to have a hundred consecutive performances;[1] the hero, William, was a sailor, and selections from Dibdin's *Naval Airs* were used appropriately. Ten years later T. E. Wilke's *Ben the Boatswain* was also successful; it borrowed nearly all the situations of *Black-Eyed Susan* and copied the songs and background music, but the audiences were quite unaware of any plagiarism. Nor would they have minded if they had noticed the similarity. It is of interest that in the latter play the midshipmen were all acted by girls, an inversion of the sixteenth-century practice.

Even a slight study of the plots of these melodramas, particularly the theme of the missing heir and the hero in disguise, immediately suggests that W. S. Gilbert may have found here his inspiration, and it may well be that *Pinafore* owes more to *Black-Eyed Susan* than is generally admitted. There is also something rather Gilbertian about the ambidextrous Sir Philip in Morton's *Speed the Plough*, which belongs to a much earlier date.[2] In the third scene of Act IV he recalls his hasty action: 'with one hand I tore the faithless woman from his damned embrace, and with the other stabbed my brother to the heart'.

The language of Morton is forceful and, although remote from ordinary human speech, it has not the flowery verbosity of most of the plays that followed. The great majority of play-goers belonged

---

[1] *Nineteenth Century Plays*, p. 2.
[2] It was first produced in 1800, repr. Oxford, 1926.

to the new industrial workers whose lives were dreary and monotonous, so it is easy to realize why they wanted something as far
as possible from reality. Improbable language, absurd situations,
crude colour, and great magnificence were what they demanded;
they did not even require continuity of plot, because many of them
took advantage of the half-price system, by which it was possible
to go into the theatres at half-price after 9 p.m. when the beer-
shops closed. For the same reasons they were delighted by farce,
and the standard of this was almost unbelievably low. Since many
members of the audience would be drunk, and most quite unedu-
cated, it was not to the interest of the management to provide them
with fare any better than they called for; if they would laugh
uproariously at simple farcical situations, such as sitting on a chair
that was not there, or at the feeblest of punning jokes, that was
what they must have. The one thing they really resented and
rejected was realism of any kind—anything, indeed, that might
remind them of their own dull lives. In these days their attitude
would be called escapist; to them it appeared, as it was, perfectly
natural.

There can be no doubt at all that London audiences really
enjoyed their theatre and that it meant more to them than the
mere passing of time. They liked factory girls marrying lords and
rapacious landlords foiled, they gasped with delight at deeds of
gallantry and with delicious fear at danger, and they wanted the
whole thing to be rendered in language nearly as foreign to them
as French or German. A character in Tom Taylor's *The Ticket-of-
Leave Man* (1863),[1] as she sits in 'the Belle Vue Tea Gardens', and
watches and listens in wide-eyed wonder, must speak for the
whole audience. Her name is Emily, and she exclaims: 'I call this
life—the music and the company, and the singing and the trapeze.
I thought the man must break his neck. It was beautiful.'

---

[1] *Nineteenth Century Plays*, p. 282. This play has lately (1957) been revived at the
Arts Theatre and has been acted and reviewed seriously—i.e. not as a burlesque.

CONCLUSION

*Among the noble cities of the world that are celebrated by Fame,
the CITY OF LONDON, seat of the Monarchy of England,
is one that spreads its fame wider, sends its wealth and wares
further, and lifts its head higher than all others.*

WILLIAM FITZSTEPHEN: *A Description of London, c.* 1182.

SEVEN centuries later the words of FitzStephen still ring true,
although London has become different in kind, as well as in
extent, from the city he knew. With the formation of the
London County Council a new phase was reached, and the passing
of the Local Government Act in 1888 meant, in principle, the
transference of some of the City's powers to the new County
Authority. Yet, in practice, it was found expedient to allow
Common Council to continue to exercise a number of its old
functions, and the City thus kept much of its character and dignity,
and also those of its former powers that it cared to retain.

The intention clearly was to create a new entity, and the London County Council marked the end of the old era as strongly as
the beginning of the new, although in some ways the City became
more formidable than ever before. Some of the London villages
still kept their special qualities, but the new Act smoothed away
many anomalies and cumbersome local rivalries, and provided
efficiency and uniformity where before its passage there had been
an unwieldy tradition of ancient custom. Yet, could John Evelyn
return to the London he knew so well, he would find many usages
familiar to him, and that the pattern of progress was a design less
intricate than repetitive.

Changes have come also in London's natural history, but here
too the continuity is seen. The kites and ravens that acted as
scavengers in Evelyn's day have been replaced in our own by
the gulls that recall to the minds of Londoners far from dockland
that the city is still a great port. In recent times, too, the pattern of
London's natural history has been repeated. A new plant has taken
charge of the waste spaces of charred earth where once stood solid

buildings—the rose-bay willow-herb riots across bombed areas, spreading its seeds at the rate of 80,000 in a single season, although a century ago botanists allowed it only eight sites in all Middlesex.[1] This flower has taken the place of the London rocket,[2] which appeared rapidly and in quantity after the fire of 1666 and within two years had smothered the ruins of Old St. Paul's. For the second time in three hundred years man-made destruction proved nature's opportunity anyone, as he mused among the quietness of the ruins, surrounded by a tangle of willow-herb and Oxford ragwort, might echo W. H. Hudson's thoughts among the felled trees in Kensington Gardens as he watched a woman collecting twigs and chips for firewood:

> It was as if she had shown me a vision of some far time, after this London, after the dust of all her people . . . had been blown about by the winds of many centuries—a vision of old trees growing again on this desecrated spot as in past ages, oak and elm, and beech and chestnut, the happy green homes of squirrel and bird and bee. It was very sweet to see London beautified and made healthy at last! And I thought, quoting Hafiz, that after a thousand years my bones would be filled with gladness, and, uprising, dance in the sepulchre.[3]

[1] R. S. R. Fitter: *London's Natural History.* London 1945, p. 231.
[2] *Sisymbrium irio.* Cf. Fitter: *loc. cit.*
[3] Written in 1898. *Birds in London* (Collected edn. 1923), p. 64.

INDEX

etc.); jobbing gardeners, 158; plant shows, 159, 161; Society of Gardeners, 161; gardening as a pastime, 69, 70; watering, 196; 'gardinage', 162, 163

Garrick, David, 1, 182, 222 n. 2, 226

Gay, John, 155; his *Trivia*, 155; *The Beggars' Opera*, 201; 281

'Gentleman Harry', 143

Gilds, 120 (*see also under* Apprentices, Crafts, Companies, etc.); religious fraternities, 19; parish gilds, 19; no gild-merchant in London, 19–20; exclusiveness of craft gilds, 33, 45, 46, 48–9, 152, 172; standards of craftsmanship, 45, 173, 188; restrictive practices, 42, 44, 45–6; 173; expulsion from, 46; military exercises of, 120, 121; conflict between Victuallers and non-Victuallers 42 (*see also* Northampton, John of); journeymen, 46, 172, 173; masters, 45, 46–8, 49, 124, 125

Gillow, Robert, shopkeeper, 182, 191

Gillray, James, caricaturist, 214, 270

Gin, 167–8, 198, 208, 209, 212 (*see also under* Drunkenness)

Gin Lane, 2; 167, 168 (*see also under* Hogarth, William)

Gipsies, 265

Government of London (*see also under* Common Council): oligarchical character of 52; commons excluded from 52; relations with the King, 13, 17, 19–20, 42, 43; attempts to control pestilence, 103, 104, 105; and theatres, 110; cancels Bartholomew Fair, 113

Grant, Roger, oculist, 156

Greene, Robert, 96, 109; *The Art of Conny-Catching*, 96; *Groatsworth of Wit*, 109

Greenwich, 219, 230 (*see also under* Fairs, Parks)

Gregory, William, chronicler, 54, 57, 58

Gresham, John, 86, 87

Gresham, Richard, 86, 87–8

Gresham, Thomas, 86, 88–9

Guildhall, 21, 52, 56, 63, 150, 219

Gurl, Leonard, nurseryman, 158 n. 2.

Hackney, 164–5, 175, 247

Hale, Richard, grocer, 100

Hammersmith, 83, 125, 160

Hampstead, 247

Hancock, John, agent, 140, 165, 214, 217, 223

Handel, George Friedrich, 130, 222

Hanseatic League, 61

Hanway, Jones, philanthropist, 206, 207–8, 255

Harley, Lady Brilliana, 68–9, 102–3

Hatton Garden, 191

Hawkers, 163, 262 (*see also* Vendors, Street): of fish ('basket people'), 125, 263; higglers, 139; Irish, 212, 262

Haymarket, 168, 192

Health Act, Public, 240

Heating, 7, 192, 261

Henry III, King, 15, 17, 25, 26, 27, 158

Henry VI, King, 53, 57, 58

Henry VIII, King, 32, 76–7, 80, 87, 96

Heppelwhite, George, 191

Herbs, 62, 158, 160, 265

Highbury Barn, 230

Highgate, 148, 175, 258

Highwaymen, 1–2, 97, 143, 170, 199, 200, 205 (*see also* 'Gentleman Harry')

Hill, Octavia, 261

Hoccleve, Thomas, poet and civil servant, 28–9

Hogarth, William, painter, 167, 215, 226; his *Harlot's Progress*, 210

Holborn, 66, 103, 162, 186, 194

Holidays, 230, 231, 266 ff. (*see also* Excursions, Festivities, etc.)

Holloway College, 278

Hollyband, Claudius, schoolmaster, 84; 85

Hooligans, 199 (*see also* Manners, Mohocks)

Hornsey, 230, 267

Horses, 18, 31, 39, 118, 140, 169, 195, 200, 230, 236, 243, 244 (*see also* Saddlery *and* Stables)

Hospitals, 103, 157; St. Bartholomew's, Smithfield, 22, 83, 100, 104, 112–13; Bedlam, 100, 219, 256–257; Foundling Hospital, 208–9; St. Giles', Holborn, 103; Hanwell Lunatic Asylum, 256; Leper Hospitals, 103–4; Magdalen Hospital, 206; pest-houses, 105

Hotels, 264, 274 (*see also* Inns)

Houndsditch, 157, 158

House-keeping, 18, 70–1, 72, 162 ff.

Houses (*see also* Almshouses, Cottages, Palaces): Roman, 6, 7; wooden, 5, 150, 193; brick and stone 152, 172, 193; pre-fabricated, 63; let to country craftsmen, 173; standing empty, 152, 173; rich men's, 20–1, 61, 62, 153, 157, 167–8, 246, 247,

Myddelton, Sir Hugh, 234–5 *(see also* Water Supply)

Nash, John, architect, 248
Nashe, Thomas, 119; his *Pierce Penilesse*, 161
National Anthem, 221, 221 n. 4, 274–5
Navy, 124, 205, 206; *(see also* Pressgang)*;* prize money, 124
Needlework, 91, 254
New Bond Street, 186
Newgate, 51, 53, 132, 256
News, 117, 118; newsletters, 178, 182; newspapers, 170, 171, 177, 178, 185
'Noonchyns', 60
Northampton, John of, 44
Nuisances, 39, 40, 41 *(see also* stench, insupportable)
Nunneries, 9, 22

Offal, 38, 39, 40, 166
Opera, *see under* Music
Overcrowding, 101, 105, 240, 251, 261
Owen, Robert, 183, 184; his *Life*, 183
Oxford Street, 114, 249

Paddington, 250, 251
Palaces, 13, 168; Savoy, 44; Whitehall, 111, 115, 147; living conditions in, 90
Pall Mall, 185
Pancras, St., 249
Panic, 76, 103, 148, 149, 205
Pantheon, 114, 249
Papists, 69, 123, 148, 212–3, 220, 264
Paris Garden, 115, 117 *(see also* Sport)
Paris, Matthew, chronicler, 16, 22
Parks, 165, 231, 276; Hyde Park, 275; St. James's, 137, 218, 231; Regent's Park, 259, 276 *(see also* Greenwich)
Parliament, Acts of, 110–11, 127, 134, 164, 167, 208, 212, 285; debates in 137, 273; petitions to, 129, 138, 208; House of Lords, 129, 174, 273; conduct of House of Commons, 174–5; parliamentary election (1710), 211; adjourned on account of pestilence, 102; county M.P.s, 174; member for Kent *(see under* Chaucer); member for the City *(see under* Rothschild)
Paston family, 66

Paternoster Row, 152
Paul's, St. *(see also under* Schools): burning of (A.D. 61, 961 and 1087), 5, 9, 147, and 1561, 119, 147; the Great Fire (1666), 146–9, 191, 286; rebuilding of, 5, 9, 150; charters of, 17; dome of, 220; weathercock of, 77; names carved on the leads, 119, 220; befogged, 145; dancing in, 21; horses stabled in, 118; no wrestling in precincts, 50; or playing of ball, 118; sale of relics in, 10, 118; St. Paul's churchyard, 80, 84, 119, 187 n. 4; Paul's Cross, 24, 110; Paul's Walk, 117–19; 176
Pavey, Salathiel, boy actor, 109
Peacham, Henry 141; his *Worth of a Penny*, 81, 153
Peasants' Revolt, 41–4
Pepys, Samuel, 1, 106, 138, 146, 147, 154, 155, 164, 176, 178–9; his *Diary*, 130, 141, 146, 149, 156; Mrs. Pepys, 154, 155, 166
Perquisites of office, 14, 15, 28, 31–2, 56, 174, 200, 203 *(see also* Bribery)
Pestilence, *see under* Plague
Philip, Matthew, goldsmith, Mayor, 57
Piccadilly, 3, 185, 195
Pictures, 6, 91, 215, 216, 217 *(see also* Royal Academy); portraits, 215, 217–8; flower pieces, 215–6; landscapes, 215, 216, 217; subject pictures, 217; prints, 215, 216, 218, 258
Pilgrims, Chaucer's, 32–3; to the shrine of St Eorcenwald, 10, 117; buy relics, 117
Pinckney, Dorcas, needlewoman, 254
Piozzi, Mrs., *see* Thrale, Mrs.
Place, Francis, tailor, 227; 228
Plague, 101–2, 105–6, 110 *(see also* Diseases)
Plate, 34, 36, 90, 91 n. 1, 92, 95, 181, 258
Platter, Thomas, his *Travels*, 97 n. 4
Playhouses, 107, 162; erected outside the City, 110; re-siting of, 128; Blackfriars, 107; Drury Lane, 154, 222, 268; Globe, 108, 115; Haymarket, 222
Plays *(see also* Theatre, *and playwrights under proper names)*: miracle plays, 113; *Antony and Cleopatra*, 281; *As You Like It*, 116; *Bartholomew Fair*, 112; *Bel and the Dragon*, 113; *Ben the Boatswain*, 126, 283; *Black-eyed Susan*, 283; *Caste*, 280; *The City Madam*, 51, 86; *Macbeth*, 281; *The*